He
At
imp
voi
for
it i
crit
     T
dis
Ch
exa
soc
dis
in
trib
anc

of
be

Christine Hallett is Professor of Social Policy in the Department of Applied Social Science at the University of Stirling. **Alan Prout** is Professor of Sociology in the Department of Applied Social Science at the University of Stirling. He was also the Director of the ESRC 'Children 5–16' Research Programme.

The Future of Childhood series

Series Editor: Alan Prout

Hearing the Voices of Children

Social Policy for a New Century

**Edited by Christine Hallett
and Alan Prout**

RoutledgeFalmer
Taylor & Francis Group

LONDON AND NEW YORK

First published 2003
by RoutledgeFalmer
2 Park Square, Milton Park, Abingdon, Oxon, OX14 4RN

Simultaneously published in the USA and Canada
by RoutledgeFalmer
270 Madison Ave, New York NY 10016

RoutledgeFalmer is an imprint of the Taylor & Francis Group

Transferred to Digital Printing 2005

Typeset in 10.5/12pt Bembo by Graphicraft Limited, Hong Kong

British Library Cataloguing in Publication Data
A catalogue record for this book is available from the British Library

Library of Congress Cataloging in Publication Data
Hearing the voices of children ; social policy for a new century / edited by
Christine Hallett and Alan Prout.
    p. cm. – (The future of childhood series)
    Includes bibliographical references and index.
    1. Children and politics. 2. Children – Political activity. 3. Children – Attitudes.
  4. Social policy. I. Hallett, Christine. II. Prout, Alan. III. Series.

HQ784.P5H36 2003
306′.083–dc21   2002044533

ISBN 0–415–27642–X (pbk)
ISBN 0–415–27641–1 (hbk)

Contents

List of illustrations

Figures

Tables

Notes on contributors

Elisabeth Backe-Hansen is Senior Researcher at Norwegian Social Research and is responsible for a Strategic Institute Programme within childhood research (2002–2006). Her present research concerns children's participation in difficult and everyday decision situations. Her former research has been about children and young people's social competence, both in a Norwegian and a Nordic context, and decision-making processes in child welfare. She has important publications within the areas of foster care, decision-making in child welfare, outcomes for young children who are placed outside their homes, children and young people's living conditions and social competence, and methodology and ethics within the field of childhood research.

Jonathan Bradshaw is Professor of Social Policy at the University of York, England and Associate Director of the Social Policy Research Unit. His research interests include poverty, social security and living standards, comparative social policy and family change. He has recently completed *The Well-being of Children in the United Kingdom* (London: Save the Children, 2002), and, with N. Finch, *A Comparison of Child Benefit Packages in 22 Countries* (HM Treasury/DWP, 2002). He is Director (Hon.) of the Family Budget Unit and represents the UK on COST Action 19: Child Welfare. More information can be found at http://www-users.york.ac.uk/~jrb1/

Doris Bühler-Niederberger is Professor in Sociology at the University of Wuppertal, Germany. Several of her recent research projects have concerned childhood as a domain of professional, moral and political interest and images of childhood and children in public and professional debates. Her teaching and research interests are mainly focused on the sociology of private life and on private strategies of production and reproduction of social status and social order.

Judy Cashmore has a Ph.D. in developmental psychology and is an Associate Professor at the University of Sydney, Australia. She has conducted a range of research projects related to children's involvement in legal proceedings and processes concerned with their care and protection, and their participation and perception of these processes. She is currently working on a research project with colleagues in law and psychology, including Patrick Parkinson at the University of Sydney, on children's involvement in family law matters.

Mairian Corker currently holds a visiting Senior Research Fellowship at King's College London, England working at the intersection of disability studies and discourse studies. Her books include *Deaf Transitions* (London: Jessica Kingsley, 1996), *Deaf and Disabled* or *Deafness Disabled* (Maidenhead: Open University Press, 1998), *Disability/Postmodernity*, co-edited with Tom Shakespeare (London: Continuum, 2002), and the forthcoming *Disabling Language: Analyzing Disability as Power and Social Practice* (London: Routledge, 2003). She is an executive editor of the leading disability studies journal *Disability and Society*.

Gary Craig is Professor of Social Justice at the University of Hull, England where he manages a wide range of research concerned with poverty, inequality, community development, local governance, the voluntary and community sectors, 'race' and ethnicity. He is President of the International Association for Community Development and worked in community development projects for many years before entering academic life in 1988. He is an Academician of the Academy of Learned Societies for the Social Sciences.

John Davis is Senior Lecturer in Childhood Studies and Disability Studies at the University of Northumbria, England. He has extensive experience of participatory research projects. As a research fellow at the University of Edinburgh, he contributed to projects on the ESRC Health Variations Programme and the ESRC Children 5–16 Programme. As a research consultant he has specialised in the area of social inclusion, carrying out projects for Alder Hey Hospital, Barnardo's North East, Liverpool Bureau for Children and Young People and Newbattle Cluster New Community School Midlothian. He is the author of a number of publications on disability and childhood, including journal articles in *Disability and Society*, *Children and Society* and the *International Journal of Children's Rights*.

Pam Foley lectures at the School of Health and Social Welfare at the Open University, England. She writes and researches on the social and political context of maternal and child health practices and systems and is co-editor *of Children in Society, Contemporary Theory, Policy and Practice* (Basingstoke: Palgrave, 2001).

Gill Hague is the joint co-ordinator of, and Senior Research Fellow in, the Domestic Violence Research Group of the School for Policy

Studies at the University of Bristol, England. She holds professional qualifications in social work and in pre-school education, and a doctorate in social policy. She has written and researched widely on violence against women and, with Ellen Malos, is a recognised authority on multi-agency work and domestic violence. Her publications include the popular overview book with Ellen Malos, *Domestic Violence: Action for Change* (2nd edition, 1998, Cheltenham: New Clarion Press). She has also written widely on the views and voices of abused women, children's issues, historical perspectives, international responses, and housing issues, all in specific relation to domestic violence.

Christine Hallett is Senior Deputy Principal at the University of Stirling, Scotland. She is also Professor of Social Policy and has researched and published extensively. Her particular research interests are in child protection, care and justice for children and young people, and gender and social policy. She is a Fellow of the Royal Society of Edinburgh.

Umme Farvah Imam is Head of Community and Youth Work Studies at the University of Durham, England. She specialises in issues of race and gender, for example the impact of abuse in the lives of south Asian children and young people, particularly young women. Born and educated in India, she worked in Roshni, Asian Women's Association, and co-founded Panah, the black women's refuge, both in Newcastle upon Tyne, prior to commencing her academic career. Her publications include 'Asian children and domestic violence' in A. Mullender and R. Morley (eds) *Children Living with Domestic Violence* (London: Whiting and Birch, 1994) and 'Black workers as mediators and interpreters' in S. Banks (ed.) *Ethical Issues in Youth Work* (London: Routledge, 1999).

Liz Kelly is Professor of Sexualised Violence and Director of the Child and Woman Abuse Studies Unit at London Metropolitan University, England. For almost thirty years, she has combined activism and campaigning with writing and research. After her ground-breaking study of women's experiences of male violence (*Surviving Sexual Violence*, Cambridge: Polity Press, 1988), she jointly undertook the key British work on the prevalence of sexual abuse in childhood. Her theorising has continually broached new territory, including the connections between woman abuse and child abuse, abuse in lesbian relationships, trafficking in women, the public focus on the term 'paedophile', and the issues surrounding 'victim' and 'survivor' status in long-term core identities. She chaired the Council of Europe expert group on violence against women and, in 2000, was awarded the CBE for services combating violence against women and children.

Ellen Malos is the joint co-ordinator of, and Senior Lecturer in, the Domestic Violence Research Group of the School for Policy Studies at the University of Bristol, England. Her work spans interests in childcare and in domestic violence and gender studies. Funded work has resulted in research reports, conference papers, chapters and articles on custodianship, adoption, domestic violence and housing, and multi-agency work. An edited book, *The Politics of Housework* (1980) was revised in 1995 for New Clarion Press, Cheltenham, and she co-authored the popular overview book with Gill Hague, *Domestic Violence: Action for Change* (2nd edition, 1998, Cheltenham: New Clarion Press). Currently, she is co-ordinating a four-university collaborative evaluation of the domestic violence multi-service interventions in the Home Office Crime Reduction Programme.

Audrey Mullender is Professor of Social Work at the University of Warwick, England where she chairs the Faculty of Social Studies and directs the Centre for the Study of Safety and Well-being (SWELL). She has over twenty years' experience of social work teaching and research, prior to which her background was in the statutory social services. Over a hundred publications include: *Children Living with Domestic Violence: Putting Men's Abuse of Women on the Child Care Agenda* (edited jointly with Rebecca Morley and published in 1994 by Whiting and Birch) and *Rethinking Domestic Violence: The Social Work and Probation Response* (London: Routledge). She is a member of the Academy of Learned Societies for the Social Sciences.

Cathy Murray is Professor and Assistant Director of the Institute of Child Care Research at Queen's University, Belfast, Northern Ireland. She has researched extensively in the area of child welfare and juvenile justice, including a three-year Scottish Executive funded study of the Scottish Children's Hearings system and 'Young People Negotiating Pathways to Welfare', as part of the ESRC's Children 5–16 programme. She is currently working on children's resistance and early desistance from crime, exploring peer-led focus groups as a method.

Nigel Parton is Professor in Child Care and Director of the Centre of Applied Childhood Studies at the University of Huddersfield, England. Over the last twenty years he has written a wide range of books, chapters and articles on the broad themes of child welfare policy and practice. He is also co-editor of the journal *Children and Society*, which is published by John Wiley in association with the National Children's Bureau.

Alan Prout is Professor of Sociology at the University of Stirling, Scotland. He was Director of the ESRC Children 5–16 Research Programme and is series editor for *The Future of Childhood*, the book series of which this volume is a part. He is co-editor of *Constructing and Reconstructing Childhood* (London: Falmer Press, 1997) and co-author of *Theorising Childhood* (Cambridge: Polity Press, 1998).

Samantha Punch is a lecturer in sociology in the Department of Applied Social Science at Stirling University, Scotland. Her research interests are in the area of the sociology of childhood and the sociology of development, looking in particular at children's work, young people's problems and household livelihoods. She has undertaken ethnographic fieldwork on rural childhoods in Bolivia and participatory research in India on household coping strategies. Her current research is on children's experiences of sibling relationships in the UK.

Moira Rayner, LLB (Hons) MA (Public Policy), is a human rights and social policy advocate and a barrister, who was the first Director of the Office of Children's Rights Commissioner for London (2000–2001) which modelled effective children's participation in the management of the Office itself and in government decision-making, as well as helping to write the first Children's Strategy for the Mayor of the Greater London Authority. She was the Chairman of the Law Reform Commission in Western Australia, and the Commissioner for Equal Opportunity for Victoria, Australia, and a Hearings Commissioner of the Australian Human Rights and Equal Opportunity Commission. She helped establish and chaired the National Children's and Youth Law Centre in Sydney for the first seven years. She has written widely on children's rights and legal advocacy and her books include *The Women's Power Handbook* (Victoria: Penguin Books Australia), with Joan Kirner (first woman Premier of Victoria); *Resilient Children and Young People*, with Meg Montague, and *Rooting Democracy: Growing the Society We Want* (Saint Leonards: Allen and Unwin), with Jenny Lee. She is completing *The A–Z of Children's Rights* for Amnesty UK. She is presently the Commissioner for Equal Opportunity (a human rights, not sex discrimination, post) in Western Australia.

Linda Regan is currently a senior research officer at the Child and Woman Abuse Studies Unit, London Metropolitan University, England where she has been based for over ten years. During that time, she has been involved in over thirty research and evaluation projects, has presented at numerous national and international conferences, and has delivered training to voluntary and statutory sector participants at home and overseas. She is a member of several advisory boards and a trustee of the Emma Humphreys Memorial Prize.

Helen Roberts is Professor of Child Health at City University, London where she leads the new Child Health Research and Policy Unit. Before that, she was head of R&D with Barnardo's. She currently works on evidence-based health and social care for children, the gap between what we know and what we do, and how we can consult with children more effectively, and work with what they tell us in policy and practice. Her most recent publication is an edited collection with Di McNeish and Tony Newman, *What Works for Children?* (Maidenhead: Open University Press, 2002).

Jeremy Roche is a lecturer in law in the School of Health and Social Welfare at the Open University, England. He writes and researches in the field of children's rights and the law and is co-editor of *Youth and Society* (1997) and *Children and Society* (2001). He is currently working on children, human rights and professional practice.

Mirja Satka is currently working as a professor of social work at the Department of Social Policy, University of Helsinki, Finland. Her doctorate in social policy was based on early welfare laws and early professional texts of social work. Her current research interests include the history of Finnish child welfare and old and new forms of knowledge production in social work. She is the author of *Making Social Citizenship. Conceptual Practices from the Finnish Poor Law to Professional Social Work* (Jyväskylä Sophi, revised edn 2002), a co-author of *Reconstructing Social Work Research. Finnish Methodological Adaptations* (Jyväskylä Sophi, 1999), and the author of numerous articles on social work history, research and education.

Hannele Sauli, Master of Political Sciences, has been acting as a senior researcher in Statistics Finland since 1975. She has mainly worked in developing, producing and reporting surveys and official statistics on general living conditions. She is also active in several national and international research projects on children's living conditions. Children's position in the socio-economic structure of the society in terms of income, consumption, education and service structure has been her main interest. *Children in Finland* (Statistics Finland: Population 2001: 9) is her latest publication (co-authored).

Tom Shakespeare is Director of Outreach at the Policy, Ethics and Life Sciences Research Institute at the University of Newcastle, England. Trained as a sociologist at Cambridge, he now works on bioethics and science engagement, with particular reference to the new genetics. His major research has been in the field of disability studies; he has published six books and many academic papers. He was principal investigator for the ESRC Life as a Disabled Child Project (1996–8) while based at the University of Leeds Centre for Disability Research.

Stanley Tucker is a senior lecturer in the School of Health and Social Welfare at the Open University, England. He has researched and written extensively in the area of children, young people and social policy. He has recently undertaken major research into children and young people's social exclusion and the support services available to young carers and those young people suffering from ME in the community. He is co-editor, with Jeremy Roche, of *Youth in Society*, and with Pam Foley and Jeremy Roche of *Children in Society*.

Nick Watson is a lecturer in the Sociology of Health and Illness, Department of Nursing Studies, University of Edinburgh, Scotland. He has a wide range of experience in researching disability and health promotion and of working with children, both as an academic and professional in the field. He is active in the disabled people's movement and was until recently convenor of Access-Ability Lothian, a leading Scottish organisation of disabled people.

Acknowledgements

The editors would like to thank the contributors for their work in preparing the individual chapters and Jackie O'Brien for her tremendous help in preparing the manuscript. Several of the contributing chapters are based on projects within the Economic and Social Research Council's Children 5–16 Research Programme and we would like to thank the Council for its support of this work.

Introduction

Alan Prout and Christine Hallett

The central concern of this volume is the emergence of 'children's voice' and the implications of this for social policy. Taken together the contributing chapters provide the fresh perspectives on social policy that hearing the voice(s) of children promises to bring about. The volume is divided into four main themes: hearing children's voices, discourses of childhood, children and services, and resources for children.

Before outlining the contribution that the different chapters make to these themes, we wish briefly to set out the orientation of this book. In essence we wish to give critical encouragement to the gathering movement for children's participation. Children's voice should, we believe, be heard much more strongly in the process of policy formation at all levels. We recognise that this is not uncontentious. Although the last twenty years have seen growing support for the idea of children as social participants in their own right, this has not been without opposition. As the chapters of Part II of this volume show, historically social policy has not thought of children as persons with a voice. Rather they have been seen as objects of concern. Contemporary societies are perhaps more ambiguous on this point, with different visions of childhood coming into play, sometimes overlapping and sometimes conflicting with each other. Nevertheless, the idea of children's voice, although more accepted, remains a contested one. One critical position is opposed to the very idea of children's rights, including their participation rights. Such a position may be argued for on a variety of grounds. It may be suggested, for example, that children's rights undermine those of parents or that they encode a culturally specific, 'northern' notion of childhood that is inappropriate to the circumstances of many children (see, for example, Pupavac 1998, 2001).

Whilst such arguments give rise to fundamental debate about the meaning of children's rights, we do not intend, in this volume, to enter into this debate or to mount a defence of the idea of children's participation. Others have set out the case for children's participation rights (see for example, Archard 1993; Franklin 2001) and, in any case, these issues continue to be debated in forums such as the *International Journal of*

Children's Rights. Rather, we take the growth in children's participation as a positive social trend. This, however, does not mean that it cannot benefit from critical analysis. The contributors to this volume, although sympathetic to the idea of children's participation, make many critical points about the current attempts to put it into practice. Often, for example, claims to children's participation are strong on rhetoric but weak in reality. As Kjorholt (2002) has recently shown in the case of Norway, local initiatives involving children's participation are often marked by the mixed motives of the adults involved and by the lack of sustained and lasting change in institutional practice. Children's participation is not necessarily easy to accomplish and many pitfalls await those who attempt it.

Hearing children's voices

In fact many of the contributors to the first section of this book document such problems, as well as recording successes. The main theme of this section is why and how children's voices need to be taken into account during the shaping of policy. It argues that more attention should be paid to fostering children's active participation in policy and practice at all levels. Contributors explore both the rationale for this claim and describe a range of different ways in which children's voices might become more influential in shaping policy. They critically but constructively examine both failures and successes of attempts to do so and draw on international comparisons.

Prout opens this section of the volume with a discussion of contemporary patterns of social change and their implications for childhood. He suggests that public discourse about children has been caught between two poles: children as in danger and children as dangerous. These are increasingly inadequate and policy discussions require new ways of thinking about childhood that focus on the possibility of children's citizenship. Contemporary childhood, he argues, is caught up and being transformed by the social transformations wrought by late modernity. He identifies five areas of childhood change: that children are a declining proportion of the population in industrialized countries; that children's living circumstances are becoming more diverse; that childhood is increasingly produced through cross-national flows of people, things, values and images that constitute children as active agents in a complex process of multiple socialization; increasing efforts on the part of government to control and regulate childhood; and, as part of wider trends towards individualization, the emergence of children's rights and voice. These changes both confirm the importance of welfare policy for children and suggest ways in which hearing children's voice is critical to creating institutions (whether statutory, voluntary, private or in the informal sector of family and community) that are responsive and flexible in their work for children.

Roberts also takes up these issues, pointing to the pressures towards greater children's participation felt by UK policy-makers, in both governmental and non-governmental organizations, and discussing a number of examples of the process in practice. Whilst positive about these, she points to a number of emerging issues and problems. Central to these is the gap between developing new methods and approaches to children's participation and 'doing something meaningful' with the results of it. Participation, she argues, is not necessarily easy or straightforward. Young people need induction, support and training. The approach of adults and children may not be the same and this must be acknowledged by developing new methods of consultation. In addition, she suggests, attempts at children's participation need long-term follow-up and evaluation to identify what works best.

A number of these points are echoed in Craig's review of the international experience of projects using a community development approach. He argues that this can be an appropriate and effective method for fostering the participation of children. In particular, the evidence from community development projects suggests that children's voice needs to be consciously articulated. It cannot be assumed that social change deriving from adult perspectives will lead to an automatic 'trickle down' of benefits to children. Whilst drawing attention to the need for age-appropriate methods and goals, Craig insists that the empowerment of children and young people should be a central objective. This may lead to a tension between general community development work and that focused specifically on children. Like Roberts, however, he suggests that more systematic evaluation is required from which to develop new initiatives. He identifies the sustainability of participation as a crucial issue.

In her chapter on the setting up of a model Children's Rights Commissioner for London, Rayner draws a series of highly practical lessons for children's participation. The principle of children's participation should be central and established from the start, even before the actual work begins. Such work needs a clear framework of values that should be developed with the children involved. The process must be given a realistic time-frame and resources, and everything within it should be made 'child-friendly'. Underlying these lessons is the commitment to non-authoritarian ways of working which respect children as participants and aim at fostering their sense of ownership.

Discourses of childhood

The second section of the volume focuses on the policy context within which children's participation might arise. It examines how assumptions about, and socially available models of, childhood interact with social policy. Whilst the first section shows the importance of challenging and rethinking conventional ideas about children, this section highlights how in both historical and contemporary societies social policy has tended to see children through notions of dependence, vulnerability, malleability and investment in the future.

Three different examples are given – from Finland, Germany and the UK. Writing from a Finnish perspective, Satka traces discourses of childhood as they have been expressed in the evolution of Finnish welfarism. She shows how shifting ideas about children have been embedded in key historical issues of twentieth-century Finland and how they shaped social policy towards young people. In particular the legacy of civil war emphasized the danger of children 'growing up deviant' and led to the surveillance of children and families. In the aftermath of the Second World War there was a shift to seeing children as a strategic target of social investment, based on the provision of universal social benefits. Alongside this ran the idea of children's development as dependent on the permanent presence of their mother and resistance to the idea of day care.

Bühler-Niederberger suggests both changes and continuities in German social policy towards children through the twentieth century. On the one hand, the explicitly racist intentions of family policy during the Nazi period have been suppressed in the post-war period. On the other hand, policy continues to be based on a male breadwinner model that discourages women from participation in the labour market. This second feature is expressed through a variety of tax and fiscal policies, such as child benefits. In part this is legitimized by the need to ensure the transmission of cultural values and by the assumption that unless socialized within the family children will grow up into crime and political extremism. Central to this process is the power of an ideological figure, 'the needy child'. Bühler-Niederberger shows how this figure is deployed by (almost) all sides of contemporary German political debate. Acceptance of the needs of children as natural is the token of entry into such debates. Alternative conceptualizations of children are effectively excluded from this discussion.

These themes find some echo in Foley and her colleagues' exploration of UK policy. They point to the underlying assumption that children are both vulnerable (and therefore in need of protection) but also liable to become unruly and threatening (and therefore in need of control). Some services, such as education and health, have become a routine part of the obligation of governments to children, whilst others, such as criminal justice, tend to focus on particular communities and families, bringing them into a network of surveillance and regulation. However, Foley *et al.* also explore some of the ambiguities of UK policy towards children. They argue that although government has been cautious about encroaching on the 'rights of the family', new conceptions of children as actors and of children's rights have impacted upon social policy, albeit in a partial and uneven manner. Although 'the voice of children' is a principle to be heard in some spheres and levels of policy (and at times is even put into practice) the overall development of policy tends in other directions: children's dependency on the family is extended and overridden by a concern for parental rights; and some children are demonized and subject to intensified surveillance and regulation.

Children and services

In the third section of this volume contributors focus upon children as service users and co-producers of their own welfare. If the chapters in the second section illustrate the gap between conventional policy thinking and ideas of children as social actors and participants, then the chapters of this section point to both the need and the opportunities for children's voices to be heard. They discuss children's experiences in these spheres, drawing particularly on studies which have sought to articulate children's views of different forms of social welfare provision and which document their active role in the processes of welfare.

This section starts, appropriately, with research about how children themselves deal with problems and issues that arise in their lives. Based on interview and other data gathered directly from children, Hallett, Murray and Punch illuminate children's coping and help-seeking behaviour, examining, *inter alia*, the role of mothers, fathers, teachers, agencies, and friends. The research shows how a variety of contextual and contingent factors make the process of help-seeking a complex one. It reveals a number of ways in which agencies might think about their image with young people, as well as the availability and accessibility of their services. It also suggests that a majority of young people anticipated that a problem could be made worse when taken to an adult, underlining the importance of trust, confidentiality and respect for the young people's experiences and views.

Mullender and colleagues gathered the views of children about domestic violence, including those who had experienced it personally. Children are shown to be active and strategic in their attempts to cope with and minimize violence and its effects. Their relationship with their mother is a central and stable feature of their often turbulent lives, although siblings, friends and peers also play an important role in finding ways of coping. Agencies and workers, however, are often seen as unwilling to listen seriously to them and to enrol them into finding solutions. Nevertheless, Mullender and her colleagues are able to point to a number of examples of working practice that do make listening to children an important part of the service offered and they urge that these become better known and more widespread.

Cashmore discusses children's participation in family courts. Whilst noting the need for much more research, she suggests that the available evidence shows that many children want to know what is going on and want to be consulted about the arrangements for themselves in the wake of divorce. At the same time it is clear that current practice often falls short of this. Reviewing various mechanisms for listening to children, she suggests that the central problem is the lack of feedback mechanisms during which adult assumptions about what children want and decisions that affect them can be checked by reference to children themselves. In this way courts could become more sensitive to and conscious of the complex and ambiguous circumstances of each child's life.

These themes of complexity and ambiguity are also reflected in Backe-Hansen's research on judgements about children's competence and problem behaviour. She shows that by treating these as relational phenomena they can only be understood within a social context and through an appreciation of the perspective of the person (children themselves, parents, teachers and peers) making the judgement. By collecting data from these different actors over time, Backe-Hansen reveals important similarities and differences in how children's competence and problem behaviours are seen by different actors in different contexts. Teachers and parents differ, for example, in their judgement about which children were showing problem behaviour – agreeing in only 16 per cent of cases. Such findings indicate the need for caution in accepting any one actor's assessment of competence and problems and suggest the need to listen to multiple voices, including those of children themselves. They also underline that children's capacities and behaviour (just like adults?) are a product of the social and interactional settings of their lives.

Sensitivity to individual circumstances is also important in Davis and his colleagues' discussion of how the voices of disabled children might be better heard in policy and practice. In part their discussion addresses the politics of disability, contrasting the social to the medical model of disability. They suggest that despite its advantages, the social model is also deficient in the attention that it gives to disabled children as actors. They argue that it encourages their complex and particular experiences to be submerged under stereotypical notions of structural exclusion, reduces their problems to ones that can be solved technically, and consequently fails to listen to their varied and diverse voices. Whilst the authors of this chapter found many examples of bad practice, they also celebrate the creativity of many practitioners who, overcoming difficult working environments, develop practices based on sensitivity to the diversity and individuality of disabled children and respect for their views.

Resources for children

The final theme of this volume concerns what is one of the most important reasons for hearing children's voice: that is, making children's interests visible in the social and political process of directing and garnering resources for children. The contributions of Bradshaw and Sauli both focus on the ways in which children's interests are revealed by and encoded in statistical techniques. Their work suggests that, whilst not all methodological problems are solved by it, indicators of poverty, well-being and the intra-familial distribution of resources all benefit from the effort to get as close as possible to the subjective experience and everyday lives of children (as well as other actors).

Bradshaw tackles the issue of widening inequality between children directly in a review of the international evidence about trends in child poverty. Looking at childhood at the 'societal level' he shows that over the last twenty years there have been marked differences between countries. In some countries (notably the UK) levels of child poverty rose dramatically, whilst in others (most of Europe, especially the Nordic countries) they did not. Instead, various forms of welfare state protected expenditure and income going to children. Bradshaw uses this background to discuss the relationship between poverty and children's health and well-being. There is an urgent need, he argues, to develop an internationally agreed set of indicators that can be used to compare children's health and well-being across countries. He points to two particularly interesting lines of development. The first derives from Richard Wilkinson's (Wilkinson, 1996) argument that health is primarily related not to absolute but to relative poverty and is mediated by socially constituted stress. The second is a suggestion arising from a thirty-country WHO study (Currie, 2001) that children and young people's *own* rating of their mental health is correlated with poverty and inequality.

Sauli looks at children's income from the perspective of the family. She approaches this through a discussion of 'equivalence scales' in determining the standard of living of families. Such scales attempt to estimate the consumption needs of differently constituted families by attaching a different weight to the cost of additional members. Sauli examines the different ways in which statistical studies of children's living standards determine the equivalence scales that they use and shows how these can affect the findings of such studies. Using new Finnish empirical data she then goes on to show that no one equivalence scale can capture the complexity of consumption patterns of real families. These are very diverse and change over the life course of their members. In particular, this new evidence shows that the ways in which resources are distributed between generations change according to the configuration of the family members. Sauli concludes by cautioning against the use of equivalence scales, suggesting that what is an imperfect statistical device, remote from the daily practice of families, becomes incorporated as a normative assumption in social policy and law.

Conclusion

The problems of building participation are, it should be remembered, not unique to children. Many of the same issues also arise in relation to adults. These are, as Birchall and Simmons (2002) point out, endemic in efforts to enrol users in the shaping of public services (such as housing and health care). Successful participation depends, they argue, on bringing together a number of factors (including the presence of individuals who are motivated to participate), clear (collective and individual) benefits to be gained from it, and the resources required to support and sustain it. The idea that children's voices should be represented in policy-making, at whatever level, is a relatively new one. It is therefore not a surprise that putting it into practice is difficult. Although there are many obstacles to be overcome, the contributors to this volume show that children's participation is possible, is needed to improve services, and is wanted by many children. That it is able to bring about beneficial changes in social policy and practice will only be demonstrated by many more attempts to put it into practice. Nevertheless, as many contributors to this volume have shown, there are already strong indications that this will be so. The next step, therefore, is to expand the range and opportunities for the successful participation of children, whilst at the same time carefully monitoring and evaluating the results.

References

Archard, D. (1993) *Children: Rights and Childhood*, London: Routledge.

Birchall, R.J. and Simmons, R.A. (2002) 'A Theoretical Model of What Motivates Public Service Users to Participate', Final Report to the ESRC Democracy and Participation Research Programme, Stirling: Stirling University.

Currie, C. (2001) 'Socio-economic Circumstances Among School Age Children in Europe and North America', in K. Vleminckx and T. Smeeding (eds) *Child Well-being, Child Poverty and Child Policy*, Bristol: Policy Press.

Franklin, B. (ed.) (2001) *The New Handbook of Children's Rights: Comparative Policy and Practice*, London: Routledge.

Kjorholt, A. (2002) 'Small is Powerful: Discourses on "children and participation" in Norway', *Childhood*, 9, 1: 63–82.

Pupavac, V. (1998) 'The Infantalisation of the South and the UN Convention on the Rights of the Child', in H.J. Steiner and P. Alston (eds) *International Human Rights in Context – Law, Politics and Morals*, New York: Oxford University Press.

Pupavac, V. (2001) 'Misanthropy without Borders: The International Children's Rights Regime', *Disasters*, 25, 2: 95–112.

Wilkinson, R. (1996) *Unhealthy Societies: The Applications of Affluence*, London: Routledge.

Part I

Hearing children's voices

1 Participation, policy and the changing conditions of childhood

Alan Prout

Introduction

During the last two decades many societies have seen an accelerating movement towards ideas about children's participation and voice. Enshrined in Article 12 of the UN Convention on the Rights of the Child, these notions have gathered both general support and efforts at practical implementation. Indeed they have become part of the rhetorical orthodoxy, even among those such as the current English government who have not otherwise been notably enthusiastic proponents of children's rights. For example, the Children and Young People's Unit, recently established to develop a 'joined up policy' in this area, states that:

> We want to hear the voices of young people, influencing and shaping local services; contributing to their local communities; feeling heard; feeling valued; being treated as responsible citizens.
>
> (Children and Young People's Unit, 2000: 27)

In this chapter I will discuss some of the sociological background to the emergence of these phenomena. My central theme is that general social changes in the last twenty-five years have shifted the conditions and experiences of childhood, destabilising ideas of what it is and what it should be.[1] These shifts are complex, often contradictory, and not necessarily beneficial for children. However, I suggest that these changes, and the destabilisation that they have provoked, provide an essential context for understanding the emergence of children's voice and participation that is the focus of many chapters in this book.

The century of the child

In a volume first published in 1900 the Swedish social reformer Ellen Key argued that the twentieth century ought to become 'the century of the child' (Key, [1900] 1909). In the decades that followed its publication this phrase came to stand for the strategic identification of children as a point of intervention in and investment for the future. Through the activities of both the state and civil society, childhood was turned into a project. In part this was concerned with protection and provision for children – very great resources were expended on all manner of services that have improved children's lives and well-being. At the same time, however, these actions also rendered children as objects of knowledge brought into the adult gaze, to be surveilled, studied and understood. In consequence, countless books and papers have been written about how children develop and how they can be shaped as future citizens and workers, such that childhood has become, as Nicholas Rose has famously put it:

> the most intensively governed sector of personal existence. In different ways, at different times, and by many different routes varying from one section of society to another, the health, welfare, and rearing of children have been linked in thought and practice to the destiny of the nation and the responsibilities of the state.
>
> (Rose 1989: 121)

And yet a century later the optimism about childhood and society that animated reformers such as Key is less pervasive and seems less convincing. On the contrary, the prevailing cultural mood about childhood in European and North American societies seems to be one that is at best puzzled and anxious, and at worst hostile. Why, many seem to ask, after all this effort and expenditure, does childhood seem to escape our purpose and intentions?

In this chapter I will explore one (partial) answer to this question. It concerns the adequacy of the socially available representations of childhood (see also Hendrick, 1997: ch. 4; Holland, 1992). Public discussion, I suggest, seems to struggle with an ambiguity about childhood, caught between two different but equally problematic images of childhood: children in danger and children as dangerous (see also Chapters 5, 6 and 7 of this volume). The first of these, children in danger, pictures childhood through ideas of dependence, vulnerability and idealised innocence. Its positive side is that it draws attention to important social problems like neglect, poverty and safety in public spaces but it often turns into a sentimentalised version of childhood that is saturated with nostalgia for an imagined past. Paradoxically it demands an ever more watchful protection and control over children as activities once routinely open to them, like playing together in the street, are seen as increasingly risky. Fuelled by deeply tragic but thankfully rare events, such as child murder and abduction, media exaggeration of the risks children experience plays an important part in raising levels of concern. As parents become ever more anxious about children's safety in public space, there is a proliferation of special locations that concentrate groups of children together so that their activities can take place under more or less constant adult surveillance and supervision (James *et al.*, 1998; McKendrick *et al.*, 2000; Furedi, 1997). From this point of view the space of childhood becomes narrower, more specialised and more under the adult gaze.

The second image, children as dangerous, is concerned with contemporary children as a threat to themselves, to others and to society at large. In it children are identified as personifying the supposed ills of contemporary society, such as crime, moral decay, consumerism and economic failure. Again sensationalist journalism seems ever ready to over-interpret statistically rare events, such as violent crime by children, with a shrillness that sometimes descends into demonisation (see Jenks, 1996: ch. 5; Davis and Bourhill, 1997). This too gives rise to an increasingly instrumental attempt to extend control *over* children. The persistence, if not the genesis, of social problems is sought in the upbringing of children and, as a result, 'early intervention' and 'prevention' policies loom large. But prevention, as the political philosopher Richard Freeman argues, is caught in an accelerating recursive cycle (Freeman, 1999). As societies become more complex, prevention becomes more difficult to engineer; but the failure of such interventions summons up merely a renewed commitment to further prevention. The cycle is one in which children, as a primary target of prevention, seem caught in a system that can respond to its own failure only by ratcheting up control.

Throughout the twentieth century, then, social concerns about childhood have been caught between ideas of children as in danger and notions of children as dangerous. Public policy in particular has had a tendency to zigzag back and forth between them, as the exponents of one or other end of the divide gain a temporary upper hand. I contend, however, that neither of these representations of childhood is adequate to understanding the position of children in contemporary society. What is required is a more adequate way of representing childhood. The seed of this, I suggest, is found in the idea of children as social persons, a notion that has also gained increasing currency, especially towards the end of the twentieth century. It is expressed, for example, through Article 12 of the UN Convention on the Rights of the Child. In many countries it is being turned into a practical reality through local and national projects that have begun to devise effective means for consulting children and involving them in decision-making (see for example, Davie *et al.*, 1996; Flekkoy and Kaufman, 1997; Franklin, 1995; Freeman *et al.*, 1999; John, 1996; Lansdown, 1995; Hart, 1992).

At the core of this movement is a gradual rethinking of ways of representing children, where 'representation' can be understood in a double sense. In its cultural sense representation refers to the socially available images and concepts through which children are thought about (and think of themselves). However, representation also points to the role of children in governance, suggesting that children might be involved in processes of decision-making and policy formation. I will suggest below that, by linking the cultural and the governance notions of childhood representation, a way out of the slot-rattling impasse between the image of children as in danger and children as dangerous might be found.

The changing conditions of childhood

Before doing that, however, I want to consider how, during the last quarter of the twentieth century, the conditions of childhood and the experience of children in Europe and North America have changed in significant ways. There is, of course, considerable variation between countries. They have, for example, different welfare state regimes, with quite distinct forms for the relationship between families, markets and the state, different conceptions of childhood and different patterns of intra-familial relations (Dahlberg *et al.*, 1999; Pringle, 1998). Whilst not ignoring these differences, five important general trends that can be seen more or less across Europe and North America can be identified.

First, there has been a general decline in the birth rate, an increase in life expectancy and an ageing population. For example, the countries of the European Union now have fertility rates below the threshold of generational replacement. As a result it has been projected that in Europe by 2025 the numbers in the 0–19 age group will fall by over 10 per cent (European Commission, 1996). It is as yet unclear what the implications of this are for children. However, some social policy analysts have argued that we have seen, and will see a further, redistribution of social resources away from children towards older people. This raises important issues about how justice in the distribution of resources between the generations can be achieved and maintained (Thompson, 1989; Sgritta, 1994: 361). These are linked to questions about how children's voice will be heard in decisions and debates about resource distribution.

Second, there is evidence of an increased differentiation of the life circumstances of children. One well-known source of this is family change. Most industrialised countries have seen a steady demographic decline in the nuclear family. This itself is the product of a number of linked trends in population and household formation. These are: a decline in the number of marriages and a rise in the number of divorces; an increase in cohabitation, especially in the northern European countries; and a diversification in family types, including the growth in stepfamilies and lone parent families (Ruxton, 1996).

There are differences between countries but the overall trend and general direction is the same. In the UK, for example, the number of nuclear families has fallen from 38 per cent of all households at the start of the 1960s to 25 per cent by the mid-1990s. Although children living in two-parent households are still the majority, the proportion living in single-parent households has doubled, to about 20 per cent, over the last thirty years (Clarke, 1996; Office for National Statistics, 1999).

Although all this has taken place against a background of generally rising living standards, there is evidence for an increasing differentiation between the children who share most in growing affluence and those who have benefited least. A recent study based on OECD data asked whether income distribution between children is becoming more un-equal. It appears that it is. Of the seventeen countries studied twelve showed growing income inequality between children (Oxley *et al.*, 2001: 378). International comparison of trends in child poverty presents a complex picture and is subject to many methodological difficulties. Nevertheless, a recent analysis of Luxemburg Income Study data sug-gests that during the last quarter of a century the proportion of children in families with less than 50 per cent of median income rose in eleven of the twenty countries studied. These included Australia, Belgium, Germany, Italy, the Netherlands, the UK and the USA (Bradshaw, 2000: 240).

This leads me to a third trend. For, although national comparisons remain useful and revealing, they also remind us that the twentieth-century notion of society as a distinct, geographically bounded entity is in decline. The nation-state as a unit has decreasing purchase on the emergent realities of the new century. 'Societies' thought of as 'national' units are less and less able to secure their increasingly porous bound-aries and more and more adopt a lower-level defensiveness that seeks to regulate and moderate the powerful new global flows of the people, information and products that penetrate and traverse them (Urry, 2000). These processes have implications for childhood. One aspect of this is well illustrated by the research on 'transnational childhoods' carried out by Thorne and her colleagues in California, raising questions about the variety and complexity of childhood in a rapidly changing and more mobile world (Orellana *et al.*, [1998] 2001). This research shows that children are moving backwards and forwards over national boundaries, forming and reforming, joining and separating from households. They have families (or are members of households) both in the USA and in another country (for example, Taiwan or the Philippines). Such flows create childhoods that are different from those often assumed by schools and other public services. These children are usually not those of the wealthy but of poor families using both kin and non-kin links within the USA as a route of social mobility. This is not a new phenomenon but it is one that seems to be increasing in scale, adding to the diversity of childhood in a given society.

However, there is another aspect of this situation that is sometimes overlooked. In addition to people, transnational mobilities also involve flows of products, information, values and images that most children routinely engage with in one way or another (see, for example, Buck-ingham, 2000). This flow of products, information, values and images has profound implications for socialisation. Contemporary social science has for some time recognised the increasing complexity of socialisation processes that occur when young children begin to spend a large part of their daily life away from the family – at school, in after-school clubs or in day care institutions. This gave rise to the idea of 'double socialisation'. The German educationalist Giesecke (1985), however, has suggested that we now also have to acknowledge that children, like adults, live in a pluralistic society. They are confronted by a range of competing, complementary and divergent values and perspectives from parents, school, the media, the consumer society and their peer relations. He suggests parents, teachers and other people with responsibility for the care of children have less power to control and steer these different factors as a whole. It becomes, therefore, important to understand children as individually and collectively trying to make coherence and sense of the world in which they live (Christensen and Prout, 2002).

The fourth trend concerns the ways in which the twentieth century has witnessed increased levels of institutional control over children. The introduction of compulsory schooling in many but not all countries and children's formal exclusion from paid work signalled a historical tendency towards children's increasing compartmentalisation in specifically designated, separate settings, supervised by professionals and structured according to age and ability. Nasman (1994) has called this process the institutionalisation of childhood. Throughout the twentieth century schooling has gradually been extended both 'upwards' (for example in incremental steps towards an older leaving age for compulsory schooling) and 'downwards' in the growing emphasis on pre-school education and nursery provision (Moss *et al.*, 2000). Even leisure time is often framed in this way for many children because activities such as sport or music increasingly take place within some kind of institutional setting. It can be seen in the provision of after-school and holiday clubs that organise and regulate children's activities under an adult gaze, channelling them into forms considered developmentally healthy and productive. Such phenomena have been noted across European societies. German sociologists, for example, have used the term 'domestication' to describe the progressive removal of children from the streets and other public spaces and their relocation in special, protected spaces. They use the term 'insularisation' to describe the decreased levels of children's autonomous mobility around cities and the creation of special 'islands' of childhood to and from which they are transported (Zeiher, 2001, 2002).

Within these institutions, but with significant variations according to national policy, it is possible to discern a tightening of the effort to regulate children and to shape more firmly the outcomes of their activities. Schooling is a good example of this. In the last decades of the twentieth century the rather instrumental schooling regimes of the 'Tiger economies' of South-East Asia were held up as the model for producing economic efficiency and were widely influential in changing educational systems in Europe. I have argued elsewhere that this phenomenon represents a refocusing of modernity's drive to control the future through children (Prout, 2000). This tightening of control over children derives from a declining faith in other mechanisms of economic control, combined with increasing competitive pressures from the world economy. The intensification of global competition and the intricate networking of national economies erode the state's capacity to control its own economic activity. In such circumstances, shaping children as the future labour force is seen as an increasingly important option. This, after all, is exactly what supply-side economics is about. As far as children are concerned it often leads to attempts to regulate and standardise what they learn and how they learn it.

Finally, and in (partial) contradiction to the last trend, we can see the emergence of the idea that children should have a voice in decision-making at all levels. This idea began to move from the margins of public debate only in the last two or three decades of the twentieth century. In part its emergence was to do with a more general shift in institutional practice that affected children and adults alike. Rapid social change has eroded and fragmented once taken-for-granted institutions and has led to a new sense of uncertainty and risk (Beck, 1992; Giddens, 1990, 1991). A widespread response to this has been the installation of techniques of reflexivity into institutional practice. Reflexivity, it is argued, is needed for the type of institutional responsiveness and flexibility demanded by the conditions of late modernity. The summoning up of the voice of a multitude of actors is the result. Political parties poll voters. Citizens are consulted through local and national panels. Consumers are plugged into the circuitry through which new products are devised, produced and marketed. Patients are asked to evaluate their treatment experiences. And, as one part of this, children are seen as having something valuable to tell the firms, service providers, courts, and so on.

This tendency towards children being given voice is underlined by another feature of late modernity: the trend towards *individualisation*. According to Beck (1998) this is a trend towards people coming to think of themselves as unique individuals with chosen rather than prescribed or standard identities. This requires not fewer but different sources of social interdependency because although such individuals are produced through collectivities (such as family, locality and class), they are not bound to them in traditional ways. It is important to understand that individualisation is the product of new *social* processes. A concatenation of factors, rather than a single cause, is said to be responsible for this shift. The emergence of consumption (especially leisure) as a source of identity, the pluralisation of family forms, the decline in the authority of expert knowledges, the distribution of norms about the value of democracy, and so on, all contribute to a process that has become self-propelling.

The concept of individualisation makes it possible to see the emergence of ideas about children as persons in their own right in a wider societal and historical context. Young people, Beck writes:

> no longer become individualized. They individualize themselves. The 'biographization' of youth means becoming active, struggling and designing one's own life.
>
> (Beck, 1998: 78)

At the same time these processes take place 'behind the backs' of social institutions, leaving them lagging behind or struggling to adapt. The widespread concern about the disengagement of young people from traditional forms of democratic participation (Wilkinson and Mulgan, 1995) and from schooling (OECD, 2001) are good examples of this.

Making sense of changing childhood

So far I have argued that the last twenty or thirty years have seen a number of social changes that have had an important impact on the conditions of childhood and the experience of children. The processes I have described have produced a growing disparity between conventional ways of representing children and the new realities of children's lives. Sociologically speaking, the emergence of new forms of childhood within late modernity requires revising what a new century of childhood may look like.

The modernist view was that childhood could be shaped and moulded through an effort of knowledge and will. This belief is embedded in a wider confidence in the power of rational understanding and the possibility of human control over nature and society. However, the *zeitgeist* at the turn of our new century is not that of the last. We live with the knowledge that modernity's project of rational control has limits. A new mood of uncertainty, risk (Beck, 1992) and ontological insecurity (Giddens, 1991) has replaced the more rigid notions of identity, authority and morality that characterised the earlier part of the twentieth century. Late modernity, as sociologists have termed this period, has seen the emergence of new patterns of family life, marriage and divorce, labour market participation, work and global economy. The mood is more cautious and reflexive about the status of knowledge, more aware of the complexity of nature and society, more alert to the unintended consequences of social actions and less sure of social institutions.

The importance of this is highlighted, for example, by John O'Neill in his book, *The Missing Child in Liberal Theory* (O'Neill, 1994). The market as a principle of social organisation will, he argues, always fail children. Its central mechanism, the contract, assumes the existence of independent and autonomous persons but has no account of how they come into being. What is required, he suggests, is a 'covenant' between the generations. This is expressed through social institutions that are committed to providing what he calls a 'standard' or 'civic' childhood. It would guarantee all children a decent level of economic, social and cultural resource. Such a view of childhood cannot be contained in social relations that are modelled on the market. Rather, it seems to require an appreciation of the network of relationships within which children, families and local communities are enmeshed and a channelling of the economic, social and cultural capital necessary to children's growth and well-being through multiple routes (see also Jack and Jordan, 1999; Smith, 1999).

Continuing high, and in some countries even increasing, levels of child poverty make this an urgent issue. So too does the tendency, outlined earlier, towards greater inequality between children. The attempt to limit such disparities in resource distribution between children rests on an acknowledgement of a covenant between society and children that is additional to the bond between parents and the child. From this point of view, O'Neill's restatement of the importance of the welfare state for children seems to me to be of fundamental importance. But in late-modern societies there are at least three problems with the notion of a civic childhood that require its modification. The first flows from the increasingly diverse conditions of children's lives and the processes of individualisation to which they, like adults, are subject. In these circumstances we would expect to find the idea of a standardised childhood less easy to accomplish. The implementation of civic childhood, therefore, faces the problem of translating a general commitment to provide children with a decent and fair share of resources into the delivery of public goods and services in ways that recognise children's increasingly diverse and complex life circumstances. In this situation treating children the *same* may have to mean *different*. This point does not necessarily index an opposition to universal services and benefits but it does require a critical reflection on the way resources are made available and flexibility in their content. It seems unlikely that the provision of a standard childhood to differentiated children will be accomplished by the routine methods of welfarism. Rather, the demand is for responsive institutions that engage in a creative dialogue with their users.

The second flows from the demographic trends outlined earlier. Children are a declining proportion of the population and the proportion of households including children is also declining (European Commission, 1996). This, combined with the emergence of political lobbies for the older generation, must provoke questions about who is to speak for children in decisions about resource allocation and how inter-generational distributive justice is to be achieved and maintained. From this point of view public institutions that give political representation to children's interests and needs are increasingly necessary.

Attempts to build procedures for children's voice and their participation in decision-making speak directly to these questions of institutional flexibility, responsiveness and engagement. Although more is needed, there is already a growing body of research suggesting that the participation of children in genuine decision-making in school and neighbourhood has many positive outcomes. For example, children's participation in genuine schools councils has been shown to improve the quality of the relationships between teachers and pupils and enable children to achieve new levels of responsibility (Alderson, 1999; Lansdown, 1995).

The third underlies and is the condition of possibility for fully achieving the first two modifications. It concerns moving away from narrow conceptions of citizenship that exclude children and young people. This is a complex but not impossible task. In 1900 concepts of citizenship were modelled on the adult, white (in northern and western societies) male property owner who was seen to embody values of independence and autonomy. This was, of course, a myth. The networks of interdependence upon which this supposed independence and autonomy depended have become clearer as throughout the twentieth century the hidden links between the public and private spheres have been revealed. For example, it was in part by making visible their hidden contribution to the maintenance of social and economic life that enabled women to make claim to citizenship (Lister, 1997). The social model of citizenship implied in this is one that has not yet been extended to children and young people (Roche, 1999). The 'century of the child' paid far more attention to the contribution of society to children than the contribution of children to society. Nevertheless, we are now beginning to recognise children and adults as bound by mutual interdependence. We are starting to notice the contribution that children make. Although our gaze avoided this for a long time, it is clear that children are, for example, both social carers and economic producers. They are also the active makers of the future. Whatever the level of investment society makes, without the active participation of children there will be no social future. It is, therefore, necessary to reconsider children's claim on citizenship.

The representation of children

It was not until the end of the century of the child that the view of children as social persons was generally accepted as a principle, encoded as Article 12 of the UN Convention on the Rights of the Child. Even today it remains far more controversial than the articles dealing with protection and provision precisely because it touches upon the question of citizenship. We have much to learn about ways of enabling children to speak for themselves and in their own way (see Chapters 2, 3, 4, 9, 10 and 12 of this volume). Too often children are expected to fit into adult ways of participating when what is needed is institutional and organisational change that encourages and facilitates children's voice. Unfortunately children's participation is a subject high in rhetoric but sometimes low in practical application. A recent study in Norway, in many ways a beacon of children's citizenship, showed that many initiatives on children's participation were short term and produced no lasting changes (Kjorholt, 2002). The Children 5–16 Research Programme in the UK showed children keen to have a voice but also eagle-eyed in spotting adult tokenism (Prout, 2001). The promise to be heard is taken seriously by children and the failure to see it through creates disappointment and even cynicism about democratic values.

Furthermore, it behoves social scientists and researchers to maintain critical reflection on the meaning of participation. As noted at the outset of this chapter, childhood is an intensively governed and regulated phase of life. Participation has the potential to become a technique of childhood government, through which children are enjoined to regulate themselves. Indeed it may well be that the active, participant child meets the requirements of late-modern society better than former, more traditional versions. For example, when both parents are involved in the labour market families often experience a sense of 'time squeeze' (even when this is not supported by statistical evidence on family members' use of time – see Christensen, 2002). The self-regulating, active and participating child may well be seen as serving the needs of the contemporary family with its complex timetables and negotiations. Furthermore, the demand on children to participate and be socially active may not suit all children and may give rise to, or reflect, new social divisions between children and new power relations between adults and children. Nevertheless, not all social issues can be reduced to power relations, nor is social change always best understood from this perspective. Whilst social scientists need to be alert to the unfolding meaning of children's voice and participation, a modest optimism seems preferable to the flattening pessimism that would always see change as only a reiteration of power. It does seem preferable, at least for the moment, to view having a voice as an improvement on being silenced or ignored.

Dealing with these issues is, I suggest, in some measure, a matter of cultural as much as political representation. I began this chapter by pointing to the paucity of the images used in public discourse about childhood and their tendency to flip between extreme stereotypes: little angels or little devils; criminals or victims. Modernity, as Bauman (1993) has pointed out, has a preference for such dualistic thinking. Many social groups (women, ethnic minorities, disabled people, older people) have found this oppressive and restricting. They have mounted deconstructive campaigns against being represented through such dualisms, making claims to personhood, equality and ideas of citizenship that respect difference. But children, like no other group within society, continue to labour against the deadweight of stereotypical and contradictory representations. In place of the self-defeating and endlessly recursive opposition of little devils and little angels, what is required are ways of thinking about the real, lived experiences of children and the complex character of childhood in a changing world. As Christensen observes:

> what may be challenged are those traditional perspectives . . . [in which)] . . . children have little or no influence over their own social representation . . . This focus leaves more or less unaddressed the child as a social person in their own right, to be understood through his or her perceptions and actions in the social and cultural world.
>
> (Christensen, 1994: 4)

This points to the reciprocal relationship between the political representation of children (that is, their citizenship) and their representation in social and cultural discourse. This requires both rethinking the exclusion and separation of children from public life and reconsidering the routine but unhelpful stereotypes of children that dominate public discussion. There is, after all, a crucial connection between the voice of children in public discourse and policy-making (their political representation) and the socially and culturally constructed ways in which children are seen (their social and cultural representations). Christensen (1994) made this connection some time ago by pointing out that arguments for greater public or political representation of children have to overcome widespread ideas about children's supposed incapacity to contribute usefully to public debate. In turn, for children's voice to be really heard, even when the institutional arrangements create a notional space for it, requires change in the way that children are seen.

Note

1 Although these changes have a global reach and meaning, in this chapter I concentrate on their impact on childhood in 'northern' and 'western' societies.

References

Alderson, P. (1999) 'Civil Rights in Schools', ESRC Children 5–16 Research Programme Briefing (http://www.esrc.ac.uk/curprog.html). Consulted 28/01/02.
Bauman, Z. (1993) *Modernity and Ambivalence*, Cambridge: Polity Press.
Beck, U. (1992) *Risk Society: Towards a New Modernity*, London: Sage.
Beck, U. (1998) *Democracy Without Enemies*, Cambridge: Polity Press.
Bradshaw, J. (2000) 'Child Poverty in Comparative Perspective', in D. Gordon and P. Townsend (eds) *Breadline Europe: The Measurement of Poverty*, Bristol: The Policy Press.
Buckingham, D. (2000) *After the Death of Childhood: Growing Up in the Age of the Electronic Media*, Cambridge: Polity Press.

Children and Young People's Unit (2000) *Tomorrow's Future: Building a Strategy for Children and Young People*, London: Children and Young People's Unit.

Christensen, P. (1994) 'Children as the Cultural Other', *KEA: Zeischrift für Kulturwissenschaften, TEMA: Kinderwelten*, 6: 1–16.

Christensen, P. (2002) 'Why More Quality Time is not at the Top of Children's Lists: the Qualities of Time for Children', *Children and Society*, 16, 2: 77–88.

Christensen, P. and Prout, A. (2002) 'Anthropological and Sociological Perspectives on the Study of Children', in S. Greene and D. Hogan, *Researching Children*, London: Sage.

Clarke, L. (1996) 'Demographic Change and the Family Situation of Children', in J. Brannen and M. O'Brien (eds) *Children in Families: Research and Policy*, London: Falmer Press.

Dahlberg, G., Moss, P. and Pence, A. (1999) *Beyond Quality in Early Childhood Education and Care: Postmodern Perspectives*, London: Falmer Press.

Davie, R., Upton, G. and Varma, V. (eds) (1996) *The Voice of the Child*, London: Falmer Press.

Davis, H. and Bourhill, M. (1997) '"Crisis": The Demonisation of Children and Young People', in P. Scraton (ed.) *'Childhood' in 'Crisis'?*, London: Falmer Press.

European Commission (1996) *The Demographic Situation in the European Union – 1995*, Brussels: European Commission.

Flekkoy, G.D. and Kaufman, N.H. (1997) *The Participation Rights of the Child: Rights and Responsibilities in Family and Society*, London: Jessica Kingsley.

Franklin, B. (1995) *Handbook of Children's Rights: Comparative Policy and Practice*, London: Routledge.

Freeman, C., Henderson, P. and Kettle, J. (1999) *Planning with Children for Better Communities*, Bristol: The Policy Press.

Freeman, R. (1999) 'Recursive Politics: Prevention, Modernity and Social Systems', *Children and Society*, 13, 4: 232–41.

Furedi, F. (1997) *The Culture of Fear: Risk Taking and the Morality of Low Expectations*, London: Cassell.

Giddens, A. (1990) *The Consequences of Modernity*, Cambridge: Polity Press.

Giddens, A. (1991) *Modernity and Self-identity*, Cambridge: Polity Press.

Giesecke, H. (1985) *Das Ende der Erziehung*, Stuttgart: Klett-Cotta-Verlag.

Hart, R. (1992) 'Children's Participation: From Tokenism to Citizenship', Florence: UNICEF.

Hendrick, H. (1997) *Children, Childhood and English Society*, Cambridge: Cambridge University Press.

Holland, P. (1992) *What is a Child? Popular Images of Childhood*, London: Virago Press.

Jack, G. and Jordan, B. (1999) 'Social Capital and Child Welfare', *Children and Society*, 13, 4: 242–56.

James, A., Jenks, C. and Prout, A. (1998) *Theorizing Childhood*, Cambridge: Polity Press.

Jenks, C. (1996) *Childhood*, London: Routledge.

John, M. (1996) *Children in Charge: The Child's Right to a Fair Hearing*, London: Jessica Kingsley.

Key, H. ([1900] 1909) *The Century of the Child* http://www.socsci.kun.nl/ped/whp/histeduc/ellenkey/index.html. Online edition based on the English translation,

9th print, as published in 1909 by G.P. Putnam's Sons, New York and London. Consulted 28/01/02.

Kjorholt, A. (2002) 'Small is Powerful: Discourses on "Children and Participation" in Norway', *Childhood*, 9, 1: 63–82.

Lansdown, G. (1995) *Taking Part: Children's Participation in Decision Making*, London: Institute for Public Policy Research.

Lister, R. (1997) *Citizenship: Feminist Perspectives*, Basingstoke: Macmillan.

McKendrick, J., Bradford, M.G. and Fielder, A.V. (2000) 'The Dangers of Safe Play', ESRC Children 5–16 Research Programme Briefing (http://www.esrc.ac.uk/curprog.html). Consulted 28/01/02.

Moss, P., Dillon, J. and Statham, J. (2000) 'The "child in need" and "the rich child": discourses, constructions and practice', *Critical Social Policy*, 20, 2: 233–54.

Nasman, E. (1994) 'Individualisation and Institutionalisation of Children', in J. Qvortrup, M. Bardy, G. Sgritta and H. Wintersberger (eds) *Childhood Matters: Social Theory, Practice and Politics*, Aldershot: Avebury.

OECD (2001) *What Schools for the Future?*, Paris: OECD.

Office for National Statistics (1999) *Social Trends 29*, London: The Stationery Office.

O'Neill, J. (1994) *The Missing Child in Liberal Theory*, Toronto: Toronto University Press.

Orellena, M.F., Thorne, B., Chee, A. and Lam, W.S.E. ([1998] 2001) 'Transnational Childhoods: The Deployment, Development and Participation of Children in Processes of Family Migration', Paper presented at the 14th World Congress of the International Sociological Association, Montreal, July 1998. Revised to appear in *Social Problems Journal*, November, 2001.

Oxley, H., Dang, T.-T., Forster, M.F. and Pellizzari, M. (2001) 'Income Inequalities and Poverty among Children and Households in Selected OECD Countries', in K. Vleminekx and T.M. Smeeding (eds) *Child Well-being, Child Poverty and Child Policy in Modern Nations*, Bristol: The Policy Press.

Pringle, K. (1998) *Children and Social Welfare in Europe*, Buckingham: Open University Press.

Prout, A. (2000) 'Children's Participation: Control and Self-realisation in British Late Modernity', *Children and Society* (September), 14, 4: 304–15.

Prout, A. (2001) 'Representing Children: Reflections on the Children 5–16 Programme', *Children and Society*, 15, 3: 193–201.

Roche, J. (1999) 'Children: Rights, Participation and Citizenship', *Childhood*, 6, 4: 475–93.

Rose, N. (1989) *Governing the Soul*, London: Routledge.

Ruxton, S. (1996) *Children in Europe*, London: National Children's Homes.

Sgritta, G. (1994) 'The Generational Division of Welfare: Equity and Conflict', in J. Qvortrup, M. Bardy, G. Sgritta and H. Wintersberger (eds) *Childhood Matters: Social Theory, Practice and Politics*, Aldershot: Avebury.

Smith, T. (1999) 'Neighbourhood and Prevention Strategies with Children and Families: What Works?', *Children and Society*, 13, 4: 265–77.

Thompson, D. (1989) 'The Welfare State and Generational Conflict: Winners and Losers', in P. Johnson, C. Conrad and D. Thompson (eds) *Workers versus Pensioners: Intergenerational Justice in an Ageing World*, Manchester: Manchester University Press.

Urry, J. (2000) *Sociology Beyond Societies: Mobilities for the Twenty-first Century*, London: Routledge.

Wilkinson, H. and Mulgan, G. (1995) *Freedom's Children*, London: Demos.

Zeiher, H. (2001) 'Children's Islands in Space and Time: The Impact of Spatial Differentiation on Children's Ways of Shaping Social Life', in M. du Bois-Reymond, H. Sunker and H.-H. Kruger (eds) *Childhood in Europe: Approaches–Trends–Findings*, New York: Peter Lang.

Zeiher, H. (2002) 'Shaping Daily Life in Urban Environments', in P. Christensen and M. O'Brien (eds) *Children in the City: Home, Neighbourhood and Community'*, London: Falmer Press.

2 Children's participation in policy matters

Helen Roberts

Using children or children as service users?

In a speech given in October 2001, some six weeks after terrorists flew two passenger planes into the twin towers of the World Trade Center in New York, UK Prime Minister Tony Blair reminded us: 'It is important we never forget how we felt watching the planes fly into the twin towers. Never forget how we felt imagining how mothers told children they were about to die' (30 October 2001, www.pm.gov.uk/news).

Children can be used to sell political messages or trainers, they can be used by terrorists in battles or wars, they can be used in propaganda by the good guys as well as the bad. They are frequently on the receiving end of a whole range of policies intended for their protection and the protection of family life. Children are important users, important consumers, important barometers and can provide impressive leverage in the purchasing decisions of households.

Drawing on recent UK research, this chapter describes some of the ways in which at project-based, local, national and international levels, children and young people are being invited (or not) to play a role in the policy process. The chapter also describes, on the basis of work conducted by the author and her colleagues, some of the problems which can arise en route. Just as in practice, research does not follow the relatively unproblematic course described or implied in textbooks; nor does the participation of young people. There is as much to learn through what goes wrong as through what goes right.

Participation in policy matters

Increasingly, children and young people are invited to participate in one way or another in policy matters (see Chapters 1, 3 and 4). McNeish and Newman (2002) identify five key issues related to the increasing participation of children in policy matters in the United Kingdom. These are:

1   *The growth of the power of the 'consumer'.* From the 'patients charter' to 'Best Value' the voice of the service user has become central to modernising public services in the UK.

2   *Pressure from young people's user groups.* Early attempts to involve user groups frequently failed to hear the voices of the most marginalised and disadvantaged groups. This was particularly true for children and young people until groups such as NAYPIC (National Association of Young people in Care) began to challenge assumptions about young people's capabilities.

3   *The United Nations Convention on the Rights of the Child.* Article 12 sets out the rights of children and young people to express their views about anything which affects them, and there are a number of other articles in the Convention (for example, concerning the rights to freedom of conscience and religion) asserting the rights of children to hold views independently of adults. The Convention has probably had its greatest impact as a rallying point for children's rights advocates who have used it to keep young people's participation firmly on the policy agenda.

4   *The 1989 Children Act and subsequent inquiry reports.* Implemented in 1991, the Children Act for England and Wales made it a legal requirement for the views of young people to be taken into account in any decision affecting them. The importance of listening to young people has been re-inforced by successive inquiries into the abuse of children, particularly those in the looked-after system. A recurring theme of these has been the failure of adults to listen to young people. This concern has led to an interest in more effective ways of empowering young people as a protective strategy, central to the Quality Protects initiative which aims to transform both the management and delivery of social services for children and requires mechanisms for children's and young people's views to be heeded.

5   *The growth of citizenship as a policy issue.* Government statements on a stakeholder democracy and the resurgence of interest in the concept of citizenship have contributed to a search for new ways of involving young people as members of their communities and as citizens, such as the development of Youth Councils and Youth Parliaments.

There is a range of ways in which children and young people may be involved in the policy process, by public, voluntary and private sector organisations and a number of policy arenas in the UK where there is an explicit commitment to attend to the voices and expertise of children and young people. The Children and Young People's Unit has identified participation as part of its core strategy (CYPU 2001a, 2001b) and has an attractive 'door' to its website for children and young people. One of the four key commitments of the Children's Task Force, established to drive forward all aspects of the National Health Service plan that relate to children, for instance, is 'to ensure that the voice of the child is heard' (Department of Health, 2001: 1) Moreover, a number of major UK research funders have a particular interest in work for or with children and young people and this has resulted in a substantial body of work, some of which is reported elsewhere in this book. What has been something of a sea change is that children and young people are not simply the objects of research but are seen as active agents. The Joseph Rowntree Foundation (JRF), for instance, as well as having a research programme on children and young people, also describes a commitment to exploring ways of ensuring that people central to the research or development project are involved in, and empowered by, the process. One key area for social and public policy on which children are expert participants is family life. An important study funded by JRF on family breakdown (Dunn and Deater-Deckard, 2001) interviewed more than 460 children and young people from different family backgrounds, including nearly 250 from stepfamilies, and more than a hundred from single-mother families. Most children had not only been confused and upset at the time of their parents' separation, but said they received little communication about what was happening or why. A quarter said no one had talked to them and only 5 per cent said they had been fully informed and encouraged to ask questions. What is interesting for those of us exploring the involvement of children and young people in policy and practice is the fact that, not surprisingly, the young people had practical suggestions for the problems they faced. Many children missed their non-resident parent (usually their father) very much and wanted to see more of them. They offered practical suggestions such as more weekend visits, rather than seeing their parent on school days when there was less time to talk. In general, those who had a say in decisions about visiting times and felt able to talk to their parents about problems were especially likely to express positive feelings.

A study of kinship care also funded by JRF and published in 2001 found that despite the scant attention given to kinship care in everyday policy and practice, and on social work courses, this appears to be an option valued by young people, and with good outcomes (Broad *et al.*, 2001). The researchers examined fifty kinship care placements, interviewing young people, carers and social workers. The young people were mostly in their teens, and nearly half were of Caribbean or Guyanese origin. Many of the young people interviewed said they felt loved, safe, and secure living with their extended family. Other advantages they identified included maintaining links with siblings and friends, sustaining their racial and cultural heritage and not being looked after by strangers. The main disadvantages were seen as limitations to freedom, financial hardship and lack of access to the specialist help available to care leavers. One young person interviewed said: 'I love to know that I belong to somebody. I'm loved by people and it's good to know that I've got somewhere to come after school that I can call home' (15-year-old girl in kinship care). Both of the above are examples of child and young people-informed work which could helpfully feed into policy and practice. At present, our understanding of the mechanisms which enable this to happen are imperfect (Barnardo's R&D Team, 2000), but a new ESRC programme on evidence-based policy and practice, one of whose components is research utilisation, may provide helpful pointers in this area for the future (www.evidencenetwork.org).

The Economic and Social Science Research Council (ESRC) funded two programmes directly related to children and young people – Children 5–16: Growing into the 21st Century, which ended in 2001, and Youth Citizenship and Social Change (www.esrc.ac.uk). Civil rights in schools, life as a disabled child and the business of children's play are among the projects which have actively involved children and young people in the Children 5–16 programme. Children as social actors was a key element to the same programme. While we know from cohort studies that parental involvement in children's education appears to be associated with good long-term outcomes for children, in particular those born into disadvantage (Pilling, 1990; Wadsworth, 1991), it is the ESRC programme which has given us an insight into children's own views of parental involvement in their schools (Edwards and Alldred, 2000; Edwards, 2002). This indicates that while children may be active facilitators or initiators of parental involvement, they may also be ambivalent about too great an overlap between home and school. This would indicate, suggest the researchers, that policy-makers and practitioners need to maintain a delicate balance between children's social and educational interests, and respect their ability and creativity to respond to parental involvement in diverse ways. In the same programme, the work of McKendrick (2000) on safe play draws attention to the balance to be struck between play being adventurous and exciting for children and being 'safe.' Children may identify dangers (older children identify younger children as such, and vice versa) which would not necessarily be identified by planners or others. In that sense, the lessons of the research programmes indicate not just that there is some special expert knowledge (or nice stories) to be collected from children, but that, carefully interpreted, these may have important policy and practice implications.

The Youth Citizenship and social change programme funded by the ESRC

> was set up to study young people aged 16 to 25, focusing both on the structural opportunities and constraints which shape their transitions to adulthood, and on young people as agents, who actively construct, negotiate with and shape their social worlds.
>
> (Catan, 2001: v)

One of the studies funded under this programme (Lister *et al.*, 2001: 57) indicates that young people are aware of their low levels of political knowledge, but most felt that formal politics was not necessarily the best avenue to contribute to society.

There is thus considerable enthusiasm in a number of quarters for 'involving' young people, listening to what they have to say and finding ways of addressing the democratic deficit which can arise when a large number of young citizens distance themselves from the political process.

Participation in the political process

Political apathy (at least in terms of vote casting) was at an exceptionally low level at the time of the 2001 General Election in the United Kingdom, with only six in ten voters turning out to vote. Figures were even lower among young people aged 18–25 with only four in ten casting a vote (Walker, 2001). Failing to vote is, not, of course, the same thing as disengagement from politics, and there is some evidence that issue-based politics (green and environmental issues, health and education, for instance) are high on the agenda for many children and young people (Walker, 1996; Park, 1999; Lister *et al.*, 2001). It is *party* politics which appears to have become less compelling to the young.

In 1970 the voting age in the UK was lowered from 21 to 18 and a number of bodies, ranging from youth organisations to the Electoral Reform Society, are currently questioning whether the voting age should be further lowered. The question of the extent of the franchise was nicely put by James Mill (father of John Stuart) in his article 'Government', written for the 1820 supplement to the *Encyclopaedia Britannica* and later reprinted as a pamphlet:

> All those individuals who are indisputably included in those of other individuals may be struck off without inconvenience. In this light may be viewed all children up to a certain age, whose interests are involved in those of their parents. In this light also, women may be regarded, the interest of almost all of whom is involved in that of their fathers or in that of their husbands.
>
> (quoted in Moller Okin, 1980: 201)

John Stuart Mill, taking a rather different view from his father (as children are sometimes inclined to), was a strong if imperfect advocate of equal rights. In 1867 he spoke in the House of Commons in favour of the admission of women to the electoral franchise (Moller Okin, 1980: 352–4). Similar arguments to those of both of the Mills are used in relation to lowering the age of franchise to include younger voters. At the end of 1999, a new Representation of the People Bill was introduced into Parliament, receiving Royal Assent on 9 March 2000. This Bill

included a range of proposals to ensure the inclusion of excluded groups
– people in mental health hospitals, prisoners on remand, homeless
people with no permanent address, and so on. Although an amendment
proposed to lower the voting age to 16 was not carried, it did receive
some support from individuals in each of the three main political parties
(CRAE, 2000). As one young person put it:

> To be a young person is to simply see life from the outside. Not
> being able to interfere or affect any action that goes on around you.
> We see things – natural disasters, wars, politics – and we are neither
> asked about them, or given the chance to change anything . . . To
> be a young person in the future is to hopefully see life from the
> inside.
>
> (Baker, 2000: 8)

While children do not have a vote, they increasingly have a voice. Early
in 2002, a UK broadsheet newspaper article began:

> From next week, there will be 30 more voices in Whitehall telling
> Ministers how to get their affairs in order . . . A team of children
> and young people have been recruited from across the country to
> give 'firm and frank' advice to government on how it is letting
> young Britain down and how it can improve.
>
> (Summerskill, 2002)

'A Whitehall source' in the same article is reported as saying: 'Letting
children and young people give advice is a big step forward for the civil
service culture' (Summerskill, 2002). In relation to the same initiative,
the Minister for Young People, in his foreword to *Learning to Listen:
Core Principles for the Involvement of Children and Young People*, suggests
that

> Ministers across departments are committed to giving young people
> a real say and real choices about the government policies and services
> that affect them. We want children and young people to feel that
> they can influence the services they receive.
>
> (CYPU, 2001b)

In an era of evidence-based policy and practice it is appropriate that the
minister implies a note of caution in terms of the fit between increased
participation and better outcomes. 'The result of effective participation
should [my emphasis] be better policies and services.' It makes good
sense that services which are responsive to people who use them, and
take account of their views, will provide better outcomes, although this
can't be guaranteed. It is reasonable that consulting people, including

children and young people, is a right in a democratic society, and that the question of outcomes is a separate one. Lansdown (1995) for instance suggests that:

> Participation is a fundamental right of citizenship. The creation of a society which combines a commitment to respect for the rights of individuals with an equal commitment to the exercise of social responsibility must promote the capacity of individuals from the earliest possible age, to participate in decisions that affect their lives.
> (Lansdown, 1995: 4)

Risks and benefits

In a climate where targets and outcomes form the political language of the day, we need to consider whether the participation of children and young people is a fundamental right (like voting for women), or whether it might also improve outcomes for children and young people. Are there any disbenefits to participation? There are risks as well as benefits to any policy, just as there are to any intervention. For some children and young people, consultation, particularly consultation which appears to be cosmetic, may well be seen as a disbenefit, drawing on one of the few resources over which children and young people exercise some direct control – namely, their time.

At present, our growing research expertise in consulting young people in innovative ways lags behind our ability to do something meaningful with what we find, making appropriate links between research findings, policy and practice. We cannot always guarantee, of course, that listening to children (or adults) will result in improved policies, or indeed will result in any change whatsoever. On occasions, consultations will come up with suggestions which for one reason or another (sometimes rather good reasons) will not be implemented. One consultation exercise with children, for instance in a large non-governmental organisation, resulted in the suggestion (or demand) that smoking be allowed on project premises. This did not result in a change of policy for either children or adults (and nor did the additional suggestion that the name of the organisation, recently changed after a re-branding exercise, revert to its original name). The same organisation (Barnardo's) now has a two-year pilot – The Voice of Children and Young People – which aims to improve children's and young people's participation in the organisation's work, create opportunities for young people to say what they think about the services they use and how they can be improved, and share their opinions and views on any issues that affect them. The initiative involved the employment of four young people, one in the London region, one in the Yorkshire region, one in the Policy Research and Influencing Unit, and one with the Marketing and Communications team. The leaflet setting out the aims of the project asks: Is there a danger of exploiting young people? and with disarming honesty replies: 'Yes. [We] recognise a duty of care to children and young people involved in this project. A Code of Practice has been devised to try and minimise the risk of exploitation. We also recognise that induction, support, training and preparation will be needed in order for employed young people . . . to operate effectively. We will be looking at appropriate accredited training courses for the young people wherever possible. There will also need to be work with Barnardo's staff to engage as much support as possible both for this pilot and the development of effective children's rights focused services.'[1]

Children's participation in, or attempts to affect, policy and practice matters is not a novelty. In the early twentieth century a group of children went on school strike in support of two of their schoolteachers who had been sacked. The schoolchildren, 66 out of 72, started a strike which was to last twenty-five years. The pupils continued their education on the village green. After a year, a national appeal for money was launched to fund a permanent building for the school and in 1917 the Strike School was opened as an independent establishment. For the next twenty-five years the school remained open (www.brickman. dircon.co.uk/burston).

One of the factors lying behind the dismissal of the teachers in the first place was the teachers' concerns about children being taken out of school at harvest time. The topic of child labour remains a contentious one. More recently child workers in other parts of the world, and children who act as interpreters for their families in the UK, have defended their right to participate fully in debates around child labour. Marcus (1998: 241), for instance, writes that despite pressure from Redd Barna, working children's organisations and other NGOs, the Norwegian government refused to make provision for the significant participation of working children in the International Conference on Child Labour held in Oslo in 1997. In the end three children were invited, and to increase the opportunities for children to make their voices heard a further twenty-one 13- to 18-year-olds were invited to a ten-day forum set up by an alliance of non-governmental organisations. Lessons were learned from this for future occasions, including the need for conflict resolution. Not only may there be differences in view between children and adults but also between children and children, coming to meetings with different expectations, different experiences and different cultures.

Differences in perspective between adults and children are not uncommon, as we found in a consultation for Camden and Islington Health Authority on children's participation in health matters (Liabo et al., 2002). A young man who had extensive experience of health service use had domiciliary physiotherapy after he had been discharged from hospital – a service which presumably had considerable benefits for his parents in terms of time, transport and convenience. His view, however, was that convalescing at home was an isolating business, and that trips to outpatients, with the associated camaraderie, would have been welcome. While practice and policy solutions which are responsive to both sets of needs can be relatively easily suggested – choice for patients and parents, and reliable patient transport which could both give parents convenience and a break, and give young people the chance to get out of the house – in practice there is a whole set of complex issues which would need to be disentangled to enable this to happen. New ways of involving patients in policy matters through PALS (patient advocacy and liaison services) do not at present have specific arrangements to involve children and young people. It will be important if children's voices are to be heard in the local health policy arenas for this to be addressed, existing good practice to be extended, and new ways of consultation tried. An experiment which we have adopted through the Camden and Islington consultation is the use of a website both to collect and to disseminate information (www.healthyfutures.org). We believe that the positive aspects to this are that children and young people can make their own decisions on when and whether to participate, and how much time to donate. They can receive information at the same time as giving it. Potential drawbacks are lack of access because of language and communication problems (the website is only in English at present), poor reading and writing skills, or poor access to IT. Our experience is that the latter is not a substantial problem in the area where we are working, with good IT access in schools, youth clubs, and other youth settings as well as in some supermarkets and community settings. We are considering the use of some form of mentoring or peer support for young people who might find using web-based technology difficult.

One of the issues which needs to be resolved in involving children and young people in the policy process is setting up structures and mechanisms which can continue and learning from what has not worked well. Woollcombe (1998: 237–8) helpfully sets out some of the problems. He writes: 'Young people can be persuaded to behave like diplomats, but the result is like watching a performance. They lose the very qualities that would have made working with them worthwhile.' He goes on to describe the closing words of the World Summit for Children: 'I address myself particularly to the children here: it is up to them to ensure that we keep the promises we've made here today . . .' The speaker, Woollcombe reminds us, is the chair of the very committee which, six months previously, had taken a decision not to allow any children to present their views at the summit. (It is unclear whether Woollcombe views the change of language – if not of heart, as positive or negative.) But it is clear from Woollcombe's account that the experience of participation may not have been entirely positive for the children involved:

When the heads of state arrived, two children were selected to meet two leaders. The kids were told to 'make it quick' . . . Nervous and flustered, the children gabbled their presentation . . . At the summit itself, children dressed up in national costumes and ushered their leaders to the stage where they signed the summit documents.

(Woollcombe, 1998: 237)

Woollcombe noted in his diary:

six children step up to microphones and read the preamble in the different UN languages – reading words that they had no hand in writing, watched by two-dimensional portraits of the kinds of impoverished children which these words are designed to assist and by three-dimensional politicians who are entirely responsible for providing that assistance. Nothing could symbolize the powerlessness of children more accurately than this – and yet these children cry out the words with a passion!

(Woollcombe, 1998: 237)

Relaying a UK experience in South Derbyshire, he describes some of the things which made the original participation of children and young people fail to work well despite huge efforts on all sides – among them, the off-putting traditional committee approach and the lack of ownership by part-time adult staff. Rather than asserting that participation doesn't work, a new approach called Power Pack was tried – a subcommittee comprised entirely of young people to which each statutory youth club has the right to send up to four representatives. Each club has one vote. There is a budget of some £60,000 a year, and chairpersonship is circulated among the young people, with adults allowed to speak if they are called upon by young people to do so.

Conclusion

A good deal of the literature on consulting children (including this chapter) is critical, or self-critical, of ways of doing things which don't quite get things right. Hart's (1997) ladder of participation, for instance, although a splendidly useful heuristic device, can be used to paralyse action if those who do not quite reach the right rung on the ladder soon enough feel that it's safer to do nothing than to get it wrong.

At the end of the day, as adults involved in research or policy, we are unlikely to be able to 'award' participation to children and young people. There is quite a lot we can do to facilitate it, but power tends to be seized by those who want it, rather than offered by those of us who feel that to a greater or lesser extent we have it in our grasp.

Meanwhile, one practical step which researchers (and funders) can take is to consider long-term follow-ups of projects designed to increase the participation of children and young people in policy matters. At present, even relatively short-term follow-up appears to be rare (or rarely reported). In order to do more, we need to know more. As Ennew (1998: xix) points out, 'records are few and there are even fewer evaluations . . . Success is generally claimed on the basis of unsubstantiated stories from agencies rather than being grounded in monitoring processes that use agreed definitions, criteria and indicators.'

Those of us who feel that the participation of children and young people is something worth encouraging, and worth researching and understanding, are likely to make mistakes along the way. Fortunately for most of us, the children and young people with whom we work are tolerant.

Piet Hein, a Danish poet and scientist, has some useful advice in this respect:

> The Road to wisdom?
> Well, it's plain and simple to express
> Err and err and err again
> But less and less and less

Note

1 For further details, contact Pam Hibbert, Policy Research and Influencing Unit, Barnardo's, Tanner's Lane, Barkingside, Ilford, Essex IG6 1QG.

References

Baker, M. (2000) Article 12 member in Carnegie Young People Initiative and National Youth Agency, in R. Frost (ed.) *Voices Unheard: Young People at the Beginning of the 21st Century*, Leicester: Youth Work Press.

Barnardo's R&D Team (2000) *Making Connections: What Works in Linking Research and Practice*, Basildon: Barnardo's.

Broad, B., Hayes, R. and Rushforth, C. (2001) *Kith and Kin: Kinship Care for Vulnerable Young People*, London: National Children's Bureau for the Joseph Rowntree Foundation.

Catan, L. (2001) New perspectives on youth transitions, Editorial introduction in R. Lister, S. Middleton and N. Smith, *Young People's Voices: Citizenship Education*, Leicester: Youth Work Press.

Children and Young People's Unit (CYPU) (2001a) *Building a Strategy for Children and Young People: a Consultation Document*, London: DfEE (www.dfee.gov.uk/cypu).

Children and Young People's Unit (CYPU) (2001b) *Learning to Listen: Core Principles for the Involvement of Children and Young People*, London: DfEE (www.dfee.gov.uk/cypu).

CRAE (Children's Rights Alliance for England) (2000) *The Real Democratic Deficit: Why 16 and 17 year olds Should be Allowed to Vote*, London: Children's Rights Alliance for England.

Department of Health (2001) *Children's Taskforce: An Introduction*, London: Department of Health.

Dunn, J. and Deater-Deckard, K. (2001) *Children's Views of their Changing Families*, York: York Publishing Services (for Joseph Rowntree Foundation).

Edwards, R. (ed.) (2002) *Children, Home and School: Regulation, Autonomy or Connection*, London: RoutledgeFalmer.

Edwards, R. and Alldred, P. (2000) A typology of parental involvement in education centring on children and young people: Negotiating familialisation, institutionalisation, and individualisation, *British Journal of Sociology of Education*, 21, 3: 435–55.

Ennew, J. (1998) Preface, in V. Johnson, E. Ivan-Smith, G. Gordon, P. Pridmore and P. Scott (eds), *Stepping Forward: Children and Young People's Participation in the Development Process*, London: Intermediate Technology Publications Ltd.

Hart, R.A. (1997) *Children's Participation: The Theory and Practice of Involving Young Citizens in Community Development and Environmental Care*, London: Earthscan publication with UNICEF.

Lansdown, G. (1995) *Taking Part: Children's Participation in Decision Making*, London: IPPR.

Liabo, K., Curtis, K., Roberts, H. and McNeish, D. (2002) *Healthy Futures?: A Consultation with Children and Young People in Camden and Islington about their Experiences of Receiving Health Services*, London: Camden and Islington Health Authority.

Lister, R., Middleton, S. and Smith, N. (2001) *Young People's Voices: Citizenship Education*, Leicester: Youth Work Press.

Marcus, R. (1998) Promoting children's participation in an international conference. What can we learn from the Save the Children alliance experience in Oslo?, in V. Johnson, E. Ivan-Smith, G. Gordon, P. Pridmore and P. Scott (eds), *Stepping Forward: Children and Young People's Participation in the Development Process*, London: Intermediate Technology Publications Ltd.

McKendrick, J.H. (2000) Children 5–16 Research Briefing, No. 22, in *The Dangers of Safe Play*, Hull: University of Hull.

McNeish, D. and Newman, T. (2002) Involving young people in decision making, in D. McNeish, T. Newman and H. Roberts (eds) *What Works for Children?*, Buckingham: Open University Press.

Moller Okin, S. (1980) *Women in Western Political Thought*, London: Virago.

Park, A. (1999) Young people and political apathy, in R. Jowell, J. Curtice, A. Park, K. Thomson and L. Jarvis (eds) *British Social Attitudes: The 15th Report*, Ashgate: Aldershot.

Pilling, D. (1990) *Escape from Disadvantage*, Brighton: Falmer Press.

Summerskill, B. (2002) Blair turns to children for answers – special advisers recruited on transport and schools – and they're all under 18, *The Observer*, 13 January: 6 (News section).

Wadsworth, M.E.J. (1991) *The Imprint of Time: Childhood History and Adult Life*, Oxford: Oxford University Press.

Walker, D. (1996) Young people, politics and the media, in H. Roberts and D. Sachdev, *Young People's Social Attitudes*, Barkingside: Barnardo's.

Walker, D. (2001) Abstentions strongest among young, *The Guardian*, June 9: 9.

Woollcombe, D. (1998) Children's conferences and councils, in V. Johnson, E. Ivan-Smith, G. Gordon, P. Pridmore and P. Scott (eds), *Stepping Forward: Children and Young People's Participation in the Development Process*, London, Intermediate Technology Publications Ltd.

3 Children's participation through community development

Assessing the lessons from international experience

Gary Craig

Introduction

Children and young people are increasingly perceived not as passive recipients of services and policies but as political actors in their own right. Other chapters in this book examine how and why this change has come about (see Chapters 1, 2 and 4). The purpose of this chapter is to review a range of experience, from different countries and policy contexts, of the use of community development techniques to promote children's involvement. Community (or social) development has been a long-standing technique for involving adults in identifying and meeting needs and shaping policy development (Craig and Mayo, 1995) in an increasingly wide range of policy arenas. There has, however, until now, been little attempt to apply its techniques and value base in working with children. Comparative study of such work with children facilitates the process of improving research, theory and action by providing insights from theory and practice elsewhere, enabling us to learn from others' experience and critically to assess our own.

Community development starts with the needs and aspirations of groups of disadvantaged people in poor and deprived communities (whether socially or geographically defined) (Craig and Mayo, 1995). It strives to give ordinary people a voice for expressing and acting on their needs and desires and, through the process of participating in this approach to social change, helps to empower people. The question then is to what extent is this a feasible and desirable approach for those who are, legally and technically, regarded as dependent on others (usually their biological or legal parents)?

The question 'what is a child?' is dealt with at greater length elsewhere (Postman, 1985; Aries, 1986; Gittins, 1998) and is therefore summarised briefly here. Given that the experience reported here comes from a range of cultural contexts, it is however critical to thinking about the transferability of practice between countries. The legal, cultural and social contexts for this work vary widely, placing different kinds of constraints on those seeking to engage with children on policy issues. Most fundamentally, the age at which 'children' are no longer formally dependent on adults also varies. A selection of experience of children participating in policy development in differing contexts is then reviewed. Finally, we address the question of what a model of good practice might look like. Whilst work with children in policy development may appear to be an indisputable 'good', it is important to know what is effective and why.

What is a child?

In discussing working with children, how far is it possible to work with children as independent actors in their own right, separate from the adults who have kinship, caring and/or legal responsibilities for them? Because of the contemporary legal frameworks which define childhood (albeit differently within particular cultures), children can never be seen as entirely autonomous. Childhood, as noted, is not a fixed concept and is, in any case, an adult construction. The boundaries of childhood (see e.g. Roll, 1990; Barnardo's, 1996; Coles and Craig, 1999; Craig, 2000) are important in defining what is appropriate and possible in working with children within a community development paradigm. Recent thinking about the child as a semi-independent actor with social and political rights legitimises the development of work with children but, at the same time, spells out the competing political and legal issues which have to be clarified in the course of such work. For example, in many Third World countries today, particularly in predominantly agrarian societies, children are perceived largely for their contribution to family labour.

A critical shift in thinking about childhood came from the 1970s onwards, particularly through the development of the notion of the rights of the child (Freeman, 1983; Ekelaar, 1986), captured in the publication of the UN Convention on the Rights of the Child and, within the UK, the enactment of Children Acts from 1989. Ekelaar's typology delineates *autonomy interests*, a recognition that children may wish to pursue interests separate from and not determined by those legally charged with caring for them (reflected in the Convention's Articles 12 and 13 which promote the rights to express views and receive information). Essentially, children came to be seen as having (negatively) rights not only to protection from harm where they are vulnerable and (more neutrally) to the conditions which would promote their effective development but (positively) to rights of autonomous action and to social and political participation. However, most adult commentators argue that a child's right to participation seems conditional on other childhood rights being maintained. This raises contradictions: is it legitimate for children to participate in situations where they may be at risk, and who should judge whether that risk is acceptable to the child? One contemporary example might be involvement of children in direct action against speeding vehicles.

There is now a burgeoning literature on the effects of policy on children and on the position of children themselves in debates about important social and political issues. Of particular significance in this discussion, it also highlights the way in which a specifically child-centred perspective on social and political issues is developing. As well as general arguments for involving young people in the life of their communities (Lightfoot, 1990; de Winter, 1997), the literature discusses the impacts on children of poverty and deprivation (Bradshaw, 1990; Kumar, 1993), public expenditure and fiscal policies (Holtermann, 1995), violence (Gulbenkian Foundation, 1995), and the impact of government structures on children (Hodgkin and Newell, 1996). General reviews of the interrelationship between UK social policy and children's lives include Hill and Tisdall (1997) and Daniel and Ivatts (1998), and of the development of children's rights (CRDU, 1994; Franklin, 1995). Interest has recently developed in rural policy issues in relation to children (CIS, 1991; Statham and Cameron, 1994; Davis and Ridge, 1997). Beyond the boundaries of the UK, writing examines the impact of social development on children's lives (SCF, 1995), the well-being of children in differing cultures, both within Europe (Ruxton, 1996) and more widely (Bellamy, 1997), and, on a cross-cultural basis, the 'participation rights of the child' (Flekkøy and Kaufman, 1997) and the European Union's stance towards involving children and young people in policy-making (CIS 1995).

Although the UN Convention defines children as all those under 18, we noted that the boundaries of childhood are culturally determined. Most countries are now signatories to the Convention, but local customs, economic and social conditions, and the impacts of the processes of globalisation mean that it is interpreted differently from state to state. This affects the context and constraints within which policy development work with children can take place. In areas where basic issues such as literacy, poverty, sanitation and adequate shelter are still highly important, it is hardly surprising that community development tends to focus on work with adults, reflected in the considerable literature on childhood education and development work (Booker, 1995; Grotberg, 1995; Sibly and Tibi, 1995). Some of this literature from the 'South' suggests that the 'way in' to issues relating to child's needs may not always be the most obvious one (Misra, 1983).

A more systematic approach to exploring the needs and interests of children is through the techniques of social research. This has made a particularly useful contribution to addressing ethical and methodological questions relevant to community development which need to be addressed in working with children. Research has much to offer practitioners, often leading where practice follows. Despite continuing anxieties about the capacities of children to 'speak for themselves', there is now a substantial body of experience of research with children as respondents (Roberts and Sachdev, 1996; Hogan and Gilligan, 1998; Greig and Taylor, 1997).

Although there has been a relatively long history of quantitative research concerning children and children's issues, most qualitative research about issues affecting children has, until recently, sought the views of children through proxies, usually their legal carers. However, research has increasingly involved children as actors with a voice and views of their own, initially in relation to child protection issues (where it was acknowledged that children might have views separate from those of their parents or guardians). Again, this has informed a wider policy framework, following growing awareness of the need to develop policies which do not have damaging effects on children. There is no doubt both that policy-makers have got it wrong – sometime disastrously so – in the past (as, for example, in the development of asphalted playgrounds which led to serious injuries to young children, or in failure to prevent abuse to children in public care) and that researchers, by failing to focus on the views of the child, have effectively – if implicitly – played a part in this process. The approach of involving children as respondents them-selves is thus part of a broader trend in policy-relevant research which is increasingly focusing not just on the views of 'end-users' of policy proposals but has also sought to engage them in other aspects of the research process, including design and dissemination, both as an import-ant part of policy development and change (Beresford and Croft, 1993) and as support for their empowerment.

This developing body of research has generally shown children to be more robust, articulate and willing to be heard (given appropriate age-related research design and sensitive researchers) than many adults assumed to be the case. This insight has undoubtedly fed into the grow-ing body of community development work and is one source of legiti-macy for research with children (Mahon *et al.*, 1996). A futher source of legitimacy is that, until recently, children often had no channel or forum for self-advocacy. The appointment of, for example, a Children's Com-missioner for Wales shows how this picture is beginning to alter.

The range of research now emerging extends from the more narrow historical concerns of childcare, parenting and child protection into many other social policy areas (a process increasingly mirrored in community development work). Until the early 1990s it remained the case, for example, that children's experience of poverty was mediated by their parents' perceptions or was limited to an assessment of quantitative data (Kumar, 1993; Burghes, 1994). By the time of Alderson's review of ethical questions raised in research with children she was able to report, in 'a survey of organisations concerned with doing, funding and pub-licising research with children' (1995: 89), that, although many still used proxies, two-thirds of the 92 research organisations responding indicated that they undertook interviews (often using tape or video) or surveys directly with children.

Recent research specifically addressing children's concerns through interviews with children themselves shows the range of policy issues where children's views have been sought:

- about their strategies for negotiating with parents (Middleton *et al.*, 1994);
- with young 'care runaways' (Rees, 1995; Strathdee, 1995);
- into their experiences of living in residential care (Sinclair and Gibbs, 1996);
- of their experiences of asthma and other health complaints (Ireland and Holloway, 1996);
- of their views of their profound disability (Appleton, 1995; Russell, 1997; Morris, 1998a, 1998b; Ward, 1998);
- about social work services (Heaton and Sayer, 1992; Butler and Williamson, 1994; Cloke and Davies, 1995; Davies and Dotchin, 1995; Hill, 1997);
- on fostering and adoption (Martin and Craig, 1992) and childcare services (Craig *et al.*, 1999);
- with physical, emotional and learning difficulties (Alderson and Goodey, 1996);
- on low incomes (Shropshire and Middleton, 1999) and in rural areas (Davis and Ridge, 1997);
- as carers (Children's Society, 1999); and
- into their perceptions of child support and parental roles (Clarke *et al.*, 1996).

The last-named, ironically, the first time children's views had been sought on legislation introduced into Parliament under the policy banner of 'Children Come First' (the title of the White Paper preceding the 1991 Child Support Act) and a study by O'Brien (1997), asked young children, through the use of vignettes and diaries, to reflect on comparatively complex issues such as the gendered nature of parental roles and the dimensions of family. Some studies have now also made use of young people themselves as researchers into children's and young people's perceptions (Broad and Saunders, 1998; see also Alderson, 1995: 93–112; France, 2000).

Important ethical and methodological issues, many of which are transferable to policy work with children more generally, and which address key issues for community development work, are raised in these studies (Alderson, 1995; Clarke *et al.*, 1996; Mahon *et al.*, 1996; Morrow and Richards, 1996; Solberg, 1996). One such, relating to the political status of the child, is the question of the validity of children's responses.

Children's views, carefully solicited, are no less valid than those of adults: however, problems may arise in the case of policy or legislative change where their views are in competition with those of adults, as it is adults who control legal and policy processes or the resources to promote policy change. In general, this research demonstrates that, given opportunities appropriate to their age, intellectual and emotional development, children are clearly competent at expressing coherent views on a very wide range of important social, economic and personal issues, including issues of a deeply sensitive kind or where the children themselves may be disadvantaged by their own social, physical, intellectual or emotional circumstances. Increasingly, too, children perceive research itself as being the basis from which action such as policy change and the creation of new structures can be developed (Liverpool 8 CRG, 1997).

Policy development with children in a community context: experience from 'North' and 'South'

There are values and principles informing both social research and community development in a policy-oriented context, in particular the importance of listening carefully to what people have to say, the need to synthesise and/or analyse a range of data (both qualitative and quantitative), and the overriding importance of respect for the views of those with whom the researcher or community development worker is working. Research is, however, not the same thing as community development. For example, community development workers – because of their general value orientation – may challenge people expressing racist or oppressive views, an option which may not be open to researchers. Nor is community development synonymous with research, although it is not uncommon that community development workers find that they need to draw on research to inform their activities. It is the process of moving across the threshold from research into action alongside individuals and community groups that differentiates the community development worker from the researcher. This raises further important issues about the capacity of children to be the subjects of community development work, again most of all because initiatives arising from community development work take its subjects into the world of political and social action – a world largely shaped by adults.

Thus, whilst research with children tells us what children are capable of achieving in terms of expressing their views, the crucial questions for those concerned with community development with children go further, asking to what extent can groups of children defined geographically or on the basis of some common interest, in however small a way, organise to change their world? Reported experience in the UK and other countries in the 'North' (countries which are economically more developed) and the 'South' indicates a very wide and growing range of activity.

Although the accounts below demonstrate the encouragingly wide range of actions which children and young people have taken to promote their own interests in policy development, it is important to remember that there are many inhibitors to their effective participation; they include dominant rural and urban planning trends, for example, and most of all the (often tacit) assumption by adults that impacts on the life of adults will 'trickle down' to affect the life of the child. This view should by now be as discredited as the view that economic prosperity for the very wealthy will trickle down to the poorest.

Given discussion earlier about the relatively recent development of a general awareness of children's rights, and the growing understanding of the need to offer children means to having a voice of their own, it is not surprising to find that the literature regarding community development with children is both recent and 'thin', much of it published in relatively inaccessible 'grey' sources such as magazines, house journals and monographs. It is also worth reiterating that, just as the language of 'community' and 'community development' is constantly changing, sometimes being hijacked for other political purposes (Craig, 1998), so is the language of children's participation and community development with children constantly changing (Smith, 1981). Language remains crucial to understanding what is happening: the boundaries between manipulation, consulting young people (e.g. Kealy, 1993) and full-blown community development with children are often ill-defined and the literature reviewed here is at times equally unclear as to these and other important boundaries.

Political and social arguments supporting the participation of children and young people, particularly within a 'Northern' context, are developed in Lansdown (1995), Willow (1997), Goodman (1997), Treseder (1997), Wellard *et al.* (1997), and NEF (1998). Most writers provide a range of case studies, including cameos of a variety of structures and mechanisms developed at local levels. Willow classifies initiatives into six approaches: corporate strategies to promote participation; permanent structures and mechanisms; long-term projects; time-limited projects; national initiatives; and European developments.

It is not surprising that the main foci of accounts of policy development work with children within the UK and other 'Northern' countries are in relation to *regeneration* and frequently to do with apparently relatively 'soft' policy issues such as the environment, play and leisure with which children can engage more easily and which relate to their more immediate and local needs. Cannan and Warren (1997), covering experience in France, Germany and the UK, include case studies of ways of integrating both a child protection and a community development approach to working with children, illustrations of involvement in a Festival on the Rights of the Child, and attempts to encourage the participation of children within long-term neighbourhood community work. Henderson (1995) provides detailed examples, organised into policy themes (such as environment, education, care and protection, and the neighbourhood), describing work with children over traffic-calming measures, planning play provision and the involvement of children in neighbourhood action. French experience is cited where local children's councils have become an accepted part of civic life in more than 700 towns. Willow (1997) reviews both the experience of French children's councils and German Children's Parliaments, parallel-ing the adult democratic forms in those countries.

Fitzpatrick *et al.*'s detailed discussion of regeneration work (1998) notes, unsurprisingly, that the intensity of support required for children was much greater than for working with adults. SCF (1998), which aimed to involve children and young people (aged 9–25) in forming mechanisms for their longer-term inclusion in the seven-year regen-eration programme in Leeds, implicitly reached a similar conclusion; and Robinson (1997) reviews Salford's regeneration strategy, premised on the involvement of local communities, and specifically including chil-dren and young people. This illustrates tensions between generalised community approaches and specific child-centred approaches.

Accounts of children's involvement at a local level in wider *environ-mental* issues and programmes are provided by Adams and Ingham (1998). The focus here is on environmental planning, with case studies of five further policy areas – Local Agenda 21 groups (pursuing issues of local environmental change); research; local plans; art, design and the environment; and school grounds (see also Davis and Jones, 1996 on play provision; Woolley *et al.*, 1996 on shopping issues; Nieuwenhuys, 1997 on Dutch experience in relation to the built environment). Hart *et al.* (1997) provide a comprehensive review of experience of the par-ticipation of children up to fourteen years of age in environmental issues, drawing largely on experience from 'Southern' settings such as Ecuador, Brazil, Nicaragua and the Philippines. The scope of 'the environment' is widely defined, covering such issues as conservation, monitoring of school grounds, planning, the conditions of working children, and health hazards, and material is used to identify ways in which it could be used within differing cultures. The focus on environmental issues arises because, as Hart notes,

> people's relationship to nature is the greatest issue facing the world at the turn of the century . . . [and] . . . the planning, design, mon-itoring and management of the physical environment is an ideal domain for the practice of children's participation . . . clearer for children to see and understand than many social problems.
>
> (Hart *et al.*, 1997: 20)

This is perhaps the case because children can approach the environment in a holistic fashion. In incorporating a community development approach to working with children on environmental issues, authors also explicitly challenge the increasingly discredited idea that development is essentially about growth (Korten, 1990), arguing that an appropriate response to the over-exploitation of the world's resources requires a strategy which links the local to the global, an approach to which the best work with children contributes (Craig, 2000).

Pearce (1998: 115) reviews experience of involving children in the life of *museums*, especially within the USA where he demonstrates that, through involving young people and older children as volunteers and through consultative exercises, 'the target age-groups of a children's museum could acquire both the right to influence and the means of influencing the organisation and the governance of the institution'. There is, however, a growing body of reporting on the involvement of children and young people in more 'difficult' policy areas, or with more 'hard-to-reach' groups. This includes work on *health* (de Groot, 1996 – providing examples such as young people's health forums, in large housing estates and small market towns, and working with young people with learning disabilities); *anti-poverty* work (Wilkinson with Craig and Alcock, 2000 – which reviews the involvement of children and young people in the development of anti-poverty initiatives under the umbrella of a strategic programme); *residential care* (Ward, 1995 – evaluating the development of regular community meetings within a residential care home); housing and homelessness amongst 'at risk' American children and young people (Good, 1992); and *community safety* in France and England (Pearce, 1995). This last, exploring the link between bullying within school and violence outside it, shows the value of comparative study as students from East London, visiting French counterparts, appreciated the ways in which older youths led initiatives within the French school, including managing a school radio station, and involvement in school management tasks and school–community relations. In their own school, the English students developed work with local immigrant communities, a school safety committee, and a mentoring scheme.

Work with *street children* (West, 1997) analyses participatory research undertaken by street children in Bangladesh to establish a policy framework for change. Other examples of developmental work with hard-to-reach groups are given by Dallape and Gilbert (1994) on working with street children in Kenya; Munene and Nambi (1996) on similar work in Uganda; and Ennew (1994). The last includes short case studies of the Metro Manila Street Children's Conference, in the Philippines, which built a major city-wide children's organising platform; children's responses to a research project in Bombay, India; children-led campaigning around health issues near a waste tip in Peru; and an investigation into the deaths of working children (carried out with help from adults) by children in India.

Other more sensitive policy areas where children and young people have been engaged effectively include work on *race relations* (Treppte,

1993, describing a community developmental approach to working with Turkish mothers and children in a German town). Similar community-focused approaches to pre-school children are reported from the Netherlands in Kieneker and Maas (1997); drawing on the example of the *Head Start* programme of the US 1960s War on Poverty, from Ireland (Kellaghan and Greaney, 1993); and in the field of *disability*, where Moore (1998) describes work to promote the involvement of children with special needs in Scotland. Russell (1998) and Beecher (1998) analyse the work of the Council for Disabled Children and other agencies promoting the views of disabled children, including minority ethnic disabled children, and McIvor (1995) provides examples of the ways in which disabled children in Morocco have been encouraged to challenge their dependent status and others' oppressive perceptions of them.

A UNESCO-funded study (MOST n.d.) includes accounts of work in eight countries, including Argentina and India, showing children engaging with local government representatives, planning resettlement from squatter camps and helping to create a young person's radio station, and the use of modelling techniques as a way of designing safe play environments (involving children as young as three or four; see also Miller, 1997). Johnson *et al.* (1998) review case-study material from many countries showing children participating in situations of *crisis*, *war* and *exploitation*, and within a number of policy settings (including school, the labour market, public services, the neighbourhood and in cultural activities). SCF (1995) provides brief accounts of children's participating in managing education and village health organisation; of a children's parliament in India; and children's involvement in participatory research in Kampuchea.

Models of good practice

Because this review largely draws on others' accounts of work, accounts which may be partial or limited, it is not possible to evaluate individual instances of work described. However, drawing on these accounts, on more general accounts of community development, analyses of the boundaries of childhood outlined here and elsewhere, and on the increasingly wide literature on the evaluation of qualitative social policy and community development interventions (e.g. Feuerstein, 1986; Craig, 1988; P. Harding, 1991; Breitenbach and Erskine, 1994; Carley, 1995; Barr *et al.*, 1995, 1996a, 1996b; McKendrick *et al.*, 1996; Connell and Kubisch, 1998; Sanderson *et al.*, 1998; Alcock *et al.*, 1999), it is possible to derive a framework against which future policy development work with children might be assessed.

It is an urgent political task to define the characteristics of effective policy development work with children within a community development context. At a time when, in many countries, and not least of all the UK (Coles and Craig, 1999), increasing numbers of young people – both of majority and of minority origins – have been driven further from participating in the life of their societies indirectly and directly by the impact of government policy, and where there is perceived to be a significant lack of interest amongst young people in traditional democratic forms, it is important to find effective means for engaging them in political life.

This chapter has reviewed a growing range of work which has engaged the participation of young people in a wide spectrum of settings, and in many different cultural contexts. The literature suggests that there are few, if any, arenas of policy, contexts, or approaches, where the involvement of children and young people in decision-making is not possible or appropriate: it encompasses work with children in situations of war, with children who are profoundly disabled, and those whose entire life has been spent on the streets, disengaged from any of the normal trappings of citizenship. There is little doubt that the scope of this work will continue and, with it, the literature will develop. Similarly, the techniques for engaging with children and young people, incorporating a range of innovative means of promoting such work (for example, the use of video and film, drama, narrative, fictionalised accounts and tape and, for very young children, through play), will multiply.

How do we know what works? Although the language and practice of evaluation has developed considerably in the past fifteen years in particular, and has challenged the dominant obsession of quantitative 'value-for-money' approaches of governments as largely irrelevant to the complex, multi-sectoral and qualitative approaches characteristic of community development, it is clear that very little of this evaluative practice has yet found its way into the arena of work with children. A preliminary review of this evaluation literature (Craig, 2000) highlights a number of key elements which can be regarded as important building blocks for the evaluation of community development, building blocks which could largely be applied to community development work with children. The key elements identified in this review are:

- the importance of *qualitative* indicators of success, used in a way which complements quantitative ones;
- the need to observe *process* goals as well as output and outcome goals – for children as much as adults, how things are done is as important as what is achieved;
- the stress on *participation* (which is not tokenistic) in all stages of programmes and not just, for example, in some early shallow forms of consultation; and
- the importance of *sustainability* in thinking about empowerment.

To this list of basic criteria should be added the particular concerns highlighted in earlier discussions of childhood and research with children;

namely, that work with children should attempt to meet the competing tensions of being, on the one hand, *age-appropriate* (a consideration which runs the risk of being shaped entirely by adult views of what is appropriate, particularly given the ethos on protection dominating much work with children), and, perhaps contradictorily, *liberating* rather than controlling. It remains an important research task to see if criteria developed in conjunction by children match this, unavoidably, very adult formulation.

Throughout this chapter we have argued that there will be contradictions and tensions in working with children within what is essentially an adult-driven framework. These tensions are apparent when assessing the extent of participation. For example, Arnstein's famous typology (1969) shows a hierarchy of participation, ranging from manipulation to control, against which one can assess the extent to which 'citizen participation' is most effective. Arnstein's ladder has been adapted by others to apply specifically to the issue of participation by children: Wellard *et al.* (1997: 10), drawing on Hart (1992), suggest that the eight rungs might be manipulation, decoration, tokenism, assigned but informed, consulted and informed, adult initiated, child/young person initiated, and equal partnership. The highest level of participation, in their view, is where 'children and young people come up with the ideas for a project, they set it up and then involve adults as equal partners in taking decisions and implementing them' (ibid.). This view, however, still incorporates an understanding of children as inevitably dependent on the participation of adults in their lives to some degree. This tension is apparent too when involving children in evaluation where the goals of evaluation are not shaped by children themselves.

Long timescales may be needed to see through effective evaluations of human service programmes, a point now beginning to be acknowledged in strategic government initiatives to combat social exclusion. This is particularly the case with interventions which privilege community development work, which must work at a pace determined by the capacity and needs of those who are the programme's subjects. Where these subjects are children this may be even more the case. The issue of sustainability is also critical. Empowerment implies the creation of sustainable structures, processes and mechanisms, over which local communities (in this case, of children) have an increased degree of control, and which themselves have a measurable impact on public and social policy affecting those communities, a definition incorporating both outcome and process goals. These structures, processes and mechanisms contribute to the goals of community development work with children beyond the initial impetus which establishes them. Given the domination of most structures by adults, it is hardly surprising that the evaluation of community development work with children has particularly to be seen as a long-term process (perhaps ending only as children cease being children).

In this vein, Ennew (1994: 125–6) suggests that evaluation should be an integral process of continuous learning in which the range of evaluative questions asked in work with children might be open to frequent review and revision. One tension apparent here is that children's interests change as they grow up through 'youth-hood' into adulthood and that timescales in work with some children, contradictorily, may have to be limited. There are also tensions derived from particular cultural contexts, for example in social development work in the 'South' where the desire for participation may be overriden by the imperatives of meeting basic needs such as ensuring the supply of adequate drinking water or food; or where the rights of a child to be seen as other than a source of labour have yet to be established.

Those promoting the development of policy with children and young people, and its evaluation, also have to accept that the outcome of such work may be not simply that the aims or methods of certain interventions are challenged but that that challenge extends also to the organisational context within which such interventions are made. Put most simply, effective work with children may increasingly challenge the power of adults both about what is done and how it is done. Children and young people, for example, are critical of traditional 'representative democratic forms', tending to favour much more participative ways of engaging their peers in policy debate.

Notwithstanding the relative lack of proper evaluation in most cases, this discussion shows the enormous potential for consulting and encouraging the participation of children and the potential benefits that it can bring, not least of all in ensuring that children become active and participating citizens as they grow into adulthood. Children cannot, and in general should not, be treated as 'little adults': their intellectual and emotional sophistication and understanding of the adult world is limited by the very fact that they are partly or even largely dependent on others for the maintenance of their lives – although adults have often been guilty of exaggerating the extent of that dependence, particularly perhaps in relation to children's ability to think critically and make informed choices.

Many of the lessons – and techniques – of research and community development are relevant, appropriately and sensitively used, to work with children, and the role of adults has to be to liberate their abilities and creativity within a negotiated framework of rights and responsibilities. This continues to be a subject of discussion and a source of tension, not least between children and young people, and adults themselves. Limits on the appropriate power of adults and the boundary between childhood and adulthood will continue to be tested through this process. Adults cannot, of course, absolve themselves from responsibility for the overall direction of children's lives, and community development with children will always have to be seen within this overarching framework.

Similarly, governments need to ensure that the context of legislation and policy within which this work takes place does not, directly or indirectly, create barriers between children and young people and important policy arenas (Craig, 1991; SEU, 1999). There is clearly much more that can be done to encourage children to take control of important aspects of their lives or to shape policies which affect them. The benefits of this will be seen in their increasing engagement as they grow to adulthood.

References

Adams, E. and Ingham, S. (1998) *Changing places: children's participation in environmental planning*, London: Children's Society/Planning Aid.

Alcock, P., Barnes, C., Craig, G., Harvey, A. and Pearson, S. (1999) *What counts? What works?*, London: Improvement and Development Agency.

Alderson, P. (1995) *Listening to children: children, ethics and social research*, Ilford: Barnardo's.

Alderson, P. and Goodey, C. (1996) 'Research with disabled children: how useful is child-centred ethics?', *Children and Society*, Vol. 10, No. 2: 106–16.

Aldridge, J. and Becker, S. (1993) *Children who care: inside the world of young carers*, Loughborough: University of Loughborough/Nottingham Association of Voluntary Organisations.

Appleton, P. (1995) 'Young people with a disability: aspects of social empowerment', in C. Cloke and M. Davies, (eds), *Participation and empowerment in child protection*, London: Wiley/NSPCC.

Aries, P. (1986) *Centuries of childhood*, Harmondsworth: Penguin (revised version of 1960 edition).

Arnstein, S. (1969) 'A ladder of citizen participation', *Journal of the American Institute of Planners*, Vol. 35, No. 4: 216–24.

Barnardo's (1996) *Transition to adulthood*, Ilford: Barnardo's.

Barr, A., Drysdale, J., Purcell, R. and Ross, C. (1995) *Strong communities: effective government*. Vol. 1, *The role of community work*, Glasgow: Scottish Community Development Centre.

Barr, A., Hashagen, S. and Purcell, R. (1996a) *Measuring community development in Northern Ireland, a handbook for practitioners*, Glasgow: Scottish Community Development Centre.

Barr, A., Hashagen, S. and Purcell, R. (1996b) *Monitoring and evaluation of community development in Northern Ireland*, Glasgow: Scottish Community Development Centre.

Beecher, W. (1998) *Having a say!: Disabled children and effective partnership in decision-making*: Section II, 'Practice initiatives and selected annotated references', London: Council for Disabled Children.

Bellamy, C. (1997) *The state of the world's children*, Oxford and Geneva: UNICEF/Oxford University Press.

Beresford, P. and Croft, S. (1993) *Citizen involvement: a practical guide for change*, Basingstoke: Macmillan.

Booker, S. (1995) *We are your children: the Kushanda early childhood education and care dissemination programme, Zimbabwe, 1985–1993*, Early Childhood Development Practice and Reflections Number 7, The Hague: Bernard van Leer Foundation.

Bradshaw, J. (1990) *Child poverty and deprivation in the UK*, London and Geneva: National Children's Bureau/UNICEF.

Breitenbach, E. and Erskine, A. (1994) *Partnership in Pilton*, Glasgow: University of Glasgow.

Broad, B. and Saunders, L. (1998) 'Involving young people leaving care as peer researchers in a health research project: a learning experience', *Research, Policy and Planning*, Social Services Research Group, Vol. 16, No. 1: 1–9.

Burghes, L. (1994) *Lone parenthood and family disruption: the outcomes for children*, London: Family Policy Studies Centre.

Butler, I. and Williamson, H. (1994) *Children speak: children, trauma and social work*, Harlow: Longman.

Cannan, C. and Warren, C. (eds) (1997) *Social action with children and families: a community development approach to child and family welfare*, London: Routledge.

Carley, M. (1995) *A community participation strategy in urban regeneration*, Edinburgh: Scottish Homes.

Children's Society (1999) *On small shoulders*, London: Children's Society.

CIS (1991) *Childcare in rural communities*, Edinburgh: Children in Scotland/HMSO.

CIS (1995) *The European Union 1996 inter-governmental conference: taking account of children and young people*, Factsheet No. 25, Edinburgh: Children in Scotland.

Clarke, K., Craig, G. and Glendinning, C. (1996) *Children's views on child support*, London: Children's Society.

Cloke, C. and Davies, M. (1995) *Participation and empowerment in child protection*, London: Pitman.

Coles, R. and Craig, G. (1999) 'Young people and the growth of begging', in H. Dean (ed.), *Begging in the UK*, Bristol: Policy Press.

Connell, J. and Kubisch, A. (eds) (1998) *Evaluating comprehensive community initiatives*, Washington, DC: Aspen Institute.

Craig, G. (1988) *Questions of value*, London: Law Centres Federation.

Craig, G. (1991) *Fit for nothing?*, London: Children's Society.

Craig, G. (1998) 'Community development in a global context', *Community Development Journal*, Vol. 33, No. 1: 2–17.

Craig, G. (2000) *What works in community development with children?*, Ilford: Barnardo's.

Craig, G. and Mayo, M. (1995) *Community empowerment: a reader in participation and development*, London: Zed Books.

Craig, G., Elliott-White, M., Kelsey, S. and Petrie, S. (1999) *Auditing children's needs*, Lincoln: University of Lincolnshire and Humberside/Lincolnshire County Council.

CRDU (1994) *UK Agenda for children*, London: Children's Rights Development Unit.

Dallape, F. and Gilbert, C. (1994) *Children's participation in action-research*, Harare: ENDA.

Daniel, P. and Ivatts, J. (1998) *Children and social policy*, Basingstoke: Macmillan.

Davies, M. and Dotchin, J. (1995) 'Improving quality through participation: an approach to measuring children's perceptions and expectations of services' in C. Cloke and M. Davies, *Participation and empowerment in child protection*, London: Pitman.

Davis, A. and Jones, L. (1996) 'The children's enclosure', *Town and Country Planning*, September: 233–5.

Davis, J. and Ridge, T. (1997) *Same scenery, different lifestyle: rural children on a low income*, London: Children's Society.

de Groot, R. (1996) 'Today and tomorrow, giving young people a voice', *Community Health Action*, No. 38: 12–15.

de Winter, M. (1997) *Children as fellow citizens: participation and commitment*, Abingdon: Radcliffe Medical Press.

Ekelaar, J. (1986) 'The emergence of children's rights', *Oxford Journal of Legal Studies*, Vol. 6: 161.

Ennew, J. (1994) *Street and working children: a guide to planning*, Development Manual 4, London: Save the Children.

Feuerstein, M.-T. (1986) *Partners in evaluation: evaluating development and community programmes with participants*, London: Macmillan/TALC.

Fitzpatrick, S., Hastings, A. and Kintrea, K. (1998) *Including young people in regeneration: a lot to learn?*, Bristol: Policy Press.

Flekkøy, M.G. and Kaufman, N.H. (1997) *Rights and responsibilities in family and society: the participation rights of the child*, London: Jessica Kingsley.

France, A. (2000) *Youth researching youth*, Leicester: National Youth Agency.

Franklin, B. (ed.) (1995) *The handbook of children's rights*, London: Routledge.

Freeman, M. (1983) *The rights and wrongs of children*, London: Frances Pinter.

Gittins, D. (1998) *The child in question*, Basingstoke: Macmillan.

Good, A.L. (1992) 'Alternatives for girls: a community development model for homeless and high-risk girls and young women', *Children and Youth Services Review*, Vol. 14: 237–52.

Goodman, H. (1997) 'Encouraging child and youth participation in community development', Report to Calouste Gulbenkian Foundation, London (unpublished).

Greig, A. and Taylor, G. (1997) *Doing research with children*, London: Sage.

Grotberg, E. (1995) *A guide to promoting resilience in children: strengthening the human spirit*, Early Childhood Development Practice and Reflections Number 7, The Hague: Bernard van Leer Foundation.

Gulbenkian Foundation (1995) *Children and violence*, Report of the Commission on Children and Violence, London: Calouste Gulbenkian Foundation.

Harding, L. Fox (1991) *Perspectives in child care policy*, Harlow: Longman.

Harding, P. (1991) 'Qualitative indicators and the project framework', *Community Development Journal*, Special Issue on Evaluation of Social Development Projects, Vol. 26, No. 4: 294–305.

Hart, R. (1992) *Children's participation: from tokenism to citizenship*, Innocenti Essays No. 4, Florence: UNICEF.

Hart, R., with Espinosa, M.F., Iltus, S. and Lorenzo, R. (1997) *Children's participation: the theory and practice of involving young citizens in community development and environmental care*, New York and London: UNICEF/Earthscan.

Heaton, K. and Sayer, J. (1992) *Community development and child welfare*, London: Community Development Foundation.

Henderson, P. (ed.) (1995) *Children and communities*, London: Pluto Press/Community Development Foundation.

Hill, M. (1997) 'What children and young people say they want from social services', *Research, Policy and Planning*, Vol. 15, No. 3: 17–27.

Hill, M. and Tisdall, K. (1997) *Children and society*, Harlow: Longman.

Hodgkin, R. and Newell, P. (1996) *Effective government structures for children*, London: Calouste Gulbenkian Foundation.

Hogan, D. and Gilligan, R. (1998) *Researching children's experiences: qualitative approaches*, Trinity College Dublin: Children's Research Centre.

Holtermann, S. (1995) *All our futures: the impact of public expenditure and fiscal policies on Britain's children and young people*, Ilford: Barnardo's.

Ireland, L. and Holloway, I. (1996) 'Qualitative health research with children', *Children and Society*, Vol. 10, No. 2: 155–64.

Johnson, V., Ivan-Smith, E., Gordon, G., Pridmore, P. and Scott, P., with Ennew, J. and Chambers, R. (1998) *Stepping forward: children and young people's participation in the development process*, London: Intermediate Technology Publications Ltd.

Kealy, L. (1993) *Consulting with young people on Sealand Manor*, Caerphilly: Wales Youth Agency.

Kellaghan, T. and Greaney, B.J. (1993) *The educational development of students following participation in a pre-school programme in a disadvantaged area in Ireland*, The Hague: Bernard van Leer Foundation.

Kieneker, N. and Maas, J. (1997) *Samenspel – mothers speaking*, The Hague: Bernard van Leer Foundation.

Korten, D. (1990) *Getting to the 21st century: voluntary action and the global agenda*, West Hartford, Conn.: Kumarian Press.

Kumar, V. (1993) *Poverty and inequality in the UK: the effects on children*, London: National Children's Bureau.

Lansdown, G. (1995) *Taking part: children's participation in decision-making*, London: Institute of Public Policy Research.

Lightfoot, J. (1990) *Involving young people in their communities*, London: Community Development Foundation.

Liverpool 8 CRG (1997) *Listen to the children*, Liverpool: Liverpool 8 Children's Research Group.

McIvor, C. (1995) 'Children and disability: rights and participation', in SCF, *In our own words: disability and integration in Morocco*, London: Save the Children.

McKendrick, J. et al. (1996) *Barnardo's anti-poverty strategy: a framework for evaluation*, Manchester: University of Manchester.

Mahon, A., Glendinning, C., Clarke, K. and Craig, G. (1996) 'Researching children: methods and ethics', *Children and Society*, Vol. 10, No. 2: 145–54.

Martin, G. and Craig, G. (1992) 'Seen but not heard', *Social Work Today*, 8 October: 15–16.

Middleton, S., Ashworth, K. and Walker, R. (1994) *Family fortunes*, London: Child Poverty Action Group.

Miller, J. (1997) *Never too young: how young children can take responsibility and make decisions*, London: National Early Years Network/Save the Children.

Misra, S. (1983) 'Do children grow better with potted plants? – clinics or community development as entry points for health in the Philippines', *Community Development Journal*, Vol. 18, No. 2: 160–3.

Moore, C. (1998) *'Onwards and upwards': Enabling the participation of children with special needs*, Edinburgh: Children in Scotland.

Morris, J. (1998a) *Don't leave us out*, York: Joseph Rowntree Foundation.

Morris, J. (1998b) *Still missing?* (2 vols), London: Who Cares Trust.

Morrow, V. and Richards, M. (1996) 'The ethics of social research with children: an overview', *Children and Society*, Vol. 10, No. 2: 90–105.

MOST (n.d.) *Growing up in cities: a project to involve young people in evaluating and improving their urban environments*, Project summary available from Centre for Children and Youth, Northampton: Nene College of Higher Education.

Munene, J.C. and Nambi, J. (1996) 'Understanding and helping street children in Uganda', *Community Development Journal*, Vol. 31, No. 4: 343–50.

NEF (1998) *Participation works! 21 techniques of community participation for the 21st century*, London: New Economics Foundation.

Nieuwenhuys, O. (1997) 'Spaces for children of the urban poor: experiences with participatory action-research', *Environment and Urbanisation*, Vol. 9, No. 1: 233–49.

O'Brien, M. (1997) *Space for children: patterns of family life for children of the 1990s*, Professorial Lecture Series Paper, London: University of North London.

Pearce, J. (1998) *Centres for curiosity and imagination: when is a museum not a museum?*, London: Calouste Gulbenkian Foundation.

Pearce, Jenny (1995) 'French lessons: young people, comparative research and community safety', *Social Work in Europe*, Vol. 3, No. 1: 32–6.

Postman, N. (1985) *The disappearance of childhood*, London: WH Allen/Comet.

Rees, G. (1995) *Hidden truths*, London: Children's Society.

Roberts, H. and Sachdev, D. (1996) *Young people's social attitudes: having their say: the views of 12 to 19 year olds*, Ilford: Barnardo's.

Robinson, A. (1997) 'Can do on consultation', *Youth Action*, No. 60, Spring: 18–19.

Roll, J. (1990) *Young people: growing up in the welfare state*, London: Family Policy Studies Centre, London.

Russell, P. (1997) *National survey of disabled children and young people in residential care*, London: Council for Disabled Children.

Russell, P. (1998) *Having a say! Disabled children and effective partnership in decision-making*: Section I, 'The report', London: Council for Disabled Children.

Ruxton, S. (1996) *Children in Europe*, London: NCH Action for Children.

Sanderson, I., Bovaird, T., Davis, P., Martin, S. and Foreman, A. (1998) *Made to measure: evaluation in practice in local government*, London: Local Government Management Board.

SCF (1995) *Towards a children's agenda: new challenges for social development*, London: Save the Children.

SCF (1998) Leeds *Single Regeneration Budget* Phase 3. Details available from Simon Cale, Save the Children, Leeds Office.

SEU (1999) *Bridging the gap*, London: Social Exclusion Unit.

Shropshire, J. and Middleton, S. (1999) *Small expectations*, York: York Publishing Services.

Sibly, N. with Tibi, R. (1995) *Empowering parents to change the future: an analysis of changes in parental attitudes in East Jerusalem*, Working Papers in Early Childhood Development No. 19, The Hague: Bernard van Leer Foundation.

Sinclair, I. and Gibbs, I. (1996) *Quality of care in children's homes*, Report to the Department of Health, York: University of York.

Smith, M. (1981) *Participation: creators not consumers, Rediscovering social education*, London: Youth Clubs UK.

Solberg, A. (1996) 'The challenge in child research: from "being" to "doing"', in J. Brannen and M. O'Brien (eds) *Children in families: research and policy*, Brighton: Falmer Press.

Statham, J. and Cameron, C. (1994) 'Young children in rural areas: implementing the Children Act', *Children and Society*, Vol. 8, No. 1: 17–30.

Strathdee, R. (1995) *No way back*, London: Centrepoint.

Treppte, C. (1993) *Multicultural approaches in education: a German experience*, The Hague: Bernard van Leer Foundation.

Treseder, P. (1997) *Empowering children and young people*, London: Children's Rights Office/Save the Children Fund.

Ward, A. (1995) 'Establishing community meetings in a children's home', *Groupwork*, Vol. 8, No. 1: 67–78.

Ward, L. (1998) *Seen and heard*, York: Joseph Rowntree Foundation.

Wellard, S., Tearse, M. and West, A. (1997) *All together now: community participation for children and young people*, London: Save the Children.

West, A. (1997) *A street children's research project*, Dhaka: Save the Children.

Wilkinson, M., with Craig, G. and Alcock, P. (2000) *Involving young people in action against poverty: the work of YAPP*, London: The Children's Society.

Willow, C. (1997) *Hear! Hear! Promoting children's and young people's democratic participation in local government*, London: Local Government Information Unit.

Woolley, H., Dunn, J. and Rowley, G. (1996) 'Shopping and the city', *Streetwise*, Issue 27, Vol. 7: 3–8.

4 Citizen child

London children's participation in the Office of the Children's Rights Commissioner for London

Moira Rayner

Children are not the people of tomorrow, but people today. They are entitled to be taken seriously. They have a right to be treated by adults with courtesy and respect, as equals. They should be allowed to grow into whoever they were meant to be.[1]

In the beginning

Late in 1999 a group of children met for the first time in a North London boardroom. Their ages ranged from 8 to 15: they came from all parts of the city, from a variety of ethnic and religious cultures, and by and large did not know one another. All they had in common was having volunteered to establish a model Children's Rights Commissioner in London.

It was a big ask. The Office of the Children's Rights Commissioner for London was supposed to be up and running to influence the election campaign for the new regional government for London, the Greater London Authority, starting just weeks later. It was also the first time that an institution devoted to advocating children's rights with government was to be 'owned' from the beginning by its stakeholders: the children themselves. The Office was intended to run as the children decided it should. Children were to decide what sort of staff to look for and help choose them; decide where and what kind of office they should create and what its priorities should be; speak on behalf of children with the media, to other groups, and with government. The children were to drive the adult business of child rights advocacy and policy development. If so, 'participation' would have to be more than a theory, a fetching art collection or a retrospective 'tick' in a box as a key performance indicator. Children's participation would have to be real.

The mission

Secretary of State the Hon. Chris Smith formally launched the Office of the Children's Rights Commissioner for London ('London Children's

Rights Commissioner' or 'OCRCL') on 24 July 2000. It was not a government initiative. The Office was funded for three years by the National Lottery Charities Board, the Calouste Gulbenkian Foundation and Bridge House Estates Trust Fund, as well as being financially and directly supported by the National Society for the Prevention of Cruelty to Children, The Children's Society and Save the Children (UK). The OCRCL was intended to demonstrate to the government in Westminster how valuable a Children's Rights Commissioner could be by, in effect, doing that job for the Greater London Authority (GLA).

There was no mention of such an office or function in the GLA's enabling legislation. The London Children's Rights Commissioner's office existed because a loose coalition of about a hundred and forty children's groups, known as the Children's Rights Alliance for England (formerly the Children's Rights Development Unit) put the proposal together, obtained its funding, recruited the children's Advisory Board and started off the staff selection process.

No single body represents the needs and rights of London's 1.65 million children. Although all government policy affects children, they are not consulted or involved in decisions that affect their lives intimately: whether through employment and social security programmes which influence their parents' capacity to care for them, or through policies which affect the quality of their housing, what and how they learn at school and whether or not there are safe pathways to school, their opportunities to play, and their access to public space and involvement in community life.

The lack of representation is one reason why children's issues are not a major public spending or planning priority. Another is the traditional view that a child might be an object for study and concern, training or even rescue, but otherwise should be cocooned and invisible in a family. We do not 'listen' to children, in public life. We do not even converse with them.[2]

In an effort to upgrade the status and importance of children's issues, several other European countries have established independent offices, children's ombudsmen or commissioners, to involve children in government decision-making and to act as watchdogs over children's human rights. None had been established in the UK in 1999, though there had been a push for such an office for at least a decade before OCRCL began. Most of this pressure came from voluntary bodies, but at least the notion of participation had been reflected in government policy, such as the 1989 Children Act emphasis on listening to children's wishes and feelings, and the UK government's ratification of the UN Convention on the Rights of the Child. Article 12 required governments to promise to involve children in the decisions that most affect them. Some government programmes required children to be 'consulted' about specific policy developments – although how this was to be done was left open, and tokenism was possible. Child abuse concerns had led to some initiatives such as the appointment of Children's Rights Officers in some boroughs, and proposals for a statutory commissioner in Wales, deflected by the Blair administration's preference for an administrative 'children's rights director' – a much more limited role – in the new Care Standards Commission.

Children's rights advocates were not to be satisfied with token offices. Effective government institutions for children require that children and their rights and interests are central, not residual or 'welfare', government business.[3] This would require economic and infrastructure planning with children in mind; a national agenda for children across portfolios; a commitment to children's participation in decisions that affect them, as any other citizen or user of a service; and child impact assessment mechanisms. Most of all, children – as completely powerless citizens – require a powerful advocate of their rights within government, to counteract the dominance of adult-driven agendas and social competence.

The purpose of establishing OCRCL was to fulfil this function for London without an incumbent 'commissioner' because it would have no given authority. OCRCL would have to earn its influence with government. In three years, it was hoped to make the case for a permanent Children's Rights Commissioner for each of the nations of the UK but especially for England.[4]

OCRCL committed itself to:

- promote a children's perspective and respect for the views of the child in government;
- work collaboratively with others within the framework of the UN Convention on the Rights of the Child;
- promote the involvement of socially excluded or marginalised children in London;
- foster relationships with organisations of children and young people in London;
- use media that children and young people watch/listen to/read and its website (www.londonchildrenscommissioner.org.uk) to raise interest and share information;
- develop creative ways of seeking children's views;
- support groups of children working on particular issues;
- consult children: constantly, creatively, and necessarily.

In addition it committed itself to realising children's rights under the UN Convention on the Rights of the Child.

In legal terms, OCRCL is a project of the Children's Rights Alliance for England (CRAE), a company limited by guarantee set up in 1992 to promote the implementation of the UN Convention on the Rights of the Child – and registered as a charity. The Office reports formally to CRAE's Management Council, which has 21 members, including professionals who work with young people and some young members. However, on a day-to-day basis the staff consciously reported to, involved and consulted with its Advisory Board of children.

The first 18 months

Children and young people were involved in all decision-making about and in the Office, because OCRCL intended to model the way that children should participate in decision-making.

Staff selection

OCRCL's five permanent staff were selected by members of the children's Advisory Board (discussed on below) who were trained in staff selection and interviewing techniques, sitting with (adult) members of the Children's Rights Alliance for England. All employees brought their own skill set. As its first director, I brought my experience as a human rights lawyer and advocate, having helped set up the National Children's and Youth Law Centre in Sydney, Australia. I had also been a Hearings Commissioner of Australia's Federal Human Rights and Equal Opportunity Commission. All staff had relevant and very different policy skills and interests, and they were all – administrative and research staff as well – expected to demonstrate a personal commitment to children's rights and a willingness and capacity to work directly with children as equals.

Establishment

The Advisory Board helped recruit the staff and find the premises and met at least monthly to guide the Office's work.

The Advisory Board of (originally) sixteen children and young people had been recruited and trained in the duties of an Advisory Board and children's rights and recruitment by the time the OCRCL staff first met together in March 2001. That training became an ongoing and shared commitment among Board members and the staff.

Its Office was set up within the Child Poverty Action Group's office in the Angel, Islington. It was a wheel-chair-accessible, child-friendly (open plan, music, colour, comfortable sofas, access to computers) light and informal room, chosen because of its centrality, proximity to public transport, relative street safety, and availability at evenings and weekends, when it is easier for children to meet.

Advisory Board development

Many of the key points set out below came from the Advisory Board's own review of the effectiveness of the project, 18 months into the work.

A fundamental principle was that the Board met and worked out its aims and identity before adults were employed. It was to be their office. This was crucial to the perception and reality that children 'owned' the project. The staff were at pains to ensure this was not lost: the Advisory Board ensured that this was a fundamental principle.

Key principle: If young people are to be involved, it should be easy to get involved, and stay involved

The Board members self-selected by filling out a child-friendly application form distributed throughout London, and created their own group identity before adults were employed. Applications were invited from places where children and young people could easily find leaflets because they already went there – in youth clubs, schools, libraries and organisations already committed to children's participation. Letter, tape, video, a magazine article or filling out the leaflet form, could make the application. They were asked to say what they thought would make a good children's rights adviser.

Key principle: Every process – from selection, to meetings, to communications – must be child-friendly

Even the application process was 'child tested' first by Article 12, a young people's self-advocacy group. It was decided to use the application as the basis of selection for the Board so that children would not have to face a nerve-racking interview: what might be 'normal' to an adult would not be acceptable to most children.

Key principle: Successfully involving young people means that they should not be asked to 'fit in' to structures that are already in place

The children decided how often to meet, and how the meetings should be run. Their first meeting was crucial. The fact that the Advisory Board was set up before the Office meant that the children and young people who were to be involved in the project did not have to be bound by structures that were already created and did not have to 'fit in' with something that might not have been appropriate.

Key principle: First impressions count

The first meeting was also critical to the initial confidence of the Advisory Board and its development. Chaired by Peter Newell, Chair of CRAE, the children at that meeting said they felt they and their views were important and that there was a great adventure ahead. It featured games and participatory activities to get to know themselves and find out what the project really meant – and the first training on children's rights, and the role of an Advisory Board. They had to feel comfortable first, to become a team that could drive the first months of the work.

Key principle: Let the children set their own ground rules
for working

This process included setting their own ground rules, 'Working Together', which were:

- Listen to each other and treat what they say seriously.
- Respect others – their views and who they are. Don't be judgmental. Look for people's good points. Don't let age make a difference.
- Share all opportunities and co-operate with each other.
- Try not to be shy, don't be put off by others, share your ideas and encourage each other.
- Ask questions and raise things if you don't understand them.
- Don't assume adults have all the answers – try to find them ourselves.
- Have fun together as well as work.
- No alcohol or swearing.
- No criticising writing or spelling.
- If you need something (drinks, going to the toilet) do it, don't ask permission.

The adult staff tried to apply something of the same spirit in their own dealings.

Key principle: Training is essential

It was one thing to say that the children had the power to determine how the project developed, and another to make this real. A fine line had to be drawn between involving children, and accepting their experience as real and essential, and giving them our own adult and 'knowledgeable' agenda. If the children were to be trained in being effective, adults should not take away their voice and impose their own. However, children had to get the skills to make them effective, and to build their confidence up.

The Advisory Board asked for training and, over the first 18 months, got it on: the UN Convention on the Rights of the Child; what children's rights commissioners are and what they should do; setting selection criteria, shortlisting and interviewing applicants for jobs; working with the media; policy development – members became 'portfolio holders' in areas they were particularly interested in, such as housing, education, poverty and religious minorities; being 'young consultants' – including participation techniques, interviewing and research methodologies;[5] being presenters of workshops and seminars – Advisory Board members became highly proficient and confident in giving presentations for adult and young people's groups; facilitation of meetings and, inevitably, conflict resolution.

Training workshops had to cater for young and older children with different experiences, which was not always easy. OCRCL used a combination of external facilitators and staff and young people themselves offering training.

Key principle: Keeping them involved takes planning

The original Board members did stay, remarkably, involved and loyal. The original sixteen young people contracted to twelve, as some children left London, and a second recruitment drive halfway through the project doubled this number. There was plenty of work to do and not enough people to do it. It was also hoped to make sure that more young children were involved in the work, and children who were not originally confident enough to put themselves forward. The new recruits had already met Advisory Board members and staff and been involved in some of the activities undertaken by the OCRCL, whether these were consultations on GLA strategies, or questionnaires, or the Big Meeting (see p. 67), or through action research. Keeping them involved was a key responsibility for all staff.

It was necessary to make sure that both Board meetings and other meetings members attended took place out of school hours in accessible central London venues – and they had to be child-friendly. That meant among other things that participants:

* knew well ahead of time what was to be discussed;
* had the opportunity of being briefed on the meeting business ahead of time, knowing what to expect;
* had meeting rules that, among other things, permitted them to speak first;
* had plenty of food and drink and breaks;
* met in a comfortable, friendly environment;
* started their meetings with games and fun;
* were not inflicted with jargon and long words or boring stuff during meetings;
* broke regularly – i.e. no business went on for more than an hour;
* wherever possible, either chaired or managed the meetings themselves with adults taking the notes;
* were given ways to make it clear when the conversation was not making sense to them, without feeling silly;
* received materials that were easy to understand, with lots of pictures, diagrams and clear explanations.

All minutes and papers were written in a child-friendly way – easy to read, large print, illustrated if appropriate, and very plain about who was expected to do or say what and when.

This rule about documentation applied to all written materials that came out of the OCRCL. We found, for example, that it was perfectly possible to translate large formal policy documents, such as the GLA's draft transport strategy and economic development strategy, into a simple consultation document, which had the space for comment on the key questions or issues.

The key issue for the staff was making sure that the time and resources were available to ensure the Advisory Board was informed and included and came to meetings. This meant ringing up in between times, sending notes and letters often, and where anyone seemed to feel left out, making sure they were included – sometimes the older boys talked over the younger ones – and making sure all felt welcome, and everyone had fun.

Key principle: Avoid creating an exclusive group?

A common problem with children's boards and consultative committees is their becoming a self-selected, exclusive or elite group. The Advisory Board itself foresaw this. It was addressed by talking it through – the Board was anxious to retain its sense of self as a group while recruiting more children, using the database of the thousands of children we had consulted or worked with or written to over the last year and a half, and making sure new members and old met and grew in confidence together. We were particularly keen on including younger children who could 'seed' other child participation opportunities (projects, consultations, school councils, etc.), as well as keeping the office child-centred.

Major projects

The business plan approved by the Advisory Board committed the OCRCL to:

1   Set up and run a three-year innovative high profile office and coordinated activities.
2   Promote community involvement and participation of children and young people in London at all levels, from central government to individual schools and residential homes.
3   Develop a children's and young people's perspective in all aspects of London government – by integrating their perspectives, concerns and agendas into policy-making and service development, and by successfully engaging them in mechanisms and structures associated with local governance.

4 Promote the interests of children and young people, in particular those who are traditionally socially excluded or marginalised.
5 Disseminate good models and pilot and test new methods of working with and for children.
6 Be a short-term demonstration project to benefit young Londoners.
7 Influence longer-term community and government structures at all levels in the capital.
8 Provide a model for cities and regions in the UK, which will also have international relevance.

Some of the ways that children participated in this work included:

The wide consultation

OCRCL initially conducted a wide consultation with London children, using a questionnaire (5,000 questionnaires, settled by the Advisory Board, were sent out and 3,000 were returned). In addition, the OCRCL worked with groups of children who might not find questionnaires easy or might have special problems – travellers, children excluded from school, in detention, asylum-seekers, disabled and chronically ill children. This wide consultation focused on the children's priorities for London, their understanding of children's rights and whether their citizenship (we did not use this term) was acknowledged, and what they liked and disliked like about their city.

The questionnaire was in a child-friendly format and workers with children – from schools to children's groups – were encouraged to meet and work with children's groups. The responses were consolidated and analysed, and formed the basis for the *Sort It Out!* report, launched on 6 April 2001 and presented to the Mayor of London.

These voices of children became an integral part of the Greater London Authority's Children's Strategy and the groundbreaking research report, *The State of London's Children*.[6] This report, published in October 2001, put together all available research on the reality of London children's lives, using children's experience as the key to future work in the city.

As well, OCRCL Advisory Board members and staff worked intensely with two groups of children on housing estates to develop a video report for the managers of their estates, on what they were really like from a child's perspective. The children – and adults – learned together how to conduct surveys, interview officials, use video equipment and put together a script and act. Their efforts were then edited and given a soundtrack and presented – to great effect. One mayor was so outraged at what he saw his own staff doing (standing the children up) and the state of their play facilities (dilapidated and closed with no maintenance date planned) that immediate action was taken. The children found this very empowering. So did OCRCL staff. These videos, and another prepared by the Advisory Board on their London, were used widely with other children's groups, conferences and presentations to parliamentary committees and with local government.

Consulting with children on GLA's policies

Children were directly consulted, through OCRCL, on the Mayor of London's strategic plans. This was consistent with the Mayor's interim children's policy: namely, that London should be a child-friendly city; that the Greater London Authority is committed to respect for the human rights of children. The UN Convention on the Rights of the Child recognises children's fundamental rights to the *provision* of the necessities of a decent life; *protection* from all forms of violence and exploitation, neglect and cruel or inhuman treatment; and *participation* in the decisions that affect them and in the life of their community; and that the policy framework underlying the Children's Strategy is the UN Convention on the Rights of the Child.

Its operating principles were that, in developing its strategies, the GLA will consider children's rights and how its decisions may affect them; make sure that children participate fully in strategic decision-making; make itself accountable to children as well as citizens of voting age, and promote positive and challenge negative attitudes to children. OCRCL demonstrated how the GLA could consult with young people early in 2001 when it held highly successful consultations on the Mayor's economic development and transport strategies.

Key factors to successful policy consultations were:

- Child-friendly translations of official documents – no more than eight pages including a response pamphlet – which were distributed widely and well in advance.
- Issuing invitations to attend.
- Adults were permitted to attend as 'helpers' but were not to be bossy!
- Allowing plenty of response time, so that arrangements could be made for travel costs to be met, parental permissions and appropriate travel arrangements with supportive adults for children's safety.
- Meetings were held in a large, open space within the GLA itself so the children knew this was a valued and important activity.
- Involvement of senior government representatives. The Deputy Mayor introduced these. Other strategy and policy advisers took part during the presentations and were available both to give information, and take it in.
- Like all the OCRCL meetings, provide games, food, music, fun, many breaks and plain communication.

- Highly visual presentation of important material, and many ways of contributing (i.e., as in the Big Meeting, building or drawing or describing children's ideal, or nightmare, London and London's leader).

This was then turned into a formal – and child-friendly – report to the GLA and its strategy staff.

OCRCL were encouraged by the activities of other groups, such as the Save the Children Fund (UK) and The Children's Society, who consulted with nursery school children on their hopes and fears for London. This consultation report was presented to the Deputy Mayor of London with song and a report, together with about forty children's creation of a large floor map of their ideal London park, before an audience of up to 150 adults. It showed that nursery-age children, too, have a valid point of view – their main concern with London streets was the amount of rubbish, drug paraphernalia and dog poo they encountered every day – and that those useful views could be obtained with relative ease.

Consulting on the GLA children's strategy

The Mayor engaged OCRCL to work in partnership with the GLA in developing his children's strategy. This required establishing a steering group of the major players in government, the London boroughs, and services, including three children. Meetings were held in the usual inclusive way, although it was necessary for the children to remind adults not to be 'boring' regularly.

In addition, OCRCL established a Children's Strategy group of about eighty organisations and individuals from the voluntary and borough level, and groups supportive of children's rights in London, and children.

Being accountable

A 'Big Meeting' of 300 children took place on 30 May 2001 – an all-day event for London's children at a nightclub. Free lunches, take-home bags, bus art and activities culminated in a workshop at the end of the day where two GLA members answered children's difficult questions about life in their city. The Advisory Board planned and managed the event, which gave children the opportunity to find out about their rights and participate in fun rights-based activities.

What did we learn?

So what did we learn from the first part of the work of the Office of the Children's Rights Commissioner for London?

Lesson 1: Establish the participation principle before you start

The children themselves said that this was fundamental to their being involved in this kind of work. Without such a principle it would be easy to drift into 'consultation', and dangerously easy to establish a feel-good but short-lived and tokenistic Advisory Board.

The adult staff found that a focus on children's own voices and experiences affected the way they worked. For example, because of the work done on the Wide Consultation, *The State of London's Children* report emphasised the 'nowness' of children's lives and the need for a different policy approach.

One serious ongoing issue came to the fore through the project: how much can be reasonably expected of volunteer children? Some of our young people worked very hard, coming into the office frequently during the week, advising on our work in progress, meeting with visitors and giving presentations. We needed their input, more than, perhaps, they benefited from it personally.

Lesson 2: Establish a clear values framework

Respect for the rights of children, and an operational principle that participation means more than consultation, changes the focus of the work. In my own case I could compare the work of the National Children's and Youth Law Centre in Sydney, which sought to involve young people on the Board well after the establishment of the Centre, with very limited success: they did not own the Centre, and they tended not to persist with their commitment to the Board. It was important not to do the same in the London office.

The OCRCL values statement said:

> Our job is to do what a statutory Children's Rights Commissioner would do. This means promoting the rights of London's children by making sure that . . . Children's views are listened to:

- in their communities
- by local government and powerful organisations
- by the Mayor and London Assembly and by the Government Office for London
- Children learn about democratic government by being involved in it
- Children are top of the list when government is planning, making policies and setting budgets.
- Everyone in London pays attention to the UN Convention on the Rights of the Child
- London becomes a top child-friendly city, and
- No children are missed out!

We are a campaigning office. We will show how good it would be to have a permanent Children's Rights Commissioner, so children in England will always have someone to stick up for their rights.

Our values are:

- Children are born with and entitled to enjoy the same human rights as adults
- Children are also entitled to extra help to claim and extra protection of their human rights
- We will always respect children's rights and expect others to
- We will treat everyone inside and outside the project with respect and dignity
- Children are entitled to learn about democracy by being involved in it as early and actively as possible
- It is important that children actively participate in the daily work of our project
- Children *and* adults have the right to play and rest
- We like diversity and value different kinds of people
- We like to . . . cooperate, share, trust, be open, consult, be generous!
- We like exciting and bold ideas!
- The voice of London's children must be heard!

Our Mission Statement is:
The Office of Children's Rights Commissioner for London works jointly with children to promote children's rights and participation in all areas of London life and London government, to link children with their city's government; and to make the case for a permanent, statutory Children's Rights Commissioner for all children.

Lesson 3: Give the task realistic time and resources

This can be really challenging. Our experience was that the two programme directors spent an average of two days a week each on servicing, communicating with and encouraging and involving the Advisory Board. Maintaining active involvement is demanding work and essential if children are to be equal partners. It cannot be skimped, and it takes resources as well as time.

Lesson 4: Everything must be child-friendly

This meant test-driving all communications before committing to them, meeting on children's turf, and speaking with children. We decided that even our formal reports should be accompanied with children's versions and be made available free of charge. We found that to assume that adults would benefit as much as children from child-friendly language was absolutely true: communicating a message requires clarity of vision and imagery.

Lesson 5: Preparation and training are crucial

It is essential that children have the skills and the confidence to participate in adult-partnered work. We also found it was important to keep parents and other caring or responsible adults informed, so that their children could be involved and grow through the process without pressure or negativity.

Finally

The two most important lessons of all are, first, that *children must feel that they own the work of a Children's Rights Commissioner*. Appoint the Advisory Board first, and give them the job, skills, confidence and resources to shape 'their' office. How else can it be shown that children can contribute to 'adult' activities? How else prove to government that listening to children's experience makes better decisions?

It is also good for adult organisations. In respecting children's rights, *we* reminded *ourselves* that children are important. If 'the other' has to be involved as a moral equal, our relationships cannot be condescending or authoritarian. A participant has to be taken seriously, with respect on terms of equality. Children should be an integral part of our world, all of it, and now. It works, and we work better.

The second lesson is that working with children can be challenging, but it is also enormously rewarding.

Notes

1 Janusz Korczak, footnote in S. Joseph (ed.) *A Voice for the Child: the inspirational words of Janusz Korczak*, London: Thorsons (HarperCollins), 1999.
2 See P. Alderson, *Young children's rights*, London: Jessica Kingsley/Save the Children, 2000.
3 P. Newell and R. Hodgkin, *Effective government institutions for children*, London: Calouste Gulbenkian Foundation, 1996.
4 The model was taken from P. Newell, *Taking children seriously: a proposal for a children's rights commissioner*, London: Calouste Gulbenkian Foundation, 2000.
5 See C. O'Kane, The development of participatory techniques, in P. Christensen and A. James (eds) *Research with children*, London: RoutledgeFalmer, 2000.
6 S. Hood, *The State of London's Children*, London: Office of the Children's Rights Commissioner for London, 2001.

Part II
Discourses of childhood

5 Finnish conceptions of children and the history of child welfare

Mirja Satka

'If we save the children today, tomorrow we have saved the nation' wrote the state inspector of poor relief and the leading developer of child welfare in the first Finnish handbook of child welfare (Helsingius, 1907: 106). His book was a contribution to a lively debate about how to deal with children who were considered to be lacking sufficient care and control. This slogan and idea, often cited by other reformers of the time, illustrates the predominant assumptions about children and childhood of that time as a decisive phase of life and a crucial investment in the future of the Finnish nation and its people. This understanding remained dominant throughout the first half of the twentieth century, although it has been slightly remodified several times over the years.

This chapter discusses how different understandings of children have contributed to the formation of national social policies and child welfare for the young generation in the first half of the twentieth century. In the Finnish case this was a period of a very rapid transformation from a dominantly agrarian society to an industrial one.[1] I consider childhood and youth, as well as the notions of them, as socially constructed and thus continuously transforming. The material organisation of childhood, similarly to social and cultural organisation, primarily occurs in children's families. Over the course of modernisation, resources outside of the family have become both increasingly important in organising children's everyday lives and a matter of adults' political will. This has had direct impact on the generational structure both in families and in society, and it has emphasised children and adults as relationally and socially – even biologically – dependent categories.

Nineteenth-century notions of children and childhood

The theory about the state and its citizens to which Helsingius is referring was developed by J.V. Snellman, a philosopher and academic who lived during the first half of the century (e.g. Snellman, [1842] 1928), and who is nowadays recognised as Finland's national philosopher. Based on the contemporary German theorising on the concept of the state, the three most important elements of his idea are the family, civil society and the state. Its starting point, like Hegel's, was the notion of the individual as a moral being, and society as a community of norms. According to Snellman, social integration is dependent upon the relationship between the individual and society. Social integration culminated in everyday life relations of the family and the state. Snellman considered the nuclear family, a civilising unit of parents and their children, as a system of generational relations. To him it was the institution of the family that actually maintained the entire society by teaching its children proper habits and values; the family's main function was to civilise future citizens of the state and thus to guarantee the morality of social life. Snellman concluded that society as a whole is based on the nuclear family and, more specifically, on mothers' child-rearing practices, which he considered to be the most important task in the nation-building project.

The ideal Finnish citizen of the late nineteenth century was sober, honest, sparing and hard-working, with strict internal control and discipline (Alapuro *et al.*, 1987). Since children were considered as helpless and wild creatures 'in natural state' and as 'acting according to their natural instincts' it was necessary that adults, and mothers in particular, introduce children to 'truth and good', whereas children were expected to be ignorant but loyal, obedient and thankful for the upbringing and education given to them. A typical aspect of the late nineteenth-century model of Finnish generational relations was a strict hierarchy between adults and children, as well as the implicit obedience of children. Children were the object of adults' well-meaning activities, and childhood was a phase of life whose importance lay in its potential for the future.

At the turn of the twentieth century Finland was a predominantly agrarian society, and the social problems of children related to the industrialisation and urbanisation being experienced in many parts of Europe were not a major concern. The continental social problems of children and the related ideas of child study and professional intervention, however, were well known in Finland due to the many existing scholarly links to Europe and the rest of Scandinavia. The emergence of similar problems related to children and youth were anticipated, and when the world's first Child Welfare Act was passed in Norway, in 1896, it was initially followed by intensive debate and later by a series of reform efforts in Finnish child welfare. At the time the implementation was mainly in the hands of various charities, local communities together with municipalities, and a few state institutions for the most difficult cases.

The first reform effort was motivated by the recognition of the increasing number of neglected and ill-mannered children, as well as by the assumption of childhood as the best possible phase to prevent the growth and development of future criminals, of which the concerned members of the ruling elite were already seeing signs. In the Finnish social conditions of the early twentieth century this conclusion must have been reached more by a new conceptualisation of children and childhood than by the actual numbers of depraved children. The new notion of children was introduced by a state committee (Committee Report, 1905: 9a) established for child welfare. The committee constructed both children and their social problems by applying a contemporary discourse called 'social defence', originally developed by Italian criminologists. Its aim was to help modern societies and nation-states to protect themselves from the new 'social ills', such as increasing criminality. The authors regarded children as an essential target in crime prevention, since according to them, intervention in children's developing moral character had long-lasting effects and prevented immorality and crime in the future.

Following the recent Norwegian model of child welfare (see Dahl, 1985), the radically new assumption of the committee was that each child is a developing, unique individual and at the same time a potential deviant, the occurrence of which can be discovered by means of an empirical child study. When a child shows indications of poor moral quality, as proved by the results of a scientific investigation, the child should be treated individually as sick; the child was to be cured or the illness prevented by means of a particular method that was to be applied individually, on a case-by-case basis. The idea of preventing 'social ills', and criminality in particular, with a special four-step procedure of social defence (including e.g. advice, surveillance, custody, and use of closed institutions), was perfectly suited to the previous ideas about educating good Finnish citizens. The new discourse helped to specify the treatment methods in practice with those particular 'developing creatures of nature', who had proved difficult to raise by the old means of disciplining. It also helped to define how it was the role of child welfare practitioners to find out which of the individual children were at risk and how to treat them in an appropriate and well-planned way, both according to individual moral characteristics and the model procedure of social defence. The new measures and institutions of child welfare were meant primarily for children who were either neglected or difficult to manage in institutions for normal children. According to the empirical evidence it was assumed that these conditions were likely to cause problems in the future.

One strategy with children was the extensive use of preventive measures targeted at the child population in general. This was not just a novelty of the social defence debate; similar activities were common in charities aimed at children. Preventive child welfare mainly provided leisure-time activities, basic education and day-care for children in need, and it was implemented in the slowly growing number of public schools and kindergartens. At the same time child welfare was developing slowly towards rational expert activity. The reformers, for example, started to regard charitable work as traditional, idealistic and religious-minded, and most importantly, according to them, charity was lacking a model for effective, individualised treatment of children.

The Finnish Civil War and two kinds of children

Finland was declared independent in 1917 in the shadow of the Russian revolution. In the following months, the radically politicised working-class movement, the social democrats (called Reds) on the one hand, and the bourgeois groups (Whites) on the other, was driven into violent conflict. The Finnish Civil War in 1918 was one of the bloodiest in European history. Most of the 30,000 people who were killed were Reds, who, incidentally, lost the war. The war left over 5,000 families in a desperate situation. Most of these families consisted of three or more children and a mother. Ultimately, the number of children in need of care and social support reached about 20,000. Over a thousand became orphaned, or were left without a parent who was able to take care of their upbringing and maintenance (Pulma, 1987: 130–3). Such being the case, the most urgent problems were the maintenance of survivors, children and mothers, and the care and upbringing of the Red children who had become orphans. The winners were also concerned with how to integrate the beaten Reds into society. In the young and divided nation, the victor's main concern and ideal was to create a united population that was physically strong, loyal and patriotic. The common belief was that only such a population would be able to successfully maximise the power of the nation (e.g. Korppi-Tommola, 1990: 18–83). Hence, the public institutions of moral regulation, such as the Church, public school, and emergent child welfare gained importance; they were the means of the hegemonic project.

The new state rested on an unstable political basis. One outcome of the war was that there existed not one, but two very different discursive understandings about what had happened. The victors thought that they had finally freed Finland from the Russian Bolshevists allied with the Finnish workers, while the latter understood the confrontation as the attempt of the working class to defend itself against the Finnish bourgeoisie. Furthermore, the winners began to emphasise that there was a deep moral division between themselves and the rebellious Reds[2] (cf. Alapuro, 1994: 305–7; Ketonen, 1983: 27–34).

The post-war social divisions were essentially rooted in the contemporary understanding of the human being, and citizenship became divided into first- and second-class citizenship following the divisions of the Whites and Reds. This division became deep and long-lasting, not least because of the fact that the violent conflict was very much a morally flavoured surprise on both sides. The educated classes experienced the conflict as incomprehensible (e.g. Alapuro, 1990). From their point of view, the masses that they had wished to rule had become the opposite of decent citizens (i.e. violent anarchists). This view extended to the contemporary assumptions of children and the meanings of childhood. Immediately after the Civil War, the child welfare texts of Red children seem to have a common plot. They present slightly different versions of the following story: the Red orphans have been raised in a morally inferior atmosphere. They have not had the chance to be educated by a reliable and educated adult and thus they have simply not received the kind of care and education that a child needs in order to develop into a healthy adult. Such being the case, children of the Reds, unlike children of the Whites, lacked all skills and moral values necessary to grow and develop into educated citizens (Satka, 1995: 86–8).

Consequently, the authors saw the future of Red children as bleak: if they were left without extensive social support and without an upbringing organised by the victors, the only future that they would have would be one filled with personal misery and ruin. The authors were convinced that these children were going to grow up to be criminals and drunkards, an extra burden on 'the civilised society' and the educated classes. Moreover, they thought that these children, being the offspring of the rebellious groups, constituted a real danger to the future of 'organised society'. Without effective social intervention, they believed, they would grow up to be a hostile new generation of horrible rebels (e.g. Satka, 1995: 86–7).

Interestingly, these assumptions were accentuated by another moral argument that underlined the moral innocence of the Red children in 'the national disaster'. The texts end up saying that the dependent Red children are not really to blame for their condition, unlike their mothers, who were mainly responsible for the war since they had chosen to neglect their most important societal duty to control the moral reproduction of decent citizenship in their families. Red children were secondary sufferers because of the sins of their parents. Thus, Red mothers came to represent 'the lost generation' of the Red rebels, whereas their innocent children were the 'citizen in potentia' for the nation and the state. According to a state committee for child welfare, every Finnish child was to be considered equally a *child of the state* (Committee Report, 1921: 15, 171). The child welfare texts brought Red mothers' parenting skills into the spotlight as the central subject of a careful moral investigation, while their children appeared as a necessary, and indeed the most legitimate, challenge of bourgeois intervention.

The post-Civil War social policies for children

These arguments legitimated the implementation of two simultaneous socio-political strategies for dealing with children. The first treated the children of the Reds and Whites differently, and was based on strict surveillance, while the second, far-reaching preventive measures were equally targeted to every Finnish child. One of the main arguments of the reformers was that a democratic nation-state can only function if the citizens are well-educated.

The control strategy was implemented as part of the procedures run by the state and municipalities in order to provide a necessary level of material support for Finland's needy children and their caregivers. Immediately following the end of the war there was unanimous political agreement that the treatment of Red and White survivors cannot be equal or identical. The arguments emphasised that respectable citizens must be separated from non-respectable citizens and, therefore, that material support for the Reds' needy children was to be given as poor relief, whereas similar assistance 'for the offspring of loyal citizens' was considered impossible (Committee Report, 1919: 11, 6–7). The economic support provided for the Whites was to be given in such a form that 'the innocent victim of the war' can receive it with self-respect and with the feeling that one is receiving well-deserved support. For this reason, the state guaranteed them a state pension corresponding to the income of the lost family member, when necessary, for the rest of their lives (Committee Report, 1918: 1a; Committee Report, 1919: 11).

That the maintenance of the Reds was given under the guise of poor relief had many negative consequences. First of all, it meant that they had no secure income at all. Even getting a dole was uncertain, dependent upon the will of the local municipal board of poor relief without consistent norms of assistance, often governed by the Whites. Second, receiving poor relief on a constant basis had many individually humiliating ramifications, like becoming an object of paternal shepherding targeted at children's upbringing and home education. In addition, those who received relief, in this case people who had until now considered themselves to be respectable and decent citizens, became socially labelled. A similar kind of control was also applied over some other groups of children with questionable moral provenance, like illegitimate children, and all children receiving poor relief (e.g. Piirainen, 1974: 63–71; Pulma, 1987: 126–36; Satka, 1994: 280–3).

The individualised maintenance of war orphans consisted of two major elements: a child's physical maintenance and moral upbringing. In the light of the increasing textual knowledge of paediatrics and child psychology, both of the elements were considered necessary and equally important for the desired objective: 'a healthy soul in a healthy body'. Since Red mothers were subject to a very particular moral surveillance, the task was given to child inspectors presumed to be familiar with children's upbringing and who preferably had some training in the field of education.

The particular duty of the new volunteer was to promote home-education. Her name was registered by the National Office of Poor

Relief, and she was to engage in continuous textual contact with the National Inspector for War Orphans. Moreover, new national regulations were made to co-ordinate her work, and an instructive handbook was written to guide her task.

The child inspector's duty was to inspect all children receiving municipal poor relief; however, the regulations put particular emphasis on war orphans. The child inspector was required to visit the homes of Red mothers three times per year. In the meantime, she was to question neighbours and other people involved in the children's upbringing. She was also expected to give a tri-annual written report concerning the child's physical and moral circumstances. The reports were then delivered to both the Municipal Board of Poor Relief and to the National Inspector of War Orphans. In addition, the care of Red children by their own biological mothers was regulated by means of a written contract. Such Red mothers, 'whose skills and motivation for child-rearing were questionable', were required to sign the contract as a precondition for receiving poor relief. The contract (Satka, 1994: 277) included several obligations to be fulfilled by the mother concerning her everyday parental practices. She had to agree that she was going to keep her home and children clean, carefully control the leisure activities of her children, and teach them industriousness and the virtues of a decent citizen in cooperation with the public school. Over all these obligations there was a threat that should she not adhere exactly to what she had signed, her children could be taken away.

The necessary minimum concerning the moral upbringing of the poor and Red children was that they regularly attend a public school. In the poor relief texts of the early 1920s, the public school appears as an integral part of child welfare with the primary aim of operating as a preventive measure (e.g. Böök, 1923: 159). Making public school compulsory after 1921 was one of the preventive measures in the child's moral upbringing and physical maintenance. Another significant effort concerning children's physical maintenance was public support for kindergartens (1927), as well as mother–child clinics, which started to provide medical services such as maternal care and child welfare. The strategy was to advise and instruct mothers in the preconditions of healthy childhood (e.g. Korppi-Tommola, 1990: 62–5). The emphasis on reorganising the practices of mothering was considerable, and it was regarded as a crucial means of improving the strength of the nation and increasing its population.

The 1950s psycho-social child

After the Second World War a new, discursively much more internationally informed understanding of children and youth began to emerge. State committees for children's issues and the increasing number of professional experts in the field of childcare began to emphasise unanimously the notion that all children were equally valuable to the state, and a key investment in the reproduction of modern, autonomous and happy individuals, who will grow up to be self-supporting and loyal qualified citizens for the state. In this conceptualisation of children the idea of the future citizen and becoming a modern individual are intertwined with a strong emphasis on a better future in one strong nation that can be planned in advance, and worked out later with particular investments in the welfare of children, in tomorrow's citizens.

This widely shared understanding was an outcome and application of the previous notion of improving society by means of social prevention that resurfaced in the 1930s and 1940s. Second, it was a result of the new universal ideas, practices and models connected to the rights and obligations of modern citizenship in a nation-state. These ideas were imported from the Scandinavian countries, Britain and the United States, accompanied by an emphasis on modern individualism. The new understanding was also a consequence of people's wartime experiences, which had heightened the 1930s concern about the quality and quantity of Finns. Efforts were taken to increase the national birth rate, since the strength of the nation was regarded as equal to the status of its people, and, therefore, the number of strong and healthy children was considered as a crucial indicator of the national power. However, wartime propagation of home, mother and family also had other aims. In the context of the post-war insecurities it was meant to strengthen the general nationalist sentiment and people's moral courage, in addition to linking their minds to the promises of a future with happy homes, many children, and loving mothers (e.g. Satka, 1993: 57–62; cf. Rose, 1990).

On the personal level, people's wartime experiences of everyday life were pathbreaking; many Finns, including evacuated children, war refugees, soldiers, and women with work obligations, were cut off from their parents and homes, localities and traditions without warning. One of the consequences was that traditionally assumed (and thus self-evident) norms could no longer be considered as self-evident. This new condition created a forum for new ideas and ideals – for example, the modern home, an independent family house associated with the nuclear family as a site of personal happiness (e.g. Jallinoja, 1984; Saarikangas, 1993). At the same time, the transformation in people's minds and the ensuing feelings of insecurity opened up a new space for expert advice, and a novel possibility for professional activities based on individualist intellectual thought, like social casework, developmental psychology and child psychiatry. All of these were imported discourses; their beginnings existed prior to the war, but it was not before the 1950s that they were powerful enough to have an impact on the reconstruction of the very notion of the child.

From the point of view of the idea of the child, the leading discourse and method in social policies dealing with children was professional social casework for families with children. The post-war extension of social casework was effective; it was organised as international social aid by the United Nations and provided via the Special European Social Welfare Programme, in particular, the Expanded Programme of Technical Assistance (EPTA), which was run by the Economic Commission for Europe in Geneva, initiated in 1949. The resources of the programme included, for example, exchange programmes in which child welfare personnel could undertake professional studies abroad, or inviting foreign scholars to act as professional experts and counsellors in the newly established child welfare agencies and clinics. The idea was to offer new ideas for social workers and 'training that placed at their disposal the working tools which had been forged during the same period in the United States for social techniques as a consequence of the progress in psychology and the social sciences' (Miihaud, 1959: 22). Over the years a considerable number of Finnish social workers studied the latest Western social work techniques abroad, and by the mid-1950s they became important advocates of the psycho-social child (Satka, 1995: 128–31).

The Finnish scholars studied social casework predominantly in such American schools and agencies which by and large represented the diagnostic social casework paradigm.[3] Its ego psychological view was well suited to the aims of international modernisation; it was a theory aimed at facilitating the birth of the autonomous person who self-regulates his or her own conduct and existence for his or her benefit, and, at the same time, for the welfare of the family and the society as a whole (cf. Rose, 1990). A central belief of the theory was that a person's 'irrational' behaviour is influenced by emotions and unconscious factors unless a decisive insight occurs. The knowledge developed by the Finnish social caseworkers, however, was not identical to the diagnostic paradigm of the American social casework. They did their best to apply what they had learned to Finnish social conditions.

One of the so-called 'American Masters' in social work was Lauri Tarvainen, the chief civil servant in the field of child welfare since 1952. Influenced both by his social casework studies and the post-war ideology of the Finnish home cult, Tarvainen began to advocate family-oriented social casework as soon as he was able to draw together an appropriate theory for it; that is, to combine the theory of social casework, the texts of John Bowlby[4] and other child psychiatrists (e.g. Bovet, 1951), some texts of the contemporary Finnish developmental psychology (e.g. Takala and Takala, 1953), and his knowledge about developing Finnish social policies for children. In his textbook, *Lapsen sosiaalinen huolto* [Child's Social Care] (Tarvainen, 1954), he introduced a new view of the child and the family, and of intergenerational relations in general. The book was particularly targeted at social workers practising in child welfare.

The child of the book is, above all, a developing individual with unique, individual developmental needs, his or her own will, opinions, and need for self-respect. According to the book, a child's behaviour is especially influenced by emotions and the psychological laws discovered by positivist child psychiatry and clinical developmental psychology. This leads the author to assume that a child's misbehaviour becomes understandable when considered as an expression of the child's invisible emotional conflicts. In addition, an essential aspect of the child's welfare and psychological development is his or her membership in a family, in a particular functionalist position characteristic for all growing beings and plants: 'A child's development and growth is decisively linked to one's family in the same way as a plant's development depends on the soil' (Tarvainen, 1954: 11). Consequently, the family is the most important social environment inhabited by the psycho-social child. According to the book, a nuclear family requires material, social and emotional support to fulfil its functions for the future generations. This was to be done by means of modern social policy.

Referring to Bowlby, the family is construed in terms of psychological relations between mother and father, parents and children, brothers and sisters, and, most of all, between the mother and the child. The author describes how a child's social problems are a result of emotional instabilities in the family, or the potential personal immaturity of a family member in his or her ability to fill a particular family role, usually for mothering (Tarvainen, 1954: 168, 172). Therefore, he urges social workers to pay particular attention to the emotional state, relations, and the emotional dynamics between family members.

However, when he moves on to illustrative case examples, the family disappears as the target of the work. A short review of the cases reveals that in 85 per cent of them the target of social work is the mother, as she is always closely connected with the child's problems (e.g. Tarvainen, 1953). This view of mothers originated in the psychodynamic belief (cf. Bowlby, 1952) that an early separation of baby and mother is dangerous for the child's emotional development. A good mother has to be present during the first years of her child's life. It is also her responsibility to create a close, warm and continuous relationship with her child. From the emotional point of view, the father plays only a supporting role. He is supposed to help the mother to satisfy her needs, and to support her in maintaining a successful emotional relationship with the child; that is, the family ideal of social casework (Tarvainen, 1954; Ahla and Tarvainen, 1959: 111).

The book introduces two new concepts in child welfare: the internal emotional structure of the family and maternal deprivation, to which the author refers using a slightly different term, 'deprivation from home'. This term emphasises the child's 'psychological home'; that is, the child's social-psychological family relations, as opposed to the material home or the child's relationship to his or her biological parents (Tarvainen, 1954: 36–45, 95). Familial forms that differ from the traditional two-parent, heterosexual couple with children, where the father earns a living and the mother takes care of the home and children, are assumed to be deviant and in need of professional treatment (e.g. unmarried mother, single-parent families, families in which the mother works).

The 1950s social policies for children

The post-war years witnessed a rapid transformation of the way in which the state related to the conditions of children's everyday lives. From the war years on, the Finnish state adopted a new, reform-oriented role; it started to exercise effective social regulation and was more active in offering support – that is, levelling family costs, delivering social benefits and providing social services for its citizens. Families with children were especially targeted by the post-war state. The principle of active state intervention was derived from the Swedish '*folkhemspolitik*' and from the idea of the British welfare state designed for the benefit of all its citizens by Lord William Beveridge (e.g. Urponen, 1994: 213–14). Both of these models were aimed at attaining a society described as a place like home, where people's needs, welfare, and social security were among the continuous concerns of the state. Following these models, the Finnish government was convinced that people in need of social support because of the war[5] should by no means receive a dole. It was a conscious decision made to avoid creating social divisions. On the contrary, the new social benefits available were primarily meant to equalise the everyday lives of those groups of the population who were suffering the most, such as war orphans.

The post-war Western strategies of governing emphasised rational social planning. A dominant vision was that the creation of a better and happier society was possible according to a fairly systematic step-by-step procedure based on modern science and professional expert knowledge. In this vision, children of the nation-state had a particular position: in the light of the recent psychological research childhood was considered a definitive phase in the development of the rest of one's life course, and when the future national success was seen as dependent on the qualities of its citizens, the welfare of every child became an equally important investment for the state. For this reason children have been accorded a central role, both in the creation of modern society and the autonomous individual. For example, a contemporary leaflet published by one of the leading associations in child welfare introduced the new policy with the following illustrative statements:

> A healthy and happy childhood is the best guarantee for a capable and useful citizen in the future.

> A rationally planned scheme of child protection promotes the general wealth of the community and the welfare of its inhabitants.

Resources sacrificed for child protection are a good investment for the local welfare practices in the future, since child protection is an effective form of preventive work among adults.

(Lastensuojelun Keskusliiton julkaisu, 1952)

The social policy of the 1950s was implemented according to three important aims. First, it was meant to be a support system for every citizen, helping them to live in a way that was considered normal and acceptable and thus emphasising normalising aims. Second, a central aim was to prevent social problems before they occurred; and third, it was to be offered in forms that provided support on a case-by-case basis for those modern individuals and families who had accidentally run into problems with their personal self-regulation, or who were unable to cope successfully with the emotional economy of the family (e.g. Rauhala, 1996: 94–7; Satka, 1995: 123, 139–48).

In the post-war programming of social policy investing in the welfare and health of the 'becoming' citizens meant support of those forms of everyday life considered 'normal' and preventive in the light of positivist science. Families with small children were the primary recipients of normalising state benefits, like child allowance (1948), free school meals (1948) and maternity benefits (1949). In addition, the programme included new forms of social assistance, socially subsidised long-term family loans, and social benefits and services targeted for particular groups of needy families, like subsidies for families with numerous healthy children (1943), state subsidies for single-mother homes (1949), and for municipal home aids for overburdened mothers caring for many small children (1950) (e.g. Rauhala, 1998: 90–2; Simonen, 1990).

Simultaneously, however, there were also social services for children, the development of which was essentially frozen, or the use of which was limited and under careful reconsideration. The most important of these social services were day care and institutional care for small children in general (e.g Tarvainen, 1954: 66–85, 133–52). The first Finnish Act for Child Protection, passed in 1936, provided that municipalities should establish institutions to support children's upbringing at home. The Act regarded day care predominantly as one form of child protection, and as a means to compensate for a child's poor domestic conditions. A state committee, appointed to develop a national day care system for children in the late 1940s, regarded day care, similarly to the Act for Child Protection, as an exceptional arrangement for those who are in need of special protection. Its firm belief was that small children should be cared for in their own homes and preferably by their own mothers, although the number of female war widows with small children was considerable, and the expanding industry needed women's labour (Välimäki and Rauhala, 2000: 391–4).

At the same time, individually tailored social services provided by highly skilled, university trained professionals or multi-professional teams, expanded rapidly. They were psycho-social or medical services based on careful, individual investigation, diagnosis, and the treatment of children and their mothers at a family counselling clinic. Ordinarily such a clinic was introduced by a private association, and it was meant for the new, emotional hardships which families, parents, children and youth were experiencing. It was common for social casework to play a major role in working with clients. Professional education for social workers, who soon defined 'saving families in trouble' as their main professional responsibility, although at the same time they remained uncertain about what it meant in practice, was an important contribution to the development of family counselling practices (Satka, 1995: 144–6). The majority of the new services were geared towards families with children, like family counselling clinics, which had spread through the whole country by the end of the 1950s. At the beginning, most of their clients were schoolchildren suffering from various difficulties at school or in relation to orderly school attendance. Over the years, as more detailed knowledge about children's psycho-social problems became available, the clients' clinical problem profiles became diversified (Linna, 1988).

In addition, Lauri Tarvainen worked hard in order to transform the local practices of child welfare into ones more individually oriented, democratic, confidential and respectful of the client, including children. He wrote:

> The purpose of child welfare is to help the child's own development by securing the satisfaction of the child's developmental needs. The starting point of child welfare is an individual child with individual problems. The measures of child welfare must be based on individual investigation and prescription. All measures must correspond to the needs of the child.
>
> (Tarvainen, 1954: 35)

He was, however, lacking the techniques with which to work with children according to these principles, although it is noteworthy that he underlined the child as a developing individual who required a certain degree of sensitivity and respect from the social worker.

From assumptions to social policies

The material, social and cultural organisation of childhood and children's everyday lives is both a result and compromise of many complicated negotiations over time. This brief historical investigation of the Finnish child welfare discourse of the early twentieth century has revealed some interesting hints about how a particular understanding of children and childhood might have contributed to the shaping of social policies for the young generation, and, more generally, how these policies impacted on the generational relations by emphasising so strongly, and with various arguments, children as dependants of their biological mothers. At the same time, the father, or the child's relationship to him, simply does not exist as a target of child protection.

After the Civil War, needy Finnish children were maintained either by means of poor relief or state pension, depending on their parents' political affiliation. The socio-political decision-making was presumably based on what the winners felt was fair according to their interpretation of the war. Obviously the early twentieth century conceptualisation of children as developing individuals and potential deviants legitimated the bipartite policy through the extensive use of control of the home education of those children who were regarded as potential criminals. In a few years the policy of strict state surveillance extended to include illegitimate children living with their mothers, as well as other children who fell under the umbrella of poor relief, whose moral upbringing was also considered to be questionable.

Conversely to the previous child welfare policies, over the two post-Second World War decades in particular the poor but healthy children's welfare and health were strategic targets of social investments by the state, in addition to financial support for their families, family housing, and community planning. At the time, the value of the future generation was considered to be significant since the country was recovering from over four years of war. It was emphasised how personal and national success in the future depends on investing in children. These ideas gave strong support to the notion of the provision of universal and needs-based social benefits for every needy family with children, and for the individually tailored psycho-social services, when needed.

In the end, in the supportive policies for families with healthy small children, there was one exception: state support for the professional nursing of small children was not expanded, and public day care remained marginal, although the number of children in need of daily caring was growing since many war widows with small children were in need of maintenance, and the growing industry in need of women's labour. Many children had to manage on their own while the mothers were at work. The then novel conceptualisation of the child as a developing small being, whose welfare crucially depends on the continuous presence of the mother, played a decisive role in this. The 'truth' was strong enough to nullify both the principle of providing universal social policy and children's needs for organised and continuous daily caring. An argument by a prominent scientist, according to which day care for small children would cause social problems in the future, was too difficult to resist in a society that relied on modern science.

Notes

1 This article is part of Research Project 41439 funded by the Academy of Finland.
2 Two corresponding White modes of speaking about the war emerged. The first called it the 'war of freedom', emphasising honour, heroism and sacrifices, while the other mode of speaking called it a 'rebellion' or a 'civil war', considering Reds as useless, miserable and deceitful, and describing the war in terms of terror and persecution.
3 In the 1950s American social casework was divided into the functional (Rankian) and diagnostic (Freudian) schools. The former stressed the casework relationship as a matrix for growth within the limits of agency function, whereas the diagnostic school was deeply influenced by psychoanalytic theory and particularly the psychology of the ego, which was the focus of Anna Freud's *The Ego and the Mechanisms of Defence* (1936). Also the British social casework originated in the contemporary theories of psychoanalysis and child psychiatry (e.g. Rose, 1990: 121–31, 151–77; Yelloly, 1980: 119–65).
4 One of Bowlby's books was translated into Finnish and published as a shortened edition (Bowlby, 1957).
5 During the war, over 85,000 Finns lost their lives, about 70,000 were wounded, and about 50,000 war orphans and 24,000 female war widows were in need of social support. In addition, by the terms of the final peace agreement, Finland ceded 12 per cent of its territory to the Soviet Union; that is, about 11 per cent of the population, 400,000 people, lost their homes. Most importantly, however, the country succeeded in maintaining its national independence.

References

Ahla, M. and Tarvainen, L. (1959) *Henkilökohtainen huolto*, Helsinki: WSOY.
Alapuro, R. (1990) 'Valta ja valtio – miksi vallasta tuli ongelma 1900-luvun vaihteessa', in P. Haapala (ed.) *Talous, valta ja valtio*, Tampere: Vastapaino.
—— (1994) *Suomen synty paikallisena ilmiönä*, Helsinki: Hanki ja Jää.
Alapuro, R., Liikanen, I., Smeds, K. and Stenius, H. (eds) (1987) *Kansa liikkeessä*, Helsinki: Kirjayhtymä.
Bovet, L. (1951) *Psychiatric Aspects of Juvenile Delinquency*, Geneva: WHO.
Bowlby, J. (1952) *Maternal Care and Mental Health*, Geneva: World Health Organization.
—— (1957) *Lasten hoivan ja hellyyden tarve*, Porvoo: WSOY.
Böök, E. (1923), 'Lasten ja nuorten huolto vuoden 1922 köyhäinhoitolaissa', *Sosiaalinen Aikakauskirja*, 17, 3: 159–69.
Committee Report 1905: 9a (1905) *Ehdoitus suojelukasvatuksen järjestämiseksi. Komitean mietintö I*, Helsinki.
—— 1918: 1a (1918) *Ehdotukset soturien tahi heidän perheidensä avustamisesta*, Helsinki.
—— 1919: 11 (1919) *v. 1918 kapinan aiheuttamien turvatonten lasten huoltamisesta*, Helsinki.
—— 1921: 15 (1921) *Yhteiskunnan lasten ja nuorison suojelu*, Helsinki.
Dahl, T.S. (1985) *Child Welfare and Social Defence*, Oslo: Norwegian University Press.
Helsingius, G.A. (1907) *Yhteiskunnan lastenhoito ja suojelukasvatus*, Helsinki: Suomen Senaatti.
Jallinoja, R. (1984) 'Familistiset ja individualistiset perheratkaisut: yleiskuva 1890–1980', in E. Haavio-Mannila, R. Jallinoja and H. Strandell (eds) *Perhe, työ ja tunteet. Ristiriitoja ja ratkaisuja*, Porvoo/Helsinki/Juva: WSOY.

Ketonen, O. (1983) *Kansakunta murroksessa. Kesää 1918 ja sen taustaa*, Porvoo: WSOY.

Korppi-Tommola, A. (1990) *Terve lapsi – kansan huomen. Mannerheimin lastensuojeluliitto yhteiskunnan rakentajana 1920–1990*, Helsinki: Mannerheimin lastensuojeluliitto.

Lastensuojelun Keskusliiton julkaisu (1952) *Mitä nykyaikaikanen lastensuojelu on?*, Helsinki: Latensuojelun Keskusliitto.

Linna, P. (1988) *Psykiatris-yhteiskunnallisesta työstä kasvatus- ja perheneuvonnaksi. Suomen kasvatusneuvolatoiminnan juurien ja kehityksen tarkastelua. Kasvatus- ja perheneuvolan asema ja tehtävät*, Helsinki: Suomen kasvatusneuvolain liitto.

Miihaud, M. (1959) 'Ten years of social work in Europe: The United Nations Special European Social Welfare Programme', *International Social Work*, 2, 3: 22–7.

Piirainen, V. (1974) *Vaivaishoidosta sosiaaliturvaan*, Hämeenlinna: Arvi A. Karisto Osakeyhtiö.

Pulma, P. (1987) 'Kerjuuluvasta perhekuntoutukseen. Lapsuuden yhteiskunnallistuminen ja lastensuojelun kehitys Suomessa', in P. Pulma and O. Turpeinen (eds) *Suomen lastensuojelun historia*, Helsinki: Lastensuojelun keskusliitto.

Rauhala, P.-L. (1996) *Miten sosiaalipalvelut ovat tulleet osaksi suomalaista sosiaaliturvaa?*, Tampere: Tampereen yliopisto.

—— (1998) *Mistä ehkäisevässä sosiaalipolitiikassa on kysymys? Käsitteellistä ja historiallista tarkastelua*, Helsinki: STAKES.

Rose, N. (1990) *Governing the Soul. The Shaping of the Private Self*, London and New York: Routledge.

Saarikangas, K. (1993) *Model Houses for Model Families. Gender, Ideology and the Modern Dwelling. The Type-planned Houses of the 1940s in Finland*, Helsinki: The Finnish Historical Society.

Satka, M. (1993) 'Sota-aika perhekäsitysten ja sukupuolten suhteiden murroksena', in P. Haapala (ed.) *Hyvinvointivaltio ja historian oikut*, Tampere: Työväen historian ja perinteen seura.

—— (1994) 'Sosiaalinen työ perääankatsojamiehestä hoivayrittäjäksi', in J. Jaakkola, P. Pulma, M. Satka and K. Urponen (eds) *Armeliaisuus, yhteisöapu, sosiaaliturva. Suomalaisten sosiaalisen turvan historia*, Helsinki: Sosiaaliturvan Keskusliitto.

—— (1995) *Making Social Citizenship. Conceptual Practices from the Finnish Poor Law to Professional Social Work*, Jyväskylä: SoPhi.

Simonen, L. (1990) *Contradictions of the Welfare State, Women, and Caring*, Tampere: University of Tampere.

Snellman, J.V. ([1842] 1928) *Kootut teokset II: Valtio-oppi. Oikea ehdoton pätevyys. Kansallisuus ja kansallisuusaate* (original, *Läran om staten*), Porvoo: WSOY.

Takala, A. and Takala, M. (1953) *Lapsuuden psykologia*, Porvoo: WSOY.

Tarvainen, L. (1953) 'Perhe ja sen käsittely', *Lapsi ja nuoriso*, 12, 9: 5–8.

—— (1954) *Lapsen sosiaalinen huolto*, Helsinki: Lastensuojelun Keskusliitto.

Urponen, K. (1994) 'Huoltoyhteiskunnasta hyvinvointivaltioon', in J. Jaakkola, P. Pulma, M. Satka and K. Urponen (eds) *Armeliaisuus, yhteisöapu, sosiaaliturva. Suomalaisten sosiaalisen turvan historia*, Helsinki: Sosiaaliturvan Keskusliitto.

Välimäki, A.-L. and Rauhala, P.-L. (2000) 'Lasten päivähoidon taipuminen yhteiskunnallisiin murroksiin Suomessa', *Yhteiskuntapolitiikka*, 65, 5: 387–405.

Yelloly, M. (1980) *Social Work Theory and Psychoanalysis*, New York/London/Melbourne: Van Nostrand Reinhold.

6 The needy child and the naturalization of politics
Political debate in Germany

Doris Bühler-Niederberger

At least since the mid-1990s, various political debates have been held in the Federal Republic of Germany about issues relating to children – particularly their needs, their value for society and the type of political decision that is appropriate to them. The central debates which took place in these years have been analysed and evaluated as part of a project which is reported on in this chapter. The content and course of the discussion have been reconstructed on the basis of official transcripts of parliamentary debates, reporting in daily and weekly newspapers and interviews with politicians.[1]

Analysis of these political discussions gives rise to four major findings. They are:

1   Of the various concepts applied to children in political debate, that of the 'needy child' is the most widely used. It occurs in many different contexts.
2   The concept of the needy child is used on both sides of the argument: to accuse a political opponent and to establish a moral victory for one's own position.
3   The concept of the needy child results in a naturalization of politics. This means that decisions and institutions are legitimated as naturally right because – and only because – they are adapted to the natural needs of children. These needs are received as an expression of 'the child's nature' and therefore as universal and unchanging.
4   Decisions made on this basis are no longer open to discussion and negotiation, even if they are evidently connected with political tactics and vested interests. In this way the 'naturalization of politics' involves a depoliticizing of what is inherently political.

Behind current strategic events, with their party political moves, one can discern a constant interest in social order. Policies related to children have been embedded in such interests from their very beginnings, and – this is a fifth and probably the most far-reaching insight – they are still immersed in this same framework, as current decisions abundantly demonstrate. In this context, for instance, it is striking that patriarchal structures are openly favoured. The argument from the natural needs of children removes both the public order interest and the question of the influence of traditional structures from serious discussion. In this way, the concept of the needy child proves an effective instrument for policies that are predominantly conservative.

Family policy and child allowances in Germany: a summary of twentieth-century history

In order to show to what extent questions of social order have continuously shaped policies related to children, it is sufficient to summarize the history of family or child allowances. Ever since the beginning of the twentieth century, child or family allowances have been paid in Germany. The question of the amount and form of these measures – whether in the shape of tax relief or as monthly payments granted to families for their children – has been discussed and modified time and again. It appears, however, that the aim has always remained the same: the creation of competent and industrious children, sufficient in number to guarantee the continued existence of the public order. Families with a male breadwinner – most particularly large families of the middle class – have clearly been favoured as a means to achieve this. This bias established itself either explicitly via argumentation connecting this type of family with an interest in the public order, or implicitly by means of regulations concerned with financial support.

Before the First World War only a few large companies like Siemens, or certain mining companies, paid family allowances. Such subsidies were based on a fundamental interest in population and public order policies. A publication written in 1918 says that families should be supported in this way in the 'interest of the growth and ennoblement of our people's strength' and as 'a basis for the rights of property and the promotion of a subservient manner in children' (Langer-El Sayed, 1980: 71).

In 1920 the state introduced family allowances for civil servants, a decision which was soon adopted by private companies as well. The support was designed to favour the family model with a male breadwinner. A so-called 'women's allowance', an extra allowance, was stopped if the wife was a wage-earner. In this way jobs were kept free for men returning from the war (Langer-El Sayed, 1980). But some years later these family allowances were repealed again, and – in comparison with other countries, like France and Belgium – Germany fell far behind in this kind of family support (Bahle, 1995).

It is readily apparent from National Socialist laws and directives that population policy was of prime importance to them. Family support was increased in a way that very clearly aimed at the racist goals of the Third Reich. Only children of racially desirable marriages were supported. Tax allowances for dependent children, which had been introduced in 1920, were increased in 1934, and in 1936 additional monthly child allowances were introduced, at first only for families with at least five children, later for families with at least three children (Bahle, 1995). Additional interventions to achieve the required number of desirable young followed. A freshly married husband, for example, received an interest-free marriage loan (provided his wife gave up her job). In order to increase the willingness of women now confined to the house (until they were urgently needed on the labour market from 1938 onwards) to have children, the marriage loan could be paid off by starting a family. The outstanding debt arising from the marriage loan was reduced by 25 per cent with the birth of every new child. The German term for this new kind of payment was '*abkindern*' (which means something like 'babying off' the loan). Mother's Day, introduced in Germany as early as 1922, now acquired a special significance. In 1938 a 'Cross of Honour for the German Mother' was introduced, following a French example from the 1920s. It was awarded on 12 August, the birthday of Hitler's mother Klara. Women received a cross in bronze if they had four or more children, in silver for six children and in gold for eight children. Each award-winner was closely examined by the state and the Nazi party in accordance with racial criteria (Mühlfeld and Schönweiss, 1989; Sieder, 1998).

In the post-war German Federal Republic child allowances – like, of course, the other family policy measures clearly aiming at racist goals – were stopped by the Allies, for they too were seen as a legacy of National Socialism. But after 1949 tax allowances for dependent children were again granted to those liable to income tax. These tax allowances were calculated according to the number of children, the allowance increasing disproportionately for the second and further children. After 1955 additional child benefits (i.e. a fixed amount paid monthly according to the number of dependent children living in a family) were paid after the birth of the third child – and after 1962 even for the second child. This so-called dual system of tax allowances and simultaneous child benefits was practised until the end of 1974. Women's wage-work was again made unattractive, this time through a splitting system. This system, applying to the tax liability of couples and introduced in 1958, meant considerable tax reductions for families with one breadwinner, but no reduction at all if husband and wife earned about the same amount of money. The system is still in place today.[2] At the time it was introduced, politicians explicitly legitimized it by the 'intention behind family policies of not furthering mothers' inclination towards wage-work and . . . with the special appreciation of women as mothers and housewives' (Langer-El Sayed, 1980: 102).

This means that we can after all say that the post-war government preferred the same family structure as its predecessors; namely, the family with a male breadwinner. Additionally, it favoured middle- and upper-class families, because tax reductions based on tax allowances for children and the tax-splitting system for couples were – and still are – more advantageous for higher- than for lower-income groups. In the 1950s, this intention was openly admitted by politicians such as F.-J. Wuermeling, for example, the first Federal Minister of Family Affairs, who said:

> The fulfilment of cultural duties should not be made impossible for our middle classes because they are the ones who are passing cultural values on to their children. This benefits the future of the whole community as these classes are the protectors of our culture.
>
> (Langer-El Sayed, 1980: 100–1)

Families were seen as the stronghold of moral attitudes and the guarantors of the moral development of children. In the 1950s and 1960s F.-J. Wuermeling spoke of 'inwardly healthy families' educating their children to 'morality and industriousness'. He then compared these children to 'stray children' raised in problematic circumstances such as single-child or single-parent families, fractured families and families with working mothers (Langer-El Sayed, 1980; Gerlach, 1996). Soundly educated children were a bulwark against moral danger in general and could even, he suggested, be instrumental in winning the Cold War. For, Wuermeling said, 'Millions of healthy families with properly educated children are at least as important for our protection against the threatening danger of the eastern nations with their many children as any military defence' (Langer-El Sayed, 1980: 99). It is evident from this that political measures supporting children have for a long time formed part of public order policy, even in post-war Germany.

The Social–Liberal Coalition, which came to power in 1969 for the first time in the post-war period, achieved some changes in policies relating to children. In 1975 the dual system of family support – tax allowances plus child benefit – was abolished. A monthly child allowance irrespective of family income was now paid after the birth of the first child. This was due to the attempt of the Social Democrats to end the preferential treatment of families with higher incomes, which the former system of child support (with tax allowances) had initiated. However, the disproportionate favouring of families with several children remained unchanged. For example, after repeated increases, the child benefit for the fourth child amounted to DM 240 in 1982 – nearly five times the amount paid for the first child, DM 50.

After 1983, when the coalition of Christian Democrats and Free Democrats (liberals) was back in office, the dual system was reintroduced. Tax allowances for children returned, and were in the course of time significantly raised in response to growing pressure from the Federal Constitutional Court. Once again the children of middle-class parents, 'the protectors of our culture', were – as indeed they still are – more strongly subsidized than other children, although the arguments legitimizing higher support for the upper-income groups had changed. The bias was now justified as a form of 'horizontal justice' between childless couples and families with children, and not any more as furtherance of what was considered the most desirable family model.

The needy child versus the useful child: the election campaign in the Year of the Family

As the above outline has already shown, the system of child and family allowances has always been a bone of contention between government and opposition. In 1994 and 1995 it became a major subject of political discussion. There were at the time at least three circumstances fuelling the debate. First, 1994 had been declared the 'Year of the Family' by the United Nations, and the media took this as a cue to attack major shortcomings and even so-called 'scandals' in family policy – policies which, they said, caused a real impoverishment of children. They illustrated this impoverishment in a series of reports about poor families, and referred to alarming statements made by welfare and family organizations. Second, several judgments of the Constitutional Court obliged the government to change the tax and duty system in a way that families with children would no longer subsidize people without children. That this was indeed how matters stood was above all due to the financing modalities of the old-age pensions system, a structure in which retirement pensions were always provided by the younger working generation. That was the argument of the court.[3] It was indeed the argumentation of the specific judgment in which the term 'horizontal justice' I have already mentioned was coined. Third, 1994 was a year of federal elections in Germany, and (unsurprisingly) family policy became an important topic for the candidates. The discussion did not end after the election, as the re-elected governing parties had difficulties transforming their promises into a concrete bill. These difficulties had their roots in the different opinions held by the government itself, as well as in general financial retrenchment and in the fact that the Social Democrats stubbornly exhausted every opportunity for opposition.

For a year and a half this gave ample opportunity to the Social Democrats to attack the governing coalition of Christian Democrats and Free Democrats and to keep public interest in the topic alive. It was undisputed in this debate that the financial support of families had to be increased – this was the Constitutional Court's stipulation. The political parties, however, were divided regarding the degree of the increase and the form child support should take. While the representatives of the governing party generally wanted to stand by the dual system – i.e. the system which consisted of tax relief (more or less profitable depending on income level) on the one hand and child allowances on the other – the Social Democrats favoured standardized child benefits. In the autumn of 1995 a compromise solution was passed. The dual system was changed in such a way that parents could now choose between either increased tax allowances or child benefits – which were increased as well. In this scenario tax allowances remained more profitable for the higher income group, which remained more generously subsidized by tax allowances than others were by child benefits, even though the difference had now decreased. It remained a matter of debate whether the amount of compensation for families had been substantially increased by these measures as, from then on, only one of the two forms of subsidy (*either* increased tax allowances *or* child benefits) could be chosen.

When in 1998 the Social Democrats won the election and formed a coalition government with the Green Party, other minor increases in child benefits followed. However, the main objectives and modalities of policy relating to the family remained unchanged. Even the tax splitting system for couples was retained, despite all the lip service paid by the Social Democrats in the earlier discussion, and despite the fact that it clearly subsidized higher incomes more heavily and thus supported the male breadwinner type of family.

If this debate deserves our attention, it is *not* for any substantial changes it achieved. I have chosen it as an illustration precisely because of the different ways in which it negotiated the concept of the child. The idea taken up by the governing party was that of the 'useful child', emphasizing the importance of the birth rate and the consequences of changes in the age-distribution curve for nursing care and old-age insurance. These systems required the younger generation to pay for the older; consequently, a drop in the birth rate meant inevitably that either the younger generation was placed under great strain or that payments to the older generation had to be cut.

The fact that representatives of the governing parties invoked the usefulness of children as an argument, however, proved problematic from the start. For in this respect there was no general consensus among the governing parties. While some prominent Christian Democrats argued that more funds had to be channelled into counteracting the decrease in the birth rate, others objected that immigration could compensate for the drop in the birth rate just as well. Furthermore, they said that jobs, not the demographic curve, were of crucial importance to the pension system anyway, and that the pension reform that had just been implemented would soon sound the all-clear.

The reaction to a proposal made in February 1994 by the then Federal Minister of Family Affairs, Hannelore Rönsch, indicates the inherent problem of arguing from a concept of the 'useful child'. Rönsch met with criticism when she proposed what she called a 'contribution to the future of society', a tax levied on the childless that was intended to improve the financial position of families as compensation for their task in safeguarding the future. Critics from the ranks of her own party declared Rönsch's proposal absurd. The media stigmatized the idea as 'extremely right-wing' and described Rönsch as having been 'punished very effectively by the media'.[4] In readers' letters the proposal was censured as 'unimaginative' and even, it was insinuated, akin to certain policies of the Third Reich. Parents who supported the politician in their letters were accused of having a calculating attitude and of acting in a manner directly 'hostile to children'.[5]

At this point one encounters a moral principle whose advocates aspire to define the true value of a child. The principle highlights the problem of regarding children as 'useful', asserting that they can only be appreciated at their true worth if one draws no benefit from them – i.e. they can only attain their unique value if they remain 'useless'. This amounts to a verdict against viewing children in any way as a source of profit. Bourgeois social reformers had pushed the idea at the turn of the nineteenth century, enacting laws that were chiefly directed against poor parents (Zelizer, 1985; Bühler-Niederberger, 1996). In the debate in the mid-1990s about family allowances it was easy for politicians to cite this principle as a way of deterring unwanted demands. If one is not allowed to reap benefits from children, then the state is not entitled to rely on them as a source of future returns either – this is what the allusions to the Third Reich in readers' letters implied. The argument, therefore, excluded parents from claiming any compensation in the form of benefit, as to do so would be to 'use' their children for profit.

Shortly after this argument over the proposal made by Rönsch, the principle was invoked by the Federal Minister for Social Affairs in a debate with a pensions expert, who maintained that the number of children had to be taken into account in calculating their parents' pensions. The Minister countered that this was to tackle the problem 'like an accountant'. He continued: 'A society in which the expenses for children are reimbursed to parents by the state is a society I do not want to live in. Children are not only a burden, but also a source of happiness.'[6]

The opposition parties at this time held steadfastly and consistently to the concept of the 'needy' child. They used the growing poverty of children as an argument, and held out the prospect of drastic consequences: growing aggressiveness, crime and political extremism. The 'needy child', they argued, was a 'child at risk' and a threat to the continued existence of public order. As a member of the Social Democrats put it in a sitting of the Bundestag on 24 June 1994:

> What it means for children and families to live on social welfare, to belong to the poor and homeless, is something we will have to work out anew elsewhere. The outcome will prove disastrous.[7]

Likewise, the Social Democrat candidate for the chancellorship, Rudolf Scharping, said in August 1994 on South West German Radio that it was 'peculiarly dangerous and potentially disastrous' for so many children to be growing up on social welfare. A life shaped by unemployment and debt would 'lead to a growing feeling of despair in the people concerned and also to growing aggressiveness'.[8]

In the Bundestag debate of 7 September 1994, the leader of the Social Democratic parliamentary party predicted the following scenario:

> and then a social climate will arise in our society which may have catastrophic consequences – and already has to a very great extent. Crime and extremism, I know, do not spring from financial causes exclusively. That need, depression and injustice are, however, the breeding-ground for cancerous violence, can hardly be denied.[9]

This rhetoric of threat was reinforced in the media by criminologists and psychologists. Figures were cited for homeless children and children living in households that received social welfare. These figures, as well as others that arose in the course of this debate, were probably based partly on reliable investigations (which were, however, rarely referred to explicitly), but also partly on misunderstandings (e.g. wrong frames of reference for percentage calculations or inadequate definition of what was being calculated). For that reason, the figures cited were sometimes ten times higher than those calculated in scientific studies carried out at the same time. According to assertions made both in parliament and in the media by members of the opposition, more than 30 per cent of children – and in the new federal states which had made up the former GDR even 44 per cent of children – were living on social welfare, and more than half a million were on the streets. Based on scientific studies, the '10th Child and Youth Report' (1998)[10] gives the following figures for children under 18 living on social welfare in 1992 and 1994: 8.7 per cent in western Germany, 3.6 per cent in the new federal states (former GDR). The exaggerated estimates of the politicians were never contradicted. On the contrary, the figures became extremely important and ultimately irrefutable within a public circle of reference in which politicians cited the media and the media the politicians. While one might argue publicly about the *usefulness* of children, both the dimensions and the drama of *need* were thus excluded from serious critical debate.

The argument from the needy child gains its strategic superiority from what I call 'complementary generational logic'. This means that the ascription of characteristics, needs and values to children implies a complementary ascription of characteristics and values to their adult counterpart. In this way, the needy child is balanced against an adult who is able to cater for its needs. Strategically, therefore, the concept of the needy child is doubly profitable. On the one hand, it offers an opportunity to accuse a political opponent of shortcomings as an adult who, in ignoring the needs of children, shows himself (or herself) unwilling to play his (her) part in the generational contract. On the other hand it enables the presentation of one's own party as a group of commendable adults trying hard to fulfil these very demands. The concept of the *needy* child serves in this way not only as a touchstone for moral qualities, but as one that pre-empts any attempt to undermine it by argument or journalistic sniping. One might add that the same complementary logic prevents an adult from drawing any kudos at all from the concept of the *useful* child.

The opposition parties, particularly the Social Democrats, missed no opportunity to accuse the governing party by means of this formula of the needy child. In an interview with the magazine *Spiegel* their candidate for the chancellorship, Rudolph Scharping, described the system of family benefits as an example of the 'cold tactics' and 'bitter social injustice' promoted by the government of the day.[11] Between December 1993 and September 1994 the Social Democrats attacked the government in no less than twelve sittings of parliament on the basis of this generational concept. A broad coalition of support came into being as a consequence of these attacks and the demands they implied. The media followed the opposition's line of argumentation, speaking of the average families with two children that were now being affected by poverty, reporting (with pictures) on poor families' everyday lives, and publishing readers' letters to the effect that 'the foundations of our future are crumbling', 'a time bomb is ticking', 'no investment ought to be more rewarding than to make a dignified childhood possible for children'.[12] Churches and welfare associations also supported the opposition campaign to improve the system of family benefits, conferring on it the force of their own moral authority.

Without intending to suggest that the needy child of political rhetoric was from the beginning nothing but calculation, one should point out that the success that can be achieved with this concept – and this is something that will not have passed unnoticed by politicians – effectively canonizes its use, and with it the generational logic of poor child vs. good adult. This is evident from interviews (held within the context of the project reported on here) with members of the Children's Commission of the Bundestag, a standing committee of members of parliament, whose task it is to advise parliament on all matters to do with children, and to act in children's interests. Thus one commission member said:

> As far as policies relating to children are concerned, actually I don't know anyone who has an ambivalent attitude toward this topic. It's a topic that appeals to people, and in this respect I can only advise anyone entertaining the idea of going into politics and

wondering what topic to choose . . . I would advise them, 'Start with this one!'

> (Christian Socialist [CSU] member of the Children's
> Commission, 13th legislative period)

A Social Democrat commented, 'Many opportunities to make one's name and to present oneself arise from the level of public interest in topics relating to children'; and he added that he didn't believe his commitment to the Commission would damage his career. He concluded, 'Well, now you have had a really honest reply' (Social Democratic member of the Children's Commission, 14th legislative period).

Another Social Democrat stated that people's willingness to become active in the Children's Commission was due to motives that were

> certainly on the one hand sincere though one has to . . . one cannot fail to recognize – though this is something I only found out later – that it has a great effect on public relations and, of course, every member of parliament is keen on that . . .

> (Social Democratic [SPD] member of the Children's
> Commission, 13th legislative period)

A representative of the Green Party described herself as 'proof of the fact that membership of the Children's Commission can be quite beneficial to one's political career'. She said she had just been promoted to foreign affairs – a sphere with considerably higher profile (Green member of the Children's Commission, 13th legislative period).

It should be added that the Children's Commission focused above all on the 'needy child'. Child protection legislation, violence against children and child pornography were the dominant subjects. The interviewees judged the real gain in these areas considerably more sceptically than the gain for their own party or person.

Besides the *needy* and the *useful* child, there were two other models occasionally used in the debate of 1994. In the first one the child is regarded as a socially integrating factor – indeed as the focal point of the social order as such. Behind this model lies a concept of social order in which the members of a society are initially integrated into the family (which has to be imagined as patriarchal, its essence being children). These families in turn are the engines of integration into wider society, a process which is conceived of in heightened terms as essentially communal and emotional. This is a profoundly conservative concept of social order, attaching more importance to the community and its institutions than to the individual, who is profoundly distrusted.[13]

The Federal Chancellor, Helmut Kohl, himself coined several phrases bearing on this model. For instance in the weekly magazine *Stern*:

'Without a healthy family there can be no healthy state . . . The family has to be given absolute priority again . . . Those who say yes to children should feel that they are supported by society.'[14] In the government statement of 23 November 1994, Kohl explained that the country needed an 'alliance for the future', and went on: 'I think particularly of the mothers and fathers who say "Yes" to children and who give them security and a future.' He concluded with the words: 'We know that the family is the place where our future is decided. We know that it is the intimate, sheltered areas of life that shape the human face of our country.'[15]

A final conceptual model is that proposed by the Democratic Socialists (PDS), the party furthest to the left of the political spectrum. They did not base their claims for higher public support for children on calculations of need or potential returns. They simply and explicitly insisted on the right of children to a decent standard of living, and to a share of the cake sufficient to provide this.[16] Their arguments were therefore not child-specific but universalist.

These two models, however, were of minor importance in the political debate – the first because it didn't provide for any concrete measures and was thus mainly rhetorical in content; the second because the PDS was insignificant to the parliamentary balance of power and had no chance of enforcing its demands (which were therefore scarcely even discussed).

The naturalization of politics

The political debate about the family initiated by the election campaign of 1994 shows how the concept of need became a universal and unquestioned premise, no matter how exaggeratedly it might be presented when it came to child poverty statistics. In the political arena the needs of children enjoyed immunity from critical reflection. The precept that excluded them from debate was formulated explicitly. We can conclude from this that any statement about a child's needs or characteristics, once it has entered the political forum, is in principle regarded as a statement about the true *nature* of the child and therefore has to be accepted as axiomatic. In order to bring out the great argumentative force of this view of the child as deeply needy by nature – and of nature in this sense as specifically and immutably defined – it will be interesting to look at some further political debates in which the argument played a formative role.

In 1988, the Children's Commission of the German Bundestag was founded as a standing parliamentary committee. Its founder was a Social Democrat – the party that was then in opposition. He saw the need for the commission, as well as the special structure he planned for it (a structure that was in parliamentary terms unique), as rooted in the specific nature of the child. In a later interview he gave the following account of the events in question:

> because we said that . . . it is precisely because we are concerned with children, who don't want to be organized according to rules either, maybe we could for once set a parliamentary example and create structures that are *quite different* . . .
>
> (Social Democratic member of the Children's Commission, 12th legislative period; emphasis added)

This was something the representatives of the other parties could also accept:

> And then, when we knew which member of the Christian Democrats was our partner, it was Mr . . . , then we noticed – although he is usually incredibly conservative – that it had some effect on him . . . And then there were, of course, many conflicts in the parliamentary advisory committee and elsewhere before we managed to get it through. But it was a really thrilling factor, the way we convinced our colleagues in the other parliamentary parties by telling them, 'Look, this is a special commission, with special topics – why not have a special structure too?'
>
> (Social Democratic member of the Children's Commission, 12th legislative period)

The special structure reflected the nature of children – in this case their peculiar spontaneity. For this commission, in contrast to usual parliamentary procedures, was not constituted on the basis of party strength, but consisted of one member from each parliamentary party. Moreover, Commission resolutions were not put to the vote, but required the consent of all members. Politicians from all parties gave as a reason for this principle the fact that political discussion was unnecessary and indeed ought not to be pursued at all when children's issues were at stake. Evidence for this can be found in the following quotations from interviews with members of the Children's Commission. The statements imply that children's needs are assumed to be universal and homogeneous. That, however, can only be the case if a certain *nature* has been ascribed to children in the first place.

Questioned in an interview, a Christian Democratic politician put it like this: 'One could say that in the sphere of child policy there should be no room for different opinions. The matter is so important and party politics so unimportant . . .' She added that this was unfortunately not the case, however, although the subject itself – as she had already stated – not only made consensus possible but demanded it. Elsewhere, this politician spoke about the 'child as fact' and later made this more precise by defining it as 'thinking about children and on their behalf that should become second nature to anyone' (CDU member of the Children's Commission, 14th legislative period).

A Christian Socialist Commission member chose an analogy to describe the way in which agreement was reached. This made it clear that a consensus had to be achieved whatever happened.

> If you take, for example . . . deployment of the Federal Armed Forces . . . Everyone quarrels beforehand, but when it comes to actual deployment, the quarrels have to be set aside, and then one stands behind the soldiers and supports them. So, definitely, there are comparable elements here.
>
> > (CSU member of the Children's Commission,
> > 14th legislative period)

A liberal member of the Children's Commission put it similarly:

> This modus operandi that there has to be agreement is something I consider very good, because this topic makes it possible for adherence to the party line to be forgotten for a while . . .

And, a little later:

> Well, I wish, irrespective of party flags, especially with topics where children are concerned, which are so important to me, that politicians would act in children's interests across party lines.
>
> > (FDP member of the Children's Commission,
> > 14th legislative period)

Political calculation was nevertheless an important factor, both in the foundation of the Children's Commission and in its institutionalization of the consensus principle. It was the opposition parties that had pushed the foundation in the first place, because it promised them a political arena with high public appeal, which they were intent on exploiting without the risk of being outvoted by the governing party within the Commission. This was quite openly admitted in interviews.

Thus the Social Democratic founder of the Commission described its establishment as an opportunity 'to create modern political working structures'. He had seen the chance 'to intensify opposition activity by engaging more intensively in certain fields, especially in niches – for at that time this still was a niche – and at the same time to arouse public attention. And this proved to be the case.' Asked about the consensus principle, he listed the following tactical considerations: he and his Green colleague had come to the conclusion that, as representatives of the opposition, they would never have a chance to put through anything if they accepted the usual voting principle of proportional parliamentary representation. They would then only be able to fulfil what the governing coalition wanted. 'So we decided at a very early stage to go for the consensus principle and above all the one-seat system, i.e. only one representative from each parliamentary party . . . and, thirdly, the rotating chairmanship' (SPD member of the Children's Commission, 12th legislative period).

It is evident from this that the Children's Commission provided a forum for an astonishingly effective combination of opposition politics with the requirements derived from the concept of the nature of the child. To put it another way, the tactical manoeuvring that lay behind the rhetorical use of the concept of nature was in this case all too evident. Nevertheless the argument was successful. It made the demands and decisions related to it entirely incontestable.

The visible interests of a politically active group, as well as an unchallenged line of argument based on the concept of the nature of the child, are discernible in a further debate which took place in the 1990s – that on the new Children's Act (*Kindschaftsrecht*). Here the concept of a child's unchanging nature fulfilled the aspirations and requirements of fathers' associations and indeed of patriarchal structures generally – structures that had been supported by family policy ever since the beginning of the century. The child's radical need was defined in explicitly biological terms: a child needed both its natural parents; and all other matters which might have been raised by individual children – and which to a considerable extent they had been able to voice under the earlier law – had to take second place to this voice of nature. 'Parents remain parents. Always', said the Federal Minister of Family Affairs, Claudia Nolte. And it seems paradoxical that she gave as a reason for this apodictic assessment that 'what is most important, is the perspective of the child'.[17]

A Free Democrat (liberal) member of the Children's Commission formulated a similar opinion:

> I am convinced that a child needs both parents, not *just* a father or *just* a mother. I find myself in agreement with educationalists and psychologists when I state that both parents, in their different roles, are of great importance to a child's development, its search for identity and also its emotional stability.[18]

In this debate on the new Children's Act the 'needy' child appeared once again as a 'child at risk', and thus as a 'dangerous child' and a threat to the social order – the sphere in which child policies had always been embedded. That the child needed both its parents was substantiated by the argument that false educational developments must at all costs be avoided, and attention was drawn to the claim that the number of young offenders who had grown up without a father was 'dispro- portionately high'.[19] This universalist definition of children's needs was transformed by politicians – with widespread consensus – into the political decision of the new Children's Act, whose centrepiece was joint custody after a divorce. No party, except for the Democratic Socialists (PDS) opposed the decision on this most critical of issues, even though the new law granted more rights to fathers, almost elimin- ated those of children, and to some degree restricted those of mothers. In this highly modern and acutely difficult situation, where a choice between the individual rights of men and women (and indeed also of children) was at stake, the argumentative recourse to a concept of universal and natural need in children made a decision possible that prevented the recognition and acceptance of conflict from the very beginning.

The politicians congratulated themselves on having performed good political work – work that went beyond politics and achieved genuinely human values. This was more than politicians could otherwise dream of accomplishing. It was in this tenor that a Commission member, speaking in the final session (which is usually devoted to mutual cross- party back-slapping) said, 'I think that with this law we haven't changed anyone. But if we have managed to dry a few tears, that'll do.'[20]

Thus the concept of the needy child once more provided proof of the moral qualities of the adults who responded to its needs. And it presented politicians as quintessential human beings who – beyond all calculation of interests or political tactics – strive to do only what is humanly right and sensible.

In a special way the concept of the needy child aligns morality with nature. Whatever is said about the needs of children, is – in connection with the notions of development and growth – not only unambiguous and universal but also imperative in moral terms, because the notion of development is derived from that of nature and is at the same time highly normative (Jordanova, 1989). It is this that grounds the peculiar power of the concept of the needy child as an instrument of accusation and as an instrument of popular mobilization. Conversely, the decisions made by politicians who, by common consent, are good adults (i.e. who fulfil the needs of children), are *ipso facto* incontestable. Anyone who attacks them does so in the face of the natural needs of children, and thus in the face of both reason and morality. It will be a lonely battle. It is this exceptional power to justify decisions that exclude all protest, indeed to justify them on the grounds of exceptional political profit, which transforms the concept of the needy child into a formula of political debate that is as effective as it is dubious.

Notes

1　Project entitled 'The Value of Children in Public Debate', supported by the DFG.
2　It means that the (high) income of the main wage-earner is divided between both spouses. This leads to a significantly lower tax payment, due to the progressive German income tax system.
3　Judgments of the Constitutional Court of 29 May 1990 (BVerfGE 82, 60 – Existenzminimum) and of 7 July 1992 (BVerfGE 87, 1 – Trümmerfrauen).
4　*Spiegel* 28.2.94 'Frommer Wunsch'; *Die Zeit* 4.3.94 'Die Last mit dem Nachwuchs'; *Stern* 10.3.94 'Wenn Kinder zum Luxus werden'.
5　*Süddeutsche Zeitung* 5/6.3.84 'Ständig neue Konzepte zum Schröpfen der Bürger'; 'Bezahlen für das Kinderglück der anderen'; *Spiegel* 14.3.94 'Brandsatz gelegt'; *Die Zeit* 25.3.94 'Kostenfaktor Kind'.
6　*Die Zeit* 30.9.94 'Ohne Kinder keine Rente'.
7　German Bundestag, 12th legislative period, 24.6.94, Christel Hanewinckel, SPD, p. 20737.
8　*Süddeutsche Zeitung* 18.8.94 '1, 5 Millionen Kinder von Armut betroffen.'
9　German Bundestag, 12th legislative period, 7.9.94, Ulrich Klose, SPD, pp. 21411–21412.
10　*Sachverständigenkommission zum Zehnten Kinder und Jugendbericht: Bericht über die Lebenssituation von Kindern und die Leistungen der Kinderhilfen in Dentschland. Mit der Stellungnahme der Bundesregierung* (Bundestag-Drucksache 13/11368; 25.8.98; Hrsg. BFSFJ), Bonn, 1998.
11　*Spiegel* 10.1.94 'Wenn ich Kanzler bin'.
12　*Focus* 3.1.94 'Familienpolitik: Eltern zahlen immer drauf'; *Die Zeit* 7.1.94 'Gefährdete Art – das "Jahr der Familie" ist angebrochen'; *Die Zeit* 18.2.94 'Teures Thema'; *Die Zeit* 4.3.94 'Die Last mit dem Nachwuchs'; *Westdeutsche Zeitung* 2.8.94 'Mehr als zwei Kinder gelten als Armutsrisiko'; *Spiegel* 17.10.94 'Bitterkeit und Wut'; *Spiegel* 31.10.94 'Notorisch verdrängt', quotations from eight readers' letters.
13　Such an assessment was worked out, for example, in a book by the president of the parliamentary party, Wolfgang Schäuble, *Turned to the Future*, which appeared in 1994 and to which the newspapers paid a lot of attention.
14　*Stern* 10.3.94 'Wenn Kinder zum Luxus werden'.
15　German Bundestag, 13th legislative period 23.11.94, Helmut Kohl, Federal Chancellor, pp. 38–39.
16　Parliamentary Session, German Bundestag, 12th legislative period, 20.1.94; minute p. 17779.
17　German Bundestag, 13th legislative period, 3.7.97, Claudia Nolte, Federal Minister of Family Affairs (CDU/CSU), pp. 17360ff.
18　German Bundestag, 13th legislative period, 3.7.97, Hildebrecht Braun (FDP), pp. 17359ff.
19　*Frankfurter Rundschau* 11.6.96 'Männer und Frauen sind auch in familienrechtlichen Angelegenheiten gleichberechtigt'.
20　German Bundestag, 13th legislative period, 3.7.97, M. von Renesse (SPD), pp. 17349ff.

References

Bahle, Th. (1995) *Familienpolitik in Westeuropa. Ursprünge und Wandel im internationalen Vergleich*: Frankfurt/Main: Campus.
Bühler-Niederberger, D. (1996) Teure Kinder – Ökonomie und Emotionen im Wandel der Zeit, in Zeiher, H., Büchner, P. and Zinnecker, H. (eds) *Kinder als*

Außenseiter? Umbrüche in der gesellschaftlichen Wahrnehmung von Kindern und Kindheit, Weinheim/München: Juventa, pp. 97–116.

Gerlach, I. (1996) *Familie und staatliches Handeln. Ideologie und politische Praxis in Deutschland,* Opladen: Leske and Budrich.

Jordanova, L.J. (1989) Children in History – concepts of nature and society, in G. Scarre (ed.) *Children, Parents, and Politics,* Cambridge: Cambridge University Press.

Langer-El Sayed, I. (1980) *Familienpolitik: Tendenzen, Chancen, Notwendigkeiten,* Frankfurt/Main: Fischer.

Mühlfeld, C., and Schönweiss, F. (1989) *Nationalsozialistische Familienpolitik,* Stuttgart: Enke.

Sieder, R. (1998) Besitz und Begehren, Erbe und Elternglück. Familien in Deutschland und Österreich, in A. Burguière *et al.* (eds) *Geschichte der Familie, 4,* Frankfurt/Main: Campus, pp. 211–84.

Zelizer, V.A. (1985) *Pricing the Priceless Child – the Changing Social Value of Children,* New York: Princeton.

7   Contradictory and convergent trends in law and policy affecting children in England

Pam Foley, Nigel Parton, Jeremy Roche and Stanley Tucker

From the nineteenth century onwards child welfare policies in England have been based on the perception of children either as vulnerable, and thus in need of protection (the child as victim) or as impulsive/ unsocialised, and thus in need of guidance and control (the child as threat) (Hendrick, 1994). Both law and policy relating to children and their families reveal an underlying ambivalence when deciding what should be done for and about children. In recent years, following the election and re-election of the New Labour government in 1997 and 2001, an extensive range of new policies and laws which affect the lives of children both directly and indirectly have been promulgated. These developments have been contradictory as well as convergent. The over-all aim of this chapter is to provide a critical analysis of the developments concerned, together with an examination of the different constructions of children and childhood from which they draw and into which they feed. We argue that, in the main, children continue to be rendered invisible by policy and professional practice. When children are visible and the focus of policy this is usually because they are located as being 'troubled' or 'troublesome'. Thus, as in the past, contemporary children and 'childhoods' are inscribed by a political dimension.

The history of children's services in England can be characterised in terms of a gradual and limited encroachment into the family in response to a nation's changing views of itself and of its needs. The assumption of certain roles and responsibilities by the state towards children, particularly in relation to education and health, have become embedded. In contrast, the more targeted services such as those concerned to protect children and the criminal justice system have needed to respond to particular problems and issues that appear urgent at that time, issues which focus on certain communities and families, while leaving the majority of communities and families unscrutinised. Complex, overlapping, and often unspoken ideas about children and childhood have both fed into and fed upon the particular kinds of educational, health and social care services and support for children and families that we see today.

However, the underlying embedded dichotomy referred to above has itself become splintered by the development of two related 'new knowledges'; first, the expanding but uneven use of a distinctive modern children's rights discourse and, second, developments in the sociology of childhood which emphasise children as constituted within their own communities, distinct but not separate, capable and constructive in arenas of social action (Freeman, 1998; Mayall, 2001). This literature has critiqued the positioning of children in law and policy whereby children's agency, in the main, is not recognised and taken seriously, save where they are involved in crime and antisocial behaviour, and where children's perspectives have been subordinated to those of adults. Thus we start off by exploring some key issues associated with children and family life, including the relationship between family privacy and children's rights, which allows us to consider the public–private divide. We then look at the new youth justice system and the contemporary nature of children's services. By way of conclusion we reflect on the impact of the modern children's rights movement on law and policy affecting children.

The family and the liberal state

Ambivalence about the nature of children and of childhood is closely reflected in a profound and abiding ambivalence about the proper relationship between the family and the state. Essentially, for UK governments the family remains the key institution both to provide for and to 'raise' children and its fundamental integrity should be supported, not undermined by state policies and interventions. The family, bestriding both the public and private sphere, maintains boundaries, which should not be breached without good cause; there are 'deep' political impulses at work here. For example Mount observes (1982: 1) 'the family is a subversive organisation'. It is 'the enduring permanent enemy of all hierarchies, churches and ideologies'. Mount views the family as the place where diversity and dissent can flourish and thus is suspicious of encroachments into the private sphere. For example, arguments around the parental right to chastise their child and to bring up their children as they see fit free from the risk of state interference, save in clearly defined circumstances, connect with wider social arguments on state power, images of 'big brother' (or the 'nanny state') and the right of families and communities to live their lives differently. The politics of identity make too prescriptive a vision of 'the good family' and 'good parenting' politically problematic.

Yet for others it is clearly within the realm of legitimate politics not only to take steps to protect children at risk of significant harm and to support families with children in need so that they can continue to bring up their own children at home but also to secure the availability of core services. The liberal state while ever anxious about the family and the boundary between the private and the public sphere in the nineteenth and twentieth centuries assumed responsibilities for functions that had been partially accepted by families – for example, in relation to health and education. By the end of the twentieth century these services were 'universal' and thus in the main were not perceived as undermining the authority of particular families. All families benefited from the development of education and health services. The political dilemma related to the private–public boundary, the contested imagery of the good family, parent and child and the terms of the governance of families.

However, the last quarter of the twentieth century witnessed substantial change in the role of women in society. In addition very significant changes in family life have taken place, including a rapid increase in relationship breakdown, 'reconstituted families' and single parenthood (Pugh, 1999). Stories of the 'decline' of the family have fed into concern about its social consequences. So Smart and Neale in their rethinking of family life observe that within New Right and Ethical Socialist writing on the family 'it is argued women cause crime by rejecting men as potential breadwinners and thus blocking young men's transition into responsible adulthood' (1999: 5). They go on to comment that you cannot separate the family from other social institutions and processes. Running alongside these contestations and shifts in thinking about children and families, not to mention changing 'family practices' (Morgan, 1996), there was anxiety about 'juvenile nuisance' (Audit Commission, 1996). The state's anxieties over juvenile crime and child abuse, however, produced institutions and practices that policed certain communities and families identifying, in modern parlance 'problem' families, leaving 'successful' families intact. Beyond the state's functioning as a universal parent, delivering non-stigmatising services, other families were caught in a different regulatory frame and experienced more coercive and invasive forms of intervention.

Children's rights

While children's rights has a long history, for much of the time it has focused on the need for policy measures and legal initiatives to better promote the welfare of children. Today, while this is still the dominant meaning, the modern children's rights movement has moved beyond a traditional concern with the protection of children inside and outside the home. Now the issue of the child's voice or participation is seen as central to the children's rights project. Some writing is explicitly hostile to the children's rights project on the basis that it undermines the integrity of the family (Burrows, 1998).[1] Just as the language of the 'best interests' of the child has been used to legitimate a range of state sanctioned interventions into family life, likewise today the language of children's rights is seen as a kind of late twentieth- to early twenty-first century 'Trojan horse'. The participation of children is not only seen as leading to better decisions which more effectively secure their welfare but also as 'a good in itself'.

Today the law imagines itself as much more child friendly and as concerned to take proper account of the views and interests of children and young people.[2] The modern children's rights movement is now able to draw on the United Nations Convention on the Rights of the Child (UNCRC) and the European Convention on Human Rights (ECHR)[3] in order to advance the claims and interests of children (Kilkelly, 2000). The European Court of Human Rights (ECtHR) has been instrumental in forcing the UK to bring to an end the corporal punishment of children in state and private schools. However, in November 2001 a group of parents, along with teachers, at Christian independent schools petitioned the High Court claiming that the ban on corporal punishment in schools contravened their religious freedom (Branigan, 2001). This challenge was unsuccessful. In *The Queen on the Application of Williamson* v. *Secretary of State for Education and Employment* [2001] *The Times* (12 December) Elias J in the High Court held that such a belief (in corporal punishment) was not a manifestation of a religion so as to bring it within the freedom of conscience provisions of Art. 9 of the ECHR.[4] In 1998 the ECtHR grappled with the defence of reasonable chastisement that is permitted to parents in English law. In *A* v. *UK* [1998] 2 FLR 959 the ECtHR ruled against the UK government deciding that a nine-year-old boy, who had been beaten with a garden cane by his stepfather, had been subjected to 'inhuman and degrading treatment or punishment' contrary to Article 3 of the ECHR.[5]

Thus increasingly we are told law and policy is child centred. This is reflected in, and further secured through, the developments of advocacy projects for children – for example, the National Youth Advocacy Service, organisations such as ChildLine and the requirement on the UK government to submit regular reports to the UN Committee on the Child on the ways in which the UK is complying with its obligations under the UNCRC. The modern children's rights movement is distinctive in its emphasis on the child's participation and perspective and the emergence of a number of relatively new organisations to advance their rights. However, the language of children's rights with the modern chorus regarding children's agency and responsibility raises awkward questions in the field of criminal justice.

Youth justice

Recently there has been a growing emphasis on children and young people as directly responsible for their own behaviour and not passing them off as 'innocent victims' of their circumstances. One case in the 1990s challenged many people's ideas regarding childhood innocence: this was the murder of two-year-old James Bulger by two ten-year-old boys. This was a key moment in changing policy responses to children and young people in England (Franklin and Petley, 1996; Goldson, 1998). In passing sentence, the judge commented that the boys' 'cunning and wicked behaviour had resulted in an act of unparalleled evil and barbarity' (Goldson, 1998: 21). There was unprecedented national and international media coverage. This case was not the first involving children killing other children (see Freeman, 1997), but it connected with a growing unease about youth and disorder. Now, even young children were seen as a source of menace and trouble and childhood itself was under threat. Freeman has observed that the case 'could not have been more timely' (1997: 116). Attention was now focused on evil children rather than on child poverty and the effects of recession and dovetailed with other instances of youth crime. Not only did this case fuel the demand for action to be taken against young criminals, which we briefly consider on p. 111, but its aftermath, including a judgment of the European Court of Human Rights, has had an impact on how the criminal justice system deals with young offenders.[6]

The new attitude to youth crime from the mid-1990s is most evident in the Crime and Disorder Act (1998) which abolished the doctrine of 'doli incapax'. This doctrine meant that when a child under the age of 14 years was being prosecuted, the prosecution had to prove not only that the child had committed the offence but also that the child knew that what they did was wrong. Now the prosecution simply has to prove that the child committed the criminal offence as charged, just as in any other prosecution. The Act also abolished the right of the child aged under 14 to remain silent since the court is now allowed to draw inferences from the failure of a juvenile to give evidence or answer questions. The Act has thus extended principles of the adult criminal justice system to all offenders aged 10 and over. New orders introduced by the Act can be seen as contributing to the construction of a new category of sub-criminal – what the Audit Commission (1996) called 'juvenile nuisance'.

The antisocial behaviour orders (ASBOs) available under section 1 of the Act can be applied for in relation to any person aged 10 years or over where that person has acted 'in a manner that caused or was likely to cause harassment, alarm or distress to one or more persons not of the same household as himself'. If the order is breached the penalty is imprisonment and/or a fine. These orders have the potential to bring more children and young people within the criminal justice net, even though no crime might have been committed. The result might be, despite the intentions of the legislature, that the children and young people involved are confirmed in their drift towards a career in crime not diverted from it. In addition Parenting Orders can be made on a number of grounds and can require the parents to comply with the requirements as specified – for example, to attend counselling and guidance sessions and to make sure their child attends school. The Act also introduced the Child Safety Order, which applies only to children under 10 years old who are deemed to be behaving in an antisocial manner and where a child has committed an act which, had she or he been aged 10 or over, would have constituted a criminal offence.

The Crime and Disorder Act 1998 can be seen as significantly extending the disciplinary reach of the criminal justice system but in such a way that the responsibility of both the parent and the child is made central. If a child is the subject of a child safety order and he or she fails to comply with any requirement contained in it, then the court can discharge the order and make a care order instead.[7] The aim of a Child Safety Order is to provide local authorities, the newly established youth offending teams, and the courts with new powers to intervene positively at an early stage with children who are seen at risk of offending. The Youth Justice and Criminal Evidence Act 1999 introduced further significant changes to youth justice law and practice, in particular via the introduction of referral orders. Now any child who pleads guilty to a first offence must be referred to the youth offender panel.[8] The youth offender panel will agree a contract with the offender and this contract can cover such matters as making financial or other reparation to the victim, carrying out unpaid work in the community, being at home at specified times and staying away from specified places.

Unfortunately, the anxiety is that such developments run the risk of criminalising and demonising children. The Crime and Disorder Act 1998 and the Youth Justice and Criminal Evidence Act 1999, taken together, are seen as heralding a significant shift in youth justice placing much greater emphasis on restorative justice; some commentators have seen these developments as invasive, undermining of children's rights, authoritarian and fundamentally punitive (see further, Muncie, 2002). The moral panic centring on children and young people also embraced those who worked with them. Part of the crisis in childhood was the perceived failure of welfare and education professionals to properly discharge their responsibilities. There was a growing mistrust of teachers, youth and community workers and social workers etc. Increasingly it seemed that there is a level of 'dual problematisation' in relation to both children and families and the professionals who worked with them (Tucker, 1999). This is the context in which we have to consider the contemporary nature of children's services.

Children's services

Children, within and outside families, carry a fundamental social and political significance. From the early years of the twentieth century, children have been spoken of as a national resource, comprising of innate or fostered abilities and talents that may be wasted or squandered. During the second half of the twentieth century, the idea of childhood as a special, prolonged and protected phase of life (despite the lived reality of many children), continued to grow and influence the direction of legislation, and of social and educational policies. Changes to the benefit system in England, the collapse of traditional apprenticeships and the expansion of higher education have combined to lengthen the dependence of children upon their parents. Yet despite the expansion of 'childhood' in the sense of their economic dependency on others, children have been said to be 'invisible'. Policies, which affect children, are subsumed within those for families, and children and young people thereby are subject to 'familialisation' (Qvortrup, 1994), reinforcing assumptions that the needs of parents and the needs of children are indivisible. Many children's services are invested with these kinds of assumptions about their needs and capabilities.

Children do remain in important ways bound up with the 'success' or 'failure' of their families and communities; in this sense some are born into 'social exclusion'. New Labour policies aim to avoid this outcome (Driver and Martell, 1998; Jordan, 1998; Powell, 1999). Social exclusion policies and strategies to reduce poverty and address a range of social problems are based upon the premise that the most effective response is an increase in labour participation rates and an improvement in educational performance to enable more young people to compete effectively in the job market. The New Deal has introduced a range of incentives underpinned by the clear message that very few people, including lone parents of school-age children, should exist outside the employment market. There remains a real concern that welfare support, restricted as it is, can still foster a 'dependency culture' which not only places a financial drain on the state but leads to 'pitiful lives', 'pain' and 'misfortune' (Young, 1999). The minimum wage and tax and benefit reforms, such as the Working Families Tax Credit, the Children's Tax Credit and the Integrated Child Tax Credit, were all aimed at making work, any work, pay. It is clear that the current reforms of the welfare state in England are based not upon addressing directly inequalities of income or wealth but upon improving inequalities of opportunity.

At the heart of these initiatives, lie long-standing concerns about the nature and implications of particular forms of family life. Targeted social and economic policies, with their concomitant scrutiny, identify particular groups seen as most likely to be troublesome and/or an economic burden on the state (for example, lone parents, particularly young women from working-class communities). Welfare and criminal justice systems also identify certain families as failing to raise and educate children successfully, whether in relation to material insufficiency or child protection or when the child or young person is posing a problem within the public sphere (because of potential, perceived or actual threatening or criminal behaviour). The 'social exclusion' approach can lead policy–makers to use 'catch-all' discursive representations of certain forms of family life that have the potential to homogenise and 'problematise' the lives of quite different groups of people, such as the unemployed, those experiencing difficulties at school and those living in poverty. The language of social exclusion can often end up amplifying the personal failings and inadequacies of specified individuals and groups. This point is illustrated by a Department for Education and Employment (DfEE) for England paper on pupil support that variously describes socially excluded children and young people as being 'disaffected' as 'children from families under stress' and having 'poor attitudes or behaviour' (DfEE, 1999). While it may be that some children and young people fall into such categories, labels such as these do little to explain the complexities of how structural conditions act to determine inclusion and exclusion.

An approach based upon the concept of social exclusion can have positive benefits and can mean support for the integrity and viability of some families and their children. These may include improving the aspirations of parents and young people, channelling economic resources towards groups or individuals, refocusing on multi-agency partnerships to tackle the layered, inter-linked factors which cause social exclusion, and widening the debate, resulting in a partial rediscovery of the benefits of more active and participative forms of community (Jones and Tucker, 2000).

Regeneration of communities through projects such as those funded by the Single Regeneration Budget are designed to encourage families to move outside potentially isolating homes into their communities. As Percy-Smith (2000) has argued, such policy developments rely upon mobilising voluntary effort and seeing community activity as in itself productive, knitting communities together, invigorating local democracy and creating greater social cohesion. However, 'social exclusion' as a concept, and as a basis for a raft of governmental policies, has not obscured the need to address child poverty directly as New Labour Prime Minister Blair's commitment to eradicate child poverty within twenty years has shown. These ways of thinking can lead to very different kinds of services for children and families. Examples of this include: Sure Start, a multi-agency initiative delivering integrated health and social services to families with young children aged 0–3 living in areas where there is a concentration of ill-health and social deprivation, and the National Childcare Strategy, making childcare more accessible and acceptable while retaining an emphasis on quality in the early years of education through such things as the expansion of OFSTED into the field.

These new economic and social policies have come into place both to support certain kinds of family and discourage others and to maintain confidence in the 'normal' family's ability to contribute positively to the lives of children. But these family policies and practices are also increasingly subject to new ideas about children and childhoods. The use of the United Nations Convention on the Rights of the Child (UNCRC), with its emphasis on the need to seek the child's opinion (Article 12), and the growth of the human rights discourse in Western societies, continue to advance the notion that within and outside the family, proper account has to be taken of the views, opinions and aspirations of children and young people. One example is the work of the Social Exclusion Unit, whose influential reports into school exclusions, teenage pregnancy and young people not in education, training or employment have involved extensive consultation with children and young people. Changes to the vision and agenda for both policy and practice are beginning to take place – such a vision has to reflect the notion that children should be active 'stakeholders' in the policy–making processes.

Within schools, the failure of individuals, genders or groups to secure a good education is clearly understood as key to determining life chances, particularly employment, as an adult. The strength of this belief has resulted in an increasingly expanded, centralised and controlled education system. Childhood has also been for a long time perceived in terms of a journey, from unfulfilled potential to fully human adulthood. The first stage of that journey, early childhood, is increasingly focused on as an important stage in the processing of an economically productive human workforce for the future (Dahlberg *et al.*, 1999). Such ideas, visualising early childhood as a first rung on the ladder to success (or failure), can be seen at work in the introduction of the Foundation stage (for the age group 3–6) with its explicit early learning goals and extensive curriculum guidance, seeking to steer a child's early years through a learning programme geared towards school entry and the national curriculum. Likewise, in the last stage of that journey to adulthood,, the teenage years, national curriculum guidance on teaching 'citizenship' and strategies such as Connexions (aimed at ages 13–19) aim to make significant contributions to the formation of the self-guiding child and citizen. But again, while old, embedded ideas about what childhood is about remain active, other ideas about children's rights and agency are surfacing in schools. Children as social agents are gaining significantly more recognition in their schools; they are increasingly seen and treated as major players in the creation and sustenance of a school ethos as expressed, for example, through the development of school councils and anti-bullying and anti-racism strategies.

Within health and social services for children, while 'children in need' remains embedded in social strategies, both at national and local levels, children's services are increasingly emphasising the importance of listening to the views and wishes of children when decisions are being made about their welfare (Department of Health, 1998). Developments, which involve listening to children, are increasingly less restricted by age, thus breaking down the exclusion of young children. Such developments provide evidence of the growing influence of a children's rights-based agenda constructed around the need for consultation and the provision of opportunities for self-advocacy (Dalrymple and Hough, 1995), and the direct involvement of children as 'stakeholders' in policy formation and decision-making about welfare, health and educational issues. Underpinning stakeholder involvement is the idea that children's voices 'must be supported through a political process that allows differing interests and values to be expressed and challenged' (Clarke and Stewart, 1991: 64).[9] The contributory influence of children on the world around them is increasingly accepted; today it is up to adults to justify intervention which denies the child's autonomy rather than the onus being on children needing to demonstrate competence.

None the less, change in services for children and families is patchy and fragile. Calls for Children's Commissioners for England, Scotland, Northern Ireland and Wales have grown stronger in recent years (Newell, 2000). Newell makes the case for a powerful and independent institution to protect and promote children's human rights, highlighting their particular vulnerability to breaches of these rights by adults and governments. Their vulnerability derives from their being unfranchised and not having the power to use the legal system in the same way as adults, their limited recognition as rights-holders leading to a measure of hostility and misunderstanding, and their still having limited means of self-advocacy. The call for Children's Rights Commissioners to monitor and improve services for children are thus rooted within calls for the development of a human rights culture across Europe. Children's Rights Commissioners would, it is argued, be consulted about and report on all laws, policies and practices which affect children; they would conduct investigations and review complaints procedures, publish information, promote research and initiate and assist legal action with children and young people. Wales secured a Children's Commissioner in 2001 and there are moves in both the Northern Ireland Assembly and the Scottish Parliament to develop special structures for children and young people; at the time of writing, English children, it seems, may well be left behind in the development of more effective and accountable services for children across the UK.

So, within key thinking currently shaping the range of family policy initiatives, and social and educational policies, we can see the erosion of some concepts but, equally, the emerging of new ideas, some of which co-exist alongside much older concerns and attitudes. Initiatives such as the education and social support provided for young children, tackling social exclusion, the utilisation of social and economic policies to shape the form and function of families, the limited democratisation of schools and the development of Children's Commissioners illustrate, we suggest, how policies in the UK are developing to simultaneously adjust to new ideas while maintaining many traditional modes of thought. These can be seen to contrast significantly with the developments in youth justice, the more corporatist or universalistic approaches towards services for children within other EU states (Pringle, 1998; Ruxton, 2001) and the more committed development of independent human rights institutions for children which are being established across Europe and world-wide (Newell, 2000).

Conclusion

Two developments of the 1990s are significant for any understanding of law and policy relating to children and families in the early twenty-first century. These are the emergence of a 'modern children's rights' movement and the new sociology of childhood. What is distinctive about the modern children's rights movement is the emphasis on the child's participation and the valuing of the child's voice. The new sociology of childhood is also concerned with considering questions of the agency and competence of children and making children more visible (James and Prout, 1997; Hutchby and Moran-Ellis, 1998; Brannen *et al.*, 2000; Alanen and Mayall, 2001). However, the children's rights movement also chimes in with echoes of earlier emancipatory movements; this is not to say, however, that the children's rights movement is the same as the women's movement or the civil rights movement. Rather, in addition to the above emphasis on voice and participation, there are new questions being asked; for example, whether children have human rights too and what it would mean to answer this in the affirmative.

This said, the official discourses are themselves contradictory. For example, as noted earlier, the use of the United Nations Convention on the Rights of the Child (UNCRC), with its emphasis on the need to seek the child's opinion, serves to advance the notion that in matters of 'participation', 'protection' and service 'provision' proper account has to be taken of the views of children. Child welfare legislation in England has increasingly emphasised the importance of listening to children when decisions are being made about their welfare. In recent times attempts have been made by various government departments to include children in decision-making – for example, when in local authority care (Department of Health, 1998) – and to strengthen children's rights through independent advocacy. However, the promotion of children's voices and their rights has been an uneven development. Children's interests are easily subordinated to the political priorities of government.

In the field of education the language of children's rights and participation is largely absent – rather, reference is made, in the main, to the importance of parental choice and school standards.

What we also find is that certain countries in the UK have advocated the principles within the UNCRC to a much greater degree than England. The Scottish Law Commission asked in 1992 'whether a parent or other person exercising parental right should be under a similar obligation to ascertain and have regard to the child's wishes and feelings as an authority was in relation to a child in its care'. It continued: 'this emphasises that the child is a person in his or her own right' their views being 'entitled to respect and consideration'. Many respondents regarded a provision requiring parents to consult with the child, bearing in mind the child's age and understanding as 'an important declaration of principle' (1992 paras 2.62 to 2.64). Section 6 of the Children (Scotland) Act 1995 imposes such a duty on parents and provides that children over 12 years of age are presumed in law to be old enough to express a view.[10]

In addition to such developments the decisions of the ECtHR will continue to have an impact on law and policy affecting children and with the incorporation of the ECHR into UK domestic law as a result of the Human Rights Act 1998, domestic courts, now seized with the jurisprudence of the ECtHR, will have to engage with human rights arguments in their deliberation in cases involving children – whether it relates to the criminal justice system or private law matters. This alerts us to the need to have regard to the different levels at which law and policy affecting children can be articulated. While in some spheres children and young people are being given the potential to have a 'voice' the overall thrust to both social and policy change has been to extend the dependency of children on adults and to 'demonise' others in quite new ways. The result is that while some children and young people may be having their views listened to, others, particularly where they are seen as posing a threat, are being subjected to increased regulation and discipline. The policy responses to the growing interest in children's rights and giving children and young people a 'voice' may have the consequence, intended or otherwise, of extending further the significance of the personal responsibility of children and young people as well as the responsibilities of their parents. In making children and young people more responsible for their actions, the sanctions imposed when they are judged – by adults – not to being doing so appropriately can be seen to be even more restrictive. Ironically, the extension of the notion of children's rights may have the effect of enlisting children and young people into actively governing their own freedom(s) and hence subjecting them to a much more sophisticated form of adult monitoring, guidance and control.

Notes

1 Hence the furore caused by the House of Lords decision in *Gillick* v. *West Norfolk and Wisbech Area Health Authority* [1986] AC 112 in which Lord Scarman held that 'the underlying principle of the law . . . is that parental right yields to the child's right to make his own decision when he reaches a sufficient understanding and intelligence to be capable of making his own mind on the matter in question'.

2 One of the items in the welfare checklist in the Children Act 1989, which courts have to consider in certain proceedings, is the 'ascertainable wishes and feelings of the child concerned (considered in the light of his age and understanding)' (section 1(3)(a) of the Children Act 1989). The Children Act 1989 introduced far-reaching changes to the law and professional practice relating to the welfare of children. Amongst other things it simplified the law, placed greater emphasis on local authority services for children in need, gave parents and children new procedural rights and created a new decision-making framework.

3 The Human Rights Act 1998 incorporates the provisions of the ECHR into domestic law so that courts and tribunals must give effect to the ECHR when making decisions. It also requires public authorities to act compatibly with the rights and freedoms of the ECHR.

4 This application also serves to remind us that the family is not necessarily the harbinger of liberal human rights values.

5 The child was awarded £10,000 in compensation. In *R* v. *H* [2001] 2 FLR 431 the father beat his son with a leather belt and during the father's trial on a charge of assault occasioning actual bodily harm, the judge made it clear that, pending a legislative response to the decision of the ECtHR in *A* v. *UK* on the part of the government, the jury should be directed in accordance with that decision. The government has completed this consultation process and has concluded that in the light of *R* v. *H* there is no need for legislative reform.

6 Following the judgment of the ECtHR, in which it held that the defendants had been denied a fair trial in breach of Art 6.1 of the ECHR, the Lord Chief Justice issued a practice direction which stated: 'The trial process should not itself expose the young defendant to avoidable intimidation, humiliation or distress. All possible steps should be taken to assist the young defendant to understand and participate in the proceedings. The ordinary trial process should so far as necessary be adapted to meet those ends. Regard should be had to the welfare of the young defendant as required by section 44 of the Children and Young Persons Act 1933' (*Times* Law Report, 17 February 2000). Other paragraphs of this practice direction concerned seating, court design, the need to remove wigs and gowns, and the number of people attending the trial, including the press.

7 Irrespective of whether or not the threshold criteria contained in section 31(2) of the Children Act 1989 are satisfied. The requirement in the Act that before a care order can be made a child must have suffered or be likely to suffer significant harm (the threshold criteria) was seen as clarifying the law and as striking the right balance between family privacy and the state's interest in the welfare of children. It seems that this consideration is no longer pivotal.

8 Unless the sentence for the offence is fixed by law, or the court was considering either an absolute discharge, custodial sentence or hospital order.

9 See further Roche (2001) for a brief discussion of the Durham Investing in Children Initiative.

10 There are no plans at present to introduce a similar provision into the law in England.

References

Alanen, L. and Mayall, B. (2001) *Conceptualizing Child–Adult Relations*, London, RoutledgeFalmer.

Audit Commission (1996) *Misspent Youth*, London, Audit Commission.

Branigan, T. (2001) 'Christian schools ask for right to hit pupils', *The Guardian*, 3 November, p. 2.

Brannen, J., Heptinstall, E. and Bhopal, K. (2000) *Connecting Children. Care and Family Life in Later Childhood*, London, RoutledgeFalmer.

Burrows, L. (1998) *The Fight for the Family. The Adults behind Children's Rights*, Oxford, Family Education Trust.

Clarke, M. and Stewart, J. (1991) *Choices for Local Government for the 1990s and Beyond*, Essex, Longman.

Dahlberg, G., Moss, P. and Pence, A. (1999) *Beyond Quality in Early Childhood Education and Care*, London, Falmer Press.

Dalrymple, J. and Hough, J. (1995) *Having a Voice: An Exploration of Children's Rights and Advocacy*, Birmingham, Venture Press.

Department for Education and Employment (DfEE) (1999) *Social Exclusion: Pupil Support*, London, DfEE.

Department of Health (1998) *Quality Protects: Transforming Children's Services*, London, Stationery Office.

Driver, S. and Martell, L. (1998) *New Labour: Politics after Thatcherism*, Cambridge, Polity Press.

Franklin, B. and Petley, J. (1996) 'Killing the age of innocence: newspaper reporting of the death of James Bulger', in J. Pilcher and S. Wagg (eds) *Thatcher's Children. Politics, Childhood and Society in the 1980s and 1990s*, London, Falmer Press.

Freeman, M. (1997) 'The James Bulger tragedy: childish innocence and the construction of guilt', in A. McGillivray (ed.) *Governing Childhood*, Aldershot, Dartmouth.

Freeman, M. (1998) 'The sociology of childhood and children's rights', *The International Journal of Children's Rights*, 6 (4), 433–44.

Goldson, B. (1998) 'Re-visiting the "Bulger case": the governance of juvenile crime and the politics of punishment – enduring consequences for children in England and Wales', *Juvenile Justice Worldwide*, 1 (1), p. 21.

Hendrick, H. (1994) *Child Welfare in England 1872–1989*, London, Routledge.

Hutchby, I. and Moran-Ellis, J. (eds) (1998) *Children and Social Competence: Arenas of Action*, London, Falmer Press.

James, A. and Prout, A. (eds) (1997) *Constructing and Reconstructing Childhood: Contemporary Issues in the Sociological Study of Childhood* (2nd edition), London, Falmer Press.

Jones, L. and Tucker, S. (2000) 'Experiencing continuity and change', in A. Brechin, H. Brown and M.A. Eby (eds) *Critical Practice in Health and Social Care*, London, Sage.

Jordan, B. (1998) *The New Politics of Welfare*, London, Sage.

Kilkelly, U. (2000) 'The impact of the Convention on the case-law of the European Court of Human Rights', in D. Fottrell (ed.) *Revisiting Children's Rights: 10 years of the UN Convention on the Rights of the Child*, The Hague, Kluwer.

Mayall, B. (2001) 'The sociology of childhood in relation to children's rights', *The International Journal of Children's Rights*, 8 (3), 243–59.

Morgan, D. (1996) *Family Connections*, Cambridge, Polity.

Mount, F. (1982) *The Subversive Family*, London, Jonathan Cape.

Muncie, J. (2002) 'Children's rights and youth justice', in B. Franklin (ed.) *The New Handbook of Children's Rights: Comparative Policy and Practice*, London, Routledge.

Newell, P. (2000) *Taking Children Seriously. A Proposal for a Children's Rights Commissioner*, London, Calouste Gulbenkian Foundation.

Percy-Smith, J. (2000) *Policy Responses to Social Exclusion*, Buckingham, Open University Press.

Powell, M. (ed.) (1999) *New Labour, New Welfare State: The 'Third Way' in British Social Policy*, Bristol, The Policy Press.

Pringle, K. (1998) *Children and Social Welfare in Europe*, Buckingham, Open University Press.

Pugh, G. (1999) 'Parents under pressure – children and families: a view at the Millennium', *Community Care*, 2–8 September, pp. I–VIII.

Qvortrup, J. (1994) 'Childhood matters: an introduction', in J. Qvortrup, M. Bardy, G. Sgritta and H. Wintersberger (eds) *Childhood Matters: Social Theory, Practice and Politics*, Aldershot, Avebury.

Roche, J. (2001) 'Quality of life for children', in P. Foley, J. Roche and S. Tucker (eds) *Children in Society: Contemporary Theory, Policy and Practice*, Basingstoke, Palgrave.

Ruxton, S. (2001) 'Towards a "children's policy" for the European Union?', in P. Foley, J. Roche and S. Tucker (eds) *Children in Society: Contemporary Theory, Policy and Practice*, Basingstoke, Palgrave.

Scottish Law Commission (1992) *Report on Family Law*, Scot. Law Com. No. 135, Edinburgh, HMSO.

Smart, C. and Neale, B. (1999) *Family Fragments?*, Cambridge, Polity.

Tucker, S. (1999) 'Making the link: dual "problematisation", discourse and work with young people', *Journal of Youth Studies*, 2 (3), 283–95.

Young, J. (1999) *The Exclusive Society*, London, Sage.

Part III
Children and services

8 Young people and welfare

Negotiating pathways

*Christine Hallett, Cathy Murray
and Samantha Punch*

This chapter explores young people's perceptions of their worries and problems, their negotiations, coping strategies and their help-seeking behaviour. It considers the contingent and contextual nature of young people's worries and their responses to them, including how they cope with them and to whom, if anyone, they turn for help. Such understandings can contribute to the provision of advice and help for young people which reflects their experience and is better tailored to their needs.

The chapter draws upon a study entitled 'Young People and Welfare: Negotiating Pathways, conducted under the ESRC Children 5–16: Growing into the 21st Century Programme'.[1] The study included two samples of young people, one living at home and the other in residential care. Eighty-six young people aged 13–14 living in Scotland were interviewed both individually and in groups.[2] The first sample comprised 22 boys and 33 girls in two mainstream schools and the second 16 boys and 15 girls in residential units, referred to in this chapter as the 'at-home' and 'residential' samples respectively. Various task-based methods, stimulus material and straightforward questioning were employed (Punch, 2002).

The study was informed by the new sociology of childhood with its focus upon children's agency (James *et al.*, 1998). It was also prompted by recent developments in social policy, including an emphasis on children's rights and the need to consult children and young people about issues of concern to them enshrined in legislation (Children Act, 1989; Children (Scotland) Act, 1995) and in Article 12 of the UN Convention on the Rights of the Child. These have led to a wide range of participatory opportunities for children and young people.

Young people's problems

Studies of problems among samples of the general child population have indicated that children perceive their problems to be connected with the all-encompassing broad domains of school, family, friends and health

Table 8.1 Problems which young people had not discussed with others

At-home sample	Residential sample
Boys	*Boys*
Sexual intercourse	If I was having sexual problems
Tried to hire sex film	I was sexually abused when I was 8 years old
Getting bullied	Sex life
If no one likes you. Like if people think you're sad and you don't get girlfriends	I hardly ever talk about my brother's death because I don't like crying in front of people
Girlfriends	Bullying of some sorts
How far to go	Being alone. Out on the streets when you are older
Smoking and drinking	Shoplifting
Addictions	Dad dying
If I had a personal problem, e.g. voice breaking etc.	
Body problems	
Girls	*Girls*
If you think there is something wrong with your body	I would not tell anyone that my boyfriend is twenty years of age. I would not tell anyone if I was pregnant but I am not
That an older person had tried to have sex with you	Having underage sex and becoming pregnant and feeling you have nowhere to go
Afraid to have sex but really want to	Sleeping with another girl
Period pains. When boys tease you about your breasts	Being sexually abused
My friends have started their periods and I haven't. They talk about theirs and I just agree	My real dad kept feeling my private parts
My papa dying on Christmas	Been raped
Parents hitting me	I have been raped two times
My parents argue. I could tell my best friend but hers don't so I'm not sure she would understand	I just want my mum to love me because I feel so empty inside
Beliefs – being different, e.g. sex before marriage, divorce. Periods	When I fell out with my aunty
I really like my best friend's boyfriend	My family troubles. Some of my feelings
Worrying about going into 3rd year	I cry at night thinking of my family
If you had done something really bad – stolen something or anything really bad	Fighting with someone really close to you

(Silverman *et al.*, 1995; ChildLine, 1996; Balding, 1997; Gordon and Grant, 1997; Ghate and Daniels, 1997). Studies focusing on children in residential or foster care have demonstrated that this group experience a range of severe problems such as drug and alcohol abuse, or sexual and physical abuse (Kerfoot and Butler, 1988; Morris and Wheatley, 1994; Butler and Williamson, 1994).

While previous studies have identified some clear gender differences, gender has been less well explored in the context of responding to problems and the role of support networks, both formal and informal. It was not the purpose of the study to add to existing descriptive information about young people's problems, but rather to take it as the starting point from which to discover what young people did in response to them. The problems identified by the young people in the study were broadly similar to those previously identified. The most commonly mentioned recent worries were schoolwork, death or ill health, parental conflict, and falling out with friends. This study confirmed the consistently emerging pattern of gender differences, that girls worry more than boys do (Dekovic and Meeus, 1995; Silverman *et al.*, 1995; Gordon and Grant, 1997). For example, asked to identify from a common list of problems those which most worried them, girls ticked on average 7.6 and boys 5.5 problems. A more unexpected finding is that this gender difference is polarised in the residential sample, with boys identifying even fewer and girls even more problems which worry them than their at-home counterparts.

Despite the frequently discussed power differential between adults and young people, previous studies have relied on young people's willingness to share their problems with adult researchers. In the current study, by means of a 'secret' box, the young people were asked to indicate on a piece of paper (anonymously, indicating only their gender) whether there was a problem which they had experienced and never told anyone. It was explained to them that this would only be read by the researcher after completion of the last interview with each sample. This assured anonymity and also that questions would not be raised by the researcher about the problem. Table 8.1 shows the problems that young people had not discussed with others, including sex, rape, sexual abuse, puberty, death of a relative, and a range of illegal activities.

Young people responding to problems

The young people indicated the ways in which they were most likely to deal with problems in their lives (see Table 8.2).

The most common response was telling someone, which is discussed in more detail on pp. 128–31. The young people also frequently used distraction and avoidance tactics, such as listening to music or

Table 8.2 Young people's most likely coping strategies in rank order of frequency and by gender and living circumstances

	Whole sample	Boys	Girls	At-home	Residential
1	Tell someone	*Tell someone *Hit something	Cry	Tell someone	Run away
2	Listen to music		Listen to music	Go off by myself; go to my bedroom	Smoke a cigarette
3	Cry	Hang out with friends	Tell someone	*Listen to music *Cry	Listen to music
4	Hit something	Watch TV	Go off by myself; go to my bedroom		Cry
5	Go off by myself; go to my bedroom	Go off by myself; go to my bedroom	Write in a diary	Hang out with friends	*Hit something *Take drugs *Tell someone *Drink alcohol *Miss school on purpose
6	Hang out with friends	*Pretend to others that everything's fine *Listen to music	Go quiet	Hit something	

*Ranked equally

going out with friends, and strategies to release their feelings, such as crying or hitting out at something. The young people's accounts of their strategies revealed that sometimes they would prefer to keep their problems to themselves or try to forget them. More boys than girls indicated that they would watch television or pretend to others that everything was fine. More girls than boys indicated that they would cry or write their problems in a diary. Examples of these varied strategies include:

> I'd tell a friend and I'd write it in my diary and then I read back on it and I can sort out a solution.

> I just tend to bottle it up and I don't tell anybody and it goes away.

> I just go out with my pals and mess about and that . . . just like get chases off the police and other folk . . . If I'm upset or angry or that they [my friends] can just tell and they say 'come on, we'll go and do something, something like unusual, like, we'll go and go up the river and get a wee like swim'.

The residential sample reported a wider range of responses, many of them more extreme than those employed by the at-home sample. The majority of the looked-after young people had absconded; this compares with almost a half of those interviewed in the Triseliotis *et al.* study (1995). Three-fifths of those who ran away spontaneously said they did so either 'for fun' and 'for something to do', and two-fifths as a strategic response to problems. The young people gave reasoned accounts of the choices they were making, for example:

> I dinnae think I would [run away in the future]. I think I realise that running away is no helping me anyway . . . I'm going home the noo, I've got nae need to run away.

Another, who described herself in the past as not being good at talking about her feelings and as a 'daft wee lassie that was wild and oot of control', described how she no longer ran away, having decided instead to:

> nae run away, kept my head down, just worked the system, got leave, just done everything that was required for me to dae.

Other strategies reportedly adopted by those in residential care much more frequently than those living at home included truancy, smoking, drinking, taking drugs, smashing things or harming themselves deliberately. Morris and Wheatley (1994), in a study of calls made to ChildLine by young people in residential care, noted that they:

> may develop sophisticated defence mechanisms to manage their feelings; for some these prove ineffective or periodically break down, and may result (for example) in bouts of anger, depression, running away or withdrawal.
>
> (Morris and Wheatley, 1994: 61)

The young people in the residential sample were also more likely to report a preference for trying to solve their problems themselves, particularly in relation to bullying both at school and in the home, believing that they should be able to stand up for themselves; for example, one such boy said: 'so I hit him and then I ended up battering him and now he doesn't annoy me any more'.

Those in the residential sample responded to problems in a context which included a number of formal mechanisms which might enable them to participate in decisions concerning them (such as children's hearings[3] and reviews). However, there is little evidence in the study that they regarded such occasions as a forum for exercising much power or influence, with a majority of respondents adapting their posture in meetings to their perception that important decisions had in effect already been made; for example:

> they ask me if I've got anything to say but with all of them sitting there you don't want to say anything, you just want to get it over with. Like 'do I agree with it?' and all that. If it's written there and the social workers told it, of course I've got to agree with it.

Nonetheless, they could still adopt strategic behaviour, for example compliance, as expressed by this young person who claimed that in a children's hearing 'I only ever say three words yip, yes and aye.'

In general young people identified particular styles of responding to problems which appeared to be gendered and to reflect whether they lived at home or in residential care and, to an extent, the kind of people they were, outgoing and chatty or quiet. Some would prefer to 'bottle up' their problems; for example, one young person who said: 'It's just I've never like been one to talk to my mum or dad or anyone about anything; I just tend to just leave it and let it sort itself out.' Others would be more likely to talk about their problems. Some said that it would also depend on the mood of the person they hoped to tell or what mood they themselves were in. Young people's responses to problems were, however, flexible and choices were made as to how to respond in specific situations.

The most common response to problems was to tell someone. The young people were asked to complete a chart of whom they were most likely to turn to for a range of twenty different problems (including problems at home, at school, relationship difficulties, problems with drugs, alcohol, etc.). When aggregated for the whole sample, the most common people to tell were best friends, both parents and mothers. For the at-home sample twice as many girls as boys said that they would go to their mothers or best friends. More at-home boys said they would go to both parents or their fathers, whereas more girls said they would go to their mothers or both parents and rarely to their fathers (cf. Balding, 1997). In both samples, some girls said that they would be more likely to talk to their mothers about what they termed 'girls' problems', boyfriends and sex, because of their shared gendered experiences. Similarly some boys felt they were closer to their fathers than to their mothers, and could go to them about 'boys' problems'. However, some boys felt that their fathers put them under pressure to be tough and hard, and to stand up for themselves, rather than being understanding about their predicaments.

The residential young people, often with disrupted patterns of contact with their families and greater contact with professionals, were most likely to go to their keyworkers and, to a lesser extent, to their social workers. However, confirming their reported reliance on solving their own problems, it is interesting to note that 33 per cent of girls and 57 per cent of boys living in residential care said they would not tell anyone about their problems.

On the whole, young people tended to go to adults in their family, particularly mothers, for a wide range of problems, confirming Ghate and Daniels's (1997) finding that mothers are seen as the main confidantes by the largest number of children in their study. Fathers were considered to be most likely to think of something that could be done and offer practical advice. Mothers were said to be more likely than fathers to notice if something was worrying their children and more likely to go to the school on their behalf to sort out a problem, such as bullying. Relatives, other than parents and siblings, were considered to be a useful source of advice for family worries, as such problems were seen as more appropriately kept within the family rather than discussed with friends. Relatives were an important part of the informal networks of the residential young people, many of whom had stayed either short term or long term with their relatives at some point in their lives. Grandparents, aunts and uncles were said by some to be particularly useful for problems which parents might get angry about:

> If I was smoking or taking drugs . . . I might tell my gran and grandpa but I wouldn't tell my parents . . . Because my mum and dad just wouldn't let me go out or anything in case I did it again or something but my grandparents would just sort of help me and they wouldn't tell my parents.

Best friends were often considered the most appropriate people to approach. Hartup suggests that we do not know 'whether stable friendships buffer children and adolescents from the adverse effects of negative events occurring in everyday life' (1992: 188). Berndt (1986) points out that most studies have examined the supports available to adults in their social networks or the degree to which adults support children rather than the supportive functions of friendships and other relationships with peers during childhood and adolescence. The young people in the ESRC study indicated clearly that their friends constituted a vital source of social support. However, the gendered nature of young people's friendship patterns (Berndt, 1986; Belle, 1989; Rutter, 1998) – in particular the larger but looser friendship groups of boys compared with the smaller more intimate ones of girls – affected the ways in which girls and boys coped with their problems, as previous studies have indicated (Archer, 1992; Hartup, 1992; Borland *et al.*, 1998). Girls' friends were considered to be more intimate and supportive towards each other and they were usually more able to talk to their friends, whereas boys were said to be more likely to make fun of each other, especially if the problem was not considered serious. Boys would be more likely to go to their friends only if they were really worried about something: 'I just think girls talk about them all the time and it's all they ever talk about is problems, but boys just usually bottle it up and then eventually if it's so bad they tell each other.' Ghate and Daniels report similar findings, stating:

> girls . . . were significantly more likely to report having 'special' friends (78% vs 59%) and that they could always find a friend to talk to if they were worried or upset (80% vs 49%). Boys, on the other hand, tended to report themselves as more isolated and distant from their friends.
>
> (1997: 34)

It was suggested in the ESRC study that one reason boys were disinclined to talk about their problems was to protect their image:

> I think boys tend to bottle it up more because they like want to seem really cool in front of their friends and I don't think they would feel comfortable talking to their friends about it.

Some boys thought that the support girls received from their friends enabled them to cope better with their problems:

> They always talk to all their friends about it and that and their friends all support them. And they never break up with friends particularly anyway so they probably deal with it a bit better than boys.

Other boys, however, disagreed with the commonly held views that boys had to bottle up their problems: 'You don't have to like hide all your problems, you can tell your friends and stuff. You don't have to be solid.'

Both boys and girls thought that boys were more likely to keep their problems to themselves and try to forget them. This was confirmed when young people indicated whom they would go to, from a list of choices which included 'nobody', for a specified range of problems. Of 794 choices made by boys, 40 per cent were for 'nobody', whereas of 1,126 choices made by girls the equivalent figure was 24 per cent.

Young people were discriminating in approaching both formal and informal support networks. Many differentiated between their best friends, siblings and their parents as being better for some things rather than others: 'The least likely person I would tell [about getting pregnant] is my dad because he'd go ballistic at me.' However, the same girl also said: 'The most likely person I would tell [about pressure of school work] is my dad because he's intellectual and would help me with a way to resolve it.' In general mothers were said to be understanding and good to turn to but not for all of the young people nor for all of their problems: 'I usually tell my mum like most stuff, not everything.'

Over half of the young people in the at-home sample and nearly all of the residential sample said that they would prefer to tell their problems to someone they know very well because they would know whether they could trust them and how they might react. A quarter of the at-home sample, however, said they would prefer to talk to a stranger, especially if their problem was personal or embarrassing and they did not want anyone else to know about it.

Formal agencies: young people's knowledge and perceptions

From a list of thirteen helping agencies (teacher, guidance teacher, head teacher, doctor, school nurse, social worker, counsellor, educational psychologist, ChildLine, other advice line/helpline, police, child law centre, solicitor/lawyer) the young people were asked to indicate which they had or had not heard of. Only two of the at-home sample said that they had heard of all of them, compared with over a third of the residential sample. In response to a question as to whom they could go to about their problems, apart from family and friends, almost all of the at-home sample said telephone helplines or school (guidance and other teachers). The residential sample indicated that – in addition – they could contact social workers, workers from Who Cares? Scotland,[4] befrienders, children's rights officers and keyworkers. The at-home sample's reported reluctance to contact formal agencies was partly explained by a lack of clarity about their roles (especially social workers and counsellors) and also by their negative image; for example, counsellors were said to 'all sound a bit weird'. Equally important was the stigma attached to the young people themselves if they use the services available, such as going to guidance staff which can be perceived as 'grassing' on someone. Particularly telling is the following comment: 'When everyone found out I was going to a psychologist they all made a fool of me . . . well they think if you go and see a psychologist you're a psycho.'

The young people identified three specific issues surrounding the accessibility of formal services. The first involved locating the person who may be able to help with the problem. Most of the at-home sample were unclear how to access social workers and counsellors at all. In contrast, the residential sample were more confident about how to access formal agencies, and many of them had contact phone numbers for social workers. The second issue involved access to these formal services once they were located. Doctors, for example, were often perceived to be too busy and not to have time for teenagers, while guidance teachers and school nurses were noted for their lack of availability:

Sometimes she's [school nurse] really hard to find. Like at lunch time and like you cannae find her. At lunch, at breaks you don't, you can't see her. And if you're like ill in class, sometimes she's like away photocopying or away somewhere else and you can't find her.

A third issue was identified only by girls. A substantial minority expressed a preference for the person providing help or support, whether informal or formal, to be female, for example:

the least likely person to go to with a problem is my brother because he's a boy and he doesn't understand as much and that. He just thinks everything's a big joke and that, so I wouldn't go to him.

a lot of my teachers are, like, male and I wouldn't go to a male teacher I don't think because they just don't understand.

I would only go to a woman counsellor: I wouldn't go to a man.

Confidentiality and trust

Confidentiality and trust were of utmost importance for the young people when deciding whether or not to tell someone about a problem. They considered that informal networks (particularly friends) could usually be relied upon more than formal agencies to provide confidentiality. If particular individuals were known to them, a better judgement could be made as to how trustworthy they were. One of the major concerns to the young people was that personal knowledge about them would be spread around. Some felt that if they really did not want a certain problem to be known it would be better not to tell anybody at all. Many said that one of the most important attributes of best friends is that they could usually be trusted to keep a secret. However, not all could be trusted completely: 'If you tell it to a best friend then they might have another best friend they might tell it to.' When best friends moved away, contact would often be maintained by letter and by phone and they could be seen as particularly useful for confiding in, because there was no risk of them telling others. Also lack of privacy could mean that they would not want to write their problems down: 'I think diaries are probably the worst ideas in the world because . . . I know that probably somebody would read it, so I wouldn't write it down.'

Generation and age

Age was an important factor influencing who the young people confided in. Lack of empathy from adults was a dominant theme throughout the study. Given this, some teenagers thought that younger people were better placed to give advice. Examples included helplines and agony aunts:

> I think it should be kids that write them or folk just a little older than them that have actually got the problem . . . I mean, when I read it I think, mmm, how long ago was it that you've had this problem.

Friends, siblings and to a lesser extent cousins were considered more likely to understand problems, largely because of their recent shared childhood experiences. As one sibling explained: 'He's had all the problems just a little while ago and he's quite a nice brother so he doesn't laugh at me or anything if I tell him stuff.' Best friends were nearly always the same age and gender as well as being at the same school. Similarly, siblings tend to go to the same school and could be an important source of help with school-related problems. Mutual sharing of problems was an important feature of the best friend and sibling relationship as young people felt it was important that they could help each other with their worries, in contrast to the one-sided problem-solving which often typifies relationships with adults.

Some young people said that although their friends could listen, empathise and give suggestions, they could not do much to sort out their more serious problems:

> If it was a serious problem I'd definitely go to my brother. If it's just something small like bad confidence I'd go to a friend. My brother would be more likely for anything serious because a friend can't do much. They'd just, like if they did think about it at all, they'd just be wondering the same as you who they should tell and stuff, so then you'd have to tell someone older.

Young people acknowledged that they may lack the experience to solve some problems, and this was reflected in their perceptions of the relative advantages and disadvantages of having peer counsellors compared to guidance teachers to turn to:

> It's [peer counselling] a good idea because they're like young still and able to understand, but I think they would not really be like that experienced. They wouldn't be like trained.

One benefit of telling adults identified by the young people was their capacity actively to solve problems in situations in which this was required – for example, when the problems were deemed by the young person to be serious. In contrast, their peers lacked experience and were less in a position to take action, but could provide a 'listening ear', empathy or advice. The key issue was that although adults' problem-solving capacity was advantageous when sought out, it was viewed negatively when young people had no control over when and how it was exercised.

Anticipated adult reactions

The young people gave more instances of negative than positive adult responses to their problems. Anticipation of adults' reactions sometimes inhibited young people from telling them certain problems. Many feared that adults would take control of their problem and insist they do something about it against their will: 'like I don't really want to do anything, I just want to tell someone about it'. For the at-home sample, the main adults perceived to have the power to control young people, at least to a certain degree, were parents and teachers. Although the residential sample had a wider range of individuals they could turn to if they had a problem, because of their greater contact with professionals, they also had a greater number of adults who could exert power over them.

Young people said that they were more likely to go to adults, particularly their parents, with their problems if they knew that they would give them advice and suggestions rather than enforce their opinions:

> They're [parents] never like really shocked or you know they always sort of keep calm and you know you can talk things through . . . They'd give suggestions and so on but in the end you know they'd leave the final decision to me.

Whilst adults may desire to sort the young person's problem out and solve it for them, young people often perceived this negatively. Adults' responses might exacerbate the problem, cause embarrassment or exaggerate something considered originally not to be very serious. For example:

> they [adults] go for like extreme things so rather than just going for a little thing to help you they like go and tell all the teachers and that – so they're a bit of a waste. You might just as well talk to the teachers in the first place.

> she [mum] was going to try and talk to the guidance teacher but I asked her not . . . I didn't want to be made like a big deal of like I was overreacting and everything.

Other examples included parents lecturing young people in front of their friends or 'storming up' to the school to speak to teachers. Waksler argues that children are particularly vulnerable to such embarrassment because they are denied access to the means of 'repairing' embarrassing encounters (1996: 88). Some young people, however, welcomed the perceived capacity of their parents to solve problems for them, as in 'I just let her [mum] sort it out because every time she sorts it oot alright', and 'I would go to mum and dad because they could just solve it.'

Adults were said to respond moralistically, particularly about certain problems such as drinking, smoking or sex. Their initial reaction was often said to be that the young people should not have been engaging in the behaviour in the first place, as the following comment illustrates:

> They [teachers] dinnae understand you . . . they're no like modern or that so they dinnae ask you nothing because they're going 'well, you shouldnae have been oot at that time'.

One respondent, when asked by the researcher why he said he would not tell his mother about 'stuff', replied:

> Because she always gives me a lecture and she, like, just gets upset if I've done something really bad, like if I've tried to set the Primary school on fire or something like and she gets really really upset . . .

Some young people felt that since their parents expected them to be 'good', they did not want to shatter their illusions: 'Well, no one wants their parents to find out like they've been naughty.' Thus young people might keep such problems to themselves.

Many young people believed that adults did not perceive teenagers' problems to be as serious as their own and would sometimes trivialise them. For example, one respondent said:

> they never seem to understand when you tell them anything so I don't think kids really go to their parents because they just . . . something that means a lot to you just means nothing to them and they just laugh at you.

This confirms the findings of (for example) Butler and Williamson (1994), Gordon and Grant (1997) and Borland *et al.* (1998). Borland *et al.*, for instance, conclude in respect of a sample of children aged 8–12 that parents do not understand the importance and complexity of children's friendships. They suggest 'it may be that parents genuinely do not appreciate the depth of feeling girls of this age have for their special friends' (1998: 108).

While parents were accused of trivialising their children's problems, the young people thought, however, that adults would often take their problem more seriously if other adults became involved. The potential for adults to deny the legitimacy of some of the worries experienced by young people suggests that the somewhat compressed and linear models of problem-solving and pathways to welfare – for example, those of

Butcher and Crosbie (1977) and D'Zurilla and Goldfried (1971) – require adaptation if they are to account for the complexity and diversity of young people's actions.

Conclusion

This chapter has explored the ways in which young people respond to what they regard as problems in their lives. The findings suggest that their responses are both contextual and contingent. Among the contextual factors, gender and the young people's living situation (whether at home or in residential care, which in turn reflect different life experiences) were found to be central. So was their social status as 'children', including structural constraints such as their relative powerlessness particularly in schools (Mayall, 1994) and in residential schools, their lack of privacy and, at times, the lack of legitimacy accorded to their worries. Various contingencies additionally affected their responses. These included the nature of the problems faced, their knowledge and perception of the role of formal agencies, the characteristics of their informal network, including the mutuality and support provided to some, particularly girls, by their friends, the anticipated reaction of adults and young people's perceptions of the problem-solving capacity of others.

To what extent can it be said that young people adopt active, autonomous or considered strategies in their responses to problems, rather than, say, 'merely' reacting to events? It is clear that some of them do so to a significant degree. Among a range of responses, which include those that are perhaps unreflexive, the young people describe themselves as making conscious decisions as to what to tell and to whom, and when to withhold information in order to retain control. Young people in the particular circumstances of residential care described a number of tactics used to make their views known or to achieve ends. Strategic responses here included absconding as a calculated attempt to influence placement; rule-breaking where the costs of doing so had been weighed and found worth incurring; and decisions (conversely) to go along with the rules in order to increase bargaining power.

The young people were able to articulate clearly their experiences of the ways in which formal and informal systems had responded to their difficulties. They made a range of suggestions of ways in which formal services could be improved so that teenagers would be more likely to use them, including the provision of more information, listening more sympathetically, maintaining confidentiality and continuity and avoiding 'lectures' and condemnation. This illustrates the valuable role which research can play in shaping social policies and practices when the research seeks to identify and learn from young people's views and experiences.

Notes

1 The study (award number L129251016) was conducted by Christine Hallett, Cathy Murray, Samantha Punch and Roger Fuller at the University of Stirling, Scotland.
2 The samples included only two children from minority ethnic groups, which reflects their distribution of 1.3 per cent in the total Scottish population (Scottish Office, 1996).
3 A children's hearing is a lay tribunal to determine issues of child welfare and juvenile justice in Scotland.
4 Who Cares? Scotland is an organisation which gives advice to looked-after young people.

References

Archer, J. (1992) 'Childhood Gender Roles: Social Context and Organisation', in H. McGurk (ed.) *Childhood Social Development: Contemporary Perspectives*, Hillsdale, N.J.: Lawrence Erlbaum Associates, 31–61.

Balding, J. (1997) *Young People in 1996*, Exeter: Schools Health Education Unit, University of Exeter.

Belle, D. (1989) *Children's Social Networks and Social Supports*, Chichester: Wiley.

Berndt, T.J. (1986) 'Children's Comments about their Friendships', in M. Perlmutter (ed.) *Cognitive Perspectives on Children's Social and Behavioral Development: The Minnesota Symposia on Child Psychology*, Volume 18, Hillsdale, N.J.: Lawrence Erlbaum Associates, 189–212.

Borland, M., Laybourn, A., Hill, M. and Brown, J. (1998) *Middle Childhood: The Perspectives of Children and Parents*, London: Jessica Kingsley.

Butcher, R. and Crosbie, D. (1977) *Pensioned Off: A Study of the Needs of Elderly People in Cleaton Moor*, Cumbria CDP Report: University of York.

Butler, I. and Williamson, H. (1994) *Children Speak: Children, Trauma and Social Work*, Harlow: Longman.

ChildLine (1996) *Stressed Out: What Children Tell ChildLine about Exams and Work Pressure*, London: ChildLine.

Dekovic, M. and Meeus, W. (1995) 'Emotional Problems in Adolescence', in M. Du Bois-Reymond, R. Diekstra, K. Hurrelmann and E. Peters (eds) *Childhood and Youth in Germany and The Netherlands: Transitions and Coping Strategies of Adolescents*, Berlin: Walter de Gruyter.

D'Zurilla, T. and Goldfried, M. (1971) 'Problem-solving and Behaviour Modification', *Journal of Abnormal Psychology*, 25: 109–16.

Ghate, D. and Daniels, A. (1997) *Talking about My Generation*, London: NSPCC.

Gordon, J. and Grant, G. (eds) (1997) *How We Feel – An Insight into the Emotional World of Teenagers*, London: Jessica Kingsley Publishers.

Hartup, W.H. (1992) 'Friendships and their Developmental Significance', in H. McGurk (ed.) *Childhood Social Development: Contemporary Perspectives*, Hillsdale, N.J.: Lawrence Erlbaum Associates, 175–205.

James, A., Jenks, C. and Prout, A. (1998) *Theorising Childhood*, Cambridge: Polity Press.

Kerfoot, M. and Butler, A. (1988) *Problems of Childhood and Adolescence*, London: Macmillan.

Mayall, B. (1994) 'Children in Action at Home and School' in B. Mayall (ed.) *Children's Childhoods Observed and Experienced*, London: Falmer Press, 114–27.

Morris, S. and Wheatley, H. (1994) *Time to Listen: The Experiences of Young People in Foster and Residential Care*, London: ChildLine.

Punch, S. (2002) 'Interviewing Strategies with Young People: The "Secret Box", Stimulus Material and Task-based Activities', *Children and Society*, 16: 45–56.

Rutter, M. (1998) *Antisocial Behaviour by Young People*, Cambridge: Cambridge University Press.

Scottish Office (1996) *Factsheet 15: Ethnic Minorities* (www.scotland.gov.uk/library/documents/ethnic.htm).

Silverman, W., La Greca, A. and Wasserstein, S. (1995) 'What Do Children Worry About? Worries and their Relation to Anxiety', *Child Development*, 66: 671–86.

Triseliotis, J., Borland, M., Hill, M. and Lambert, L. (1995) *Teenagers and the Social Work Services*, London: HMSO.

Waksler, F.C. (1996) *The Little Trials of Childhood and Children's Strategies for Dealing with Them*, London: Falmer Press.

9 'Could have helped but they didn't'

The formal and informal support systems experienced by children living with domestic violence

*Audrey Mullender, Gill Hague,
Umme Farvah Imam, Liz Kelly,
Ellen Malos and Linda Regan*

they didn't bother to help. Nothing really helped very much when Dad was at home . . . For me, being with my mum really helped – that was very important, that we were not separated from my mum. Workers helped at the refuge by giving us time, taking us out and helping us to forget about things.

(8-year-old South Asian girl)

Introduction

The frequent silencing of children's voices has been further magnified in relation to domestic violence. This is due, first, to the traditionally sanctioned 'legitimacy' of the abuse of women by their husbands so that what is seen as 'normal' does not count (see Dobash and Dobash, 1979; Hague and Malos, 1998) and, second, to the emphasis on direct physical and sexual abuse as opposed to the trauma of living with domestic violence (Farmer and Owen, 1995). Over the past decade, the realisation has begun to grow that living with abuse can be as damaging as experiencing it directly (Jaffe *et al.*, 1990; Mullender and Morley, 1994; Hester *et al.*, 2000), though this was initially greeted with a tendency to regard the children involved as 'silent witnesses' or 'passive victims' (terms frequently used in conference titles, for example).

This chapter will explore how children themselves understand and experience domestic violence and will discuss the implications for both formal and informal networks of help. The former, so as to emphasise how much agencies could be doing in an ideal world, will be organised into three levels of prevention: primary, secondary and tertiary – that is, stopping the violence from ever happening, stopping it from happening again, and preventing its worst effects.

Methodology

We conducted the study (Mullender *et al.*, forthcoming) from a basically feminist ethos in that we understood that power and control issues between men and women form a key part of domestic violence (Pence and Paymar, 1990, 1996). Within this overarching concern, we also pursued an approach that would place children centre-stage and highlight their own understandings and coping strategies. The multi-methodological, multi-stage research design combined quantitative and qualitative research methods and was conducted in two phases. Phase One was a questionnaire-based survey of 1,395 children, aged 8 to 16, in primary and secondary schools, designed to discover what they knew and understood about domestic violence, as well as their attitudes towards it. Difference and diversity were built in by utilising three research sites spanning urban and rural areas and a range of ethnic communities, and by making particular efforts to include disabled children. Owing to the sensitivity of the topic, issues of consent, confidentiality and child protection received particular attention.

The second phase of the study specifically focused on the experiences and perceptions of children who were known to have lived with domestic violence. It consisted of in-depth individual interviews with 45 children and 24 mothers, as well as group interviews with a further nine children. Wherever possible (given that some families were still moving around), the children seen individually were interviewed on two occasions, with a gap ranging from 6 to 18 months between interviews. Just under half the children had recently been through a refuge, the rest being invited to take part via a range of other agencies. Minority ethnic children were deliberately over-represented in the sample so as to be able to say something meaningful about their particular experiences, still a little-researched area (Imam, 1994). As with Phase One, special efforts also went into including disabled children, including one 13-year-old girl with Down's syndrome and a 13-year-old boy with a hearing impairment. Indeed, in both phases of the research, the proportion of disabled children was comparable with estimates for the general population of children in the UK (Gordon *et al.*, 2000).

How children understand domestic violence

Children in the survey demonstrated considerable confusion as to what they understood by domestic violence. Only 9 per cent of primary and 28 per cent of secondary school children restricted those they thought it implied to parents and/or adults at home. Only 5 per cent overall combined this with some mention of arguing, fighting or hitting into a definition resembling that now commonly used by service providers and in the legislation. The in-depth interviews, on the other hand, revealed that children who have lived with domestic violence have a very clear understanding of what it involves. They have typically seen and heard far more than their parents know and, over time, have made sense of this for themselves. Although only one-third of mothers thought their children were aware of the violence, almost all the children demonstrated awareness of what had been happening:

> When we were young, they tried to keep it away from us and argued in a separate room, not in front of us . . . As the fighting and arguing got worse, we could hear them arguing even when they were in a separate room.
>
> (13-year-old South Asian boy)

While mothers in our study had tried as hard as they could to protect their children, the children had simultaneously sought on many occasions to protect their mothers from awareness of how much they knew, and how unhappy the violence had made them feel. This often resulted in a silence between them in which everyone attempted to shield everyone else from what they were feeling and thinking. An important finding from our study, then, is that developing ways to enable more open and honest communication between mothers and their children is an important element in any attempts at early intervention in domestic violence, and in the process of coping with its aftermath.

What the children remembered

Between them, the children in the in-depth sample had seen virtually every aspect of the pattern of power and control that is understood to constitute domestic violence (Pence and Paymar, 1990, 1996). They had often directly witnessed or overheard physical violence:

> He was grabbing her by the hair and trying to push her down the stairs . . . I was scared.
>
> (9-year-old South Asian boy)

> I heard this massive wallop . . . Mum was lying on the floor.
>
> (12-year-old white girl)

Only four children said they had not really been aware at all of what was happening. Over a third were able to say immediately that they could recall seeing and hearing violent incidents, and others remembered these later. The violence against the children's mothers had often been persistent and brutal. It included an attempted hanging and an attempted poisoning with bleach. Children remembered bloodstained beds and walls. There was a constant atmosphere of intimidation and threats:

> He used to say he was going to put petrol in the house and burn it while we were asleep. We were always frightened he might do that.
>
> (8-year-old Asian girl)

Emotional and verbal abuse, against both the women and the children, was clearly remembered by both:

> I think he did that by getting at them all the time – screaming and shouting – he never hit them. Mostly terrorized them – mental torture, you know.
>
> (South Asian mother)

> dirty language . . . from a father who should be protecting you.
>
> (16-year-old South Asian girl)

The overlap with child abuse, now well established in the literature (see, for example, Hester and Pearson, 1998, and Hester *et al.*, 2000, for a summary) was once again confirmed:

> He was using his fists on me.
>
> (12-year-old African boy)

> I have seen him hit all the members of the family at least once.
>
> (17-year-old dual heritage girl)

The direct abuse carried over into punishing the children inappropriately, with mothers recalling children being hit around the head and a 5-year-old dragged from the room by his hair after becoming overexcited at his own birthday party. Other ways in which the children were directly involved in the domestic violence included being forced to watch, or being used by men to threaten or hurt their partners:

> He would also starve the children to get at me. He was using them to torment and abuse me.
>
> (South Asian mother)

Women and children were often cut off from friends and family by the abuser, both through jealousy and to block sources of help. Financial abuse was also recalled in this context, being kept short of money again being a way of reducing women's options or opportunities to leave. Children could recall rows over money spent on them and even money stolen from them by the perpetrator. Only sexual abuse of the woman and marital rape were not referred to by children, although at least two women recalled having been raped with a child present. Some children were aware, though, of sexual possessiveness and morbid jealousy:

> My mum wasn't even allowed to hang washed clothes outside because he would say she was going out so she could look at other men in the front street.
>
> (8-year-old South Asian girl)

Thus children had lived with the full range of abusive behaviours that make up what adults understand by domestic violence. Not everything was grim, though. One child loved school as a place to escape. Mothers did their best to create good times when the abuser was not around. Children also used all their inventiveness and resilience to find ways to survive. But, overall, there is no escaping the fact that large numbers of children are living with horrifying levels of violence.

What had helped: sources of informal support

It came through strongly from the study that children and young people living with domestic violence or coping with its legacy drew more extensively on informal than on formal sources of help. This strongly confirmed that they, their families and friends, are at least co-producers, if not primary producers, of their own welfare.

Mothers

Most children's key source of help had been their mothers:

> My mum has helped me the most . . . I can't really think of anyone else who has really helped me apart from my mum . . . Mum has helped us the most at the time we left and she helps now.
>
> (13-year-old South Asian boy)

There is a paradox here because, as we have seen, half the children said they had not discussed the abuse in detail with their immediate family while it was happening. For them, it was about having someone there for more general support.

> Mum. Knew she would always be with us, keep us safe – everything will be OK.
>
> (14-year-old South Asian boy)

Children who leave home to escape domestic violence may lose all their other social and community support structures and supportive family relationships, just at the time when they need them most to help them cope emotionally (Garmezy and Rutter, 1983; Kashani and Allan, 1998). It is hard for them to build new sources of support because of the need for secrecy and confidentiality, with South Asian children in particular being constantly reminded not to besmirch their family's honour or *izzat*. The one constant protective factor in their lives is a secure attachment to a non-abusing parent, their mother. Yet abused women, whose partners have often drummed into them they are bad mothers, may live in fear of social workers removing the children from them – and not without reason:

> I think they finally made my mum see how risky it was for all of us to be living with him. They threatened that we would be taken into care if she stayed on after he had hit me so badly and hit her.
>
> (16-year-old South Asian girl)

Not only does this lack of partnership with a non-abusing mother fail to offer her any additional options that could help her keep herself and her children safe (let alone to tackle the violent man), it also places at risk the most important source of support in the children's life, and sometimes the only one left after the violence has taken its toll. Listening to children throws down a challenge to find a new approach.

Siblings

The importance of siblings to one another is frequently overlooked by the helping agencies (Mullender, 1999), even though, in this study, it was graphically demonstrated by one boy, aged 8 at the time, who revealed that he used to climb out of one window and in at another to be with his 13-year-old brother at night when the violence was happening. Others also spoke about the crucial support they had derived from brothers and sisters:

> M would come and calm me down and when he was feeling bad I'd go up and calm him down. Sometimes, we'd just stick together – we'd talk together about what was going on, how we felt about it.
>
> (13-year-old African girl talking about her brother,
> one year younger)

> we used to talk together and sometimes we used to hug each other. And stay together when it was happening. I look after him. We cuddle each other sometimes, like when they were arguing.
>
> (10-year-old white girl talking about her brother,
> two years younger)

Friends

Older girls, in particular, had found support within their peer group. In the sample as a whole, the most likely person a child would have told about the violence, who did not already know by virtue of being involved in some way, was a friend. It was important to find someone who could be trusted to keep a secret and to understand, for example, a long-standing friend or someone who had had a similar experience:

> In this school, now, there used to be a girl . . . we used to know each other from nursery . . . She's the only person I've told where I am. She really understands . . . She's the only one I can talk to about it and she's really calm and she doesn't tell anybody.
>
> (9-year-old white girl)

> My best friend, A, she was having a similar problem. Her mum had run away from her dad's house because he used to beat her up . . . So we could share what was going on and try to keep each other going. We are really close friends because of that.
>
> (13-year-old African girl)

The schools survey showed that children know others who are living with domestic violence, so there are more children carrying this burden than we may think (see also Burton *et al.*, 1998; Regan and Kelly, 2001). Adults tend only to think about child–adult relationships when they consider help and support for younger people, but children themselves put peer support high on their agenda in many different life circumstances (e.g. in the care system: Horrocks and Milner, 1999). Practice is slowly catching up with this realisation. Peer counselling schemes and pupils being trained to help others with conflict resolution are part of a whole-school non-violence strategy in parts of Canada, for example (Mullender, 1994; Hague *et al.*, 2001). Furthermore, recognising how important friends are to young people casts new light on the way that moving around and changing schools to escape the violence too often destroys children's peer support networks and challenges us to do more to preserve these where possible.

Other family members

Informal support had also been forthcoming for some children from the wider family:

> Q. Did you ever try talking to someone else?
> A. Only when we were at my auntie's – then we all used to talk about it.
>
> (10-year-old white girl)

> I wouldn't have minded going to live with my granddad . . . I used
> to escape there. We used to go there every summer.
>
> > (17-year-old dual heritage girl)

Grandmothers were the most commonly mentioned:

> I used to sneak away from school to see my grandmother.
>
> > (16-year-old South Asian girl)

South Asian children, in particular, had a positive expectation that
relatives would help, notably on their father's side of the family (see the
quote with which we opened this chapter). This traditional source of
support was sometimes impeded by the father's family taking his side.
When this happened, it left the woman and her children potentially
isolated from her entire family and community and particularly desper-
ately in need of help. Children did not necessarily expect their trusted
adults to be able to do anything active to help. As with mothers and
siblings, it was often just the fact of them being there that was important:

> Even though I could talk to my nani [maternal grandmother], she
> could do nothing – not even tell her sons what was happening
> because there would be trouble.
>
> > (16-year-old South Asian girl)

Once again, there is a message here for agencies to listen to children and
learn from them who is important in their lives. Forms of intervention
that cut across these vital lines of support will not be experienced as
helpful. Where they are inevitably cut, as in situations where a family
flees to a refuge, we also need to recognise the extent of the loss this
imposes on children.

Formal support: levels of preventative work in the voluntary and statutory sectors

Now that society is more aware of the negative impact of domestic
violence on children, there is an enormous task potentially ahead of us
in responding to their needs. We will tease out what children had to say
about their experience of services and about what they thought would
help under the three headings of primary, secondary and tertiary prevention where primary prevention means stopping domestic violence
from happening in the first place, secondary means ensuring it does not
recur once it has been discovered, and tertiary means preventing its
worst effects from causing as much damage as they otherwise might.
Formal organisations were often experienced by children as offering an
unsatisfactory service. Only refuges and specialist domestic violence

projects received accolades and, even here, there were suggestions for improvement.

Primary prevention

The most desirable goal in domestic violence prevention must clearly be to stop it from ever happening in the life of any given young person. This is the aim of preventative programmes in schools and youth settings.

A major finding from Phase One of the study is that awareness-raising needs to start early – preferably in junior school or very early in secondary school – since a third of teenage boys and a fifth of girls agree with a statement that some women deserve to be hit. It also needs to target boys for the most intensive work since they emerge as less likely than girls to gain a better understanding of domestic violence as they grow up. At all ages, boys have a less good understanding than girls as to who is responsible for domestic violence, even when presented with scenarios in which there is a clear perpetrator and no physical trigger or retaliation from the victim. They are more likely than girls to excuse the abuser. They get less clear, rather than more, about these matters as they get older. At around 13–14 years of age, boys' attitudes start to diverge from girls and continue to move adrift from then on. By the age of 15, girls are far more likely than boys to realise that it is difficult for a woman to leave a violent situation and that pregnant women also experience violence.

The good news from the survey is that over 80 per cent of secondary school children and just over half of primary children would like lessons on domestic violence in school. They want these to cover issues such as what causes it, what can be done about it, and how to stop it if you are on the scene. In an evaluation of a preventative youthwork programme, young people further shared that they prefer discussion-based lessons to having adults telling them what to do and think. They could ideally learn about domestic violence through case studies, speakers, theatre groups and ensuing discussion. Preparation and training for teachers must naturally precede any educational work in schools and not only amongst those who run the actual sessions. Children who have lived with violence, or whose friends have, may wish to disclose this to a trusted adult once they see the issue being raised in school. Links also need to be in place with children's and women's services, including social services and Women's Aid. Displaying the ChildLine (0800 1111) and other helpline numbers in school is also a sensible measure.

A fascinating link can be made between the two phases of the study in that it has revealed one group of young people (the general population in school, particularly of teenagers) with a great thirst to know more about domestic violence and another brimming with expertise to offer. Those who have experienced domestic violence in their own lives can describe it in detail, explain what impact it has in children's lives, and tell us a great deal about what others can do to help. Those who develop materials for educational use in schools and elsewhere should think about consulting them. While the use of such packs (e.g. London Borough of Islington, 1995) in the UK is patchy, their wider-scale use in the USA and Canada has resulted in a problem of a different kind. There, the tendency to develop general anti-violence curricula to teach non-violent conflict resolution and respectful, healthy relationships has led to a watering down of any gender content (AFRCV, 1999; Hague *et al.*, 2001). It would be highly desirable to see gendered content on violence against women and girls introduced into the UK National Curriculum in the context of broader anti-violence work.

Secondary prevention

Most of the work currently undertaken by both voluntary and statutory sector agencies can be classed as secondary prevention because it takes place after domestic violence has already started (or, indeed, become entrenched) and aims to stop it in its tracks.

Refuges

Refuges exist primarily to help women and children get to a place where the violence will stop. Children were full of praise for how it felt to be safe at last:

> you weren't scared of anything. You didn't have to be worried that, like, your dad was going to find you or anything like that.
>
> (9-year-old white girl)

Refuges are naturally not perfect in children's eyes. There is the annoyance of younger children making a noise and being a nuisance. South Asian children and their mothers thought there should be more funding for specialist Asian refuges since these met their needs better than mixed refuges. A particular problem was the devastating and recurrent losses in children's lives caused by the need to leave home and to move on if they were traced by the abuser:

> We weren't allowed to take a lot of stuff with us because . . . we'd be moving around a lot so we wouldn't be able to carry it a lot . . . I had, like, one big rucksack on my back and one big handbag. My brother had one big bag and my mum had . . . two black bags and a big bag.
>
> (10-year-old black British girl who has not seen any of her friends since that day and has had to change schools at least twice)

Children talked with much feeling about the distress and annoyance these moves and losses had caused them, in a way which, again, challenges us to ask whether it is women and children who are made to pay because of gaps in our law and policy that mean we fail to control and tackle violent men. While the policy of moving families on when they are tracked down makes absolute sense in keeping both them and other residents safe, it is not the only possible approach. In some countries, such as Denmark, the justice system works well enough to offer refuges a cordon of safety, even though their addresses are made public. This means that the onus moves away from women and children – and, indeed, refuge staff and residents – keeping themselves safe and on to the perpetrator to stop placing them in danger or face the consequences. There is no doubt that children suffer less from this latter approach, provided it can be made to work; but that would be a very real challenge to our currently less than reliable civil and criminal justice system.

Civil and criminal justice

Occasionally, the criminal and civil justice systems do combine to control the behaviour of a domestic violence perpetrator:

> The police were helpful, very helpful . . . arrested him. Then we got a court order saying he couldn't come within one hundred yards of my mum . . . He'd get arrested if he came near my mum now. So we're safe now.
>
> (11-year-old white boy)

It should be emphasised, though, that the violence in the above example had gone on for a considerable period of time before this effective action was taken and that it had become very severe, with the woman and children still terrified of a recurrence when the interviewers met them. It only just counts as a success story. Also, the police generally did not receive a vote of support from children in the study. In interview, they recalled numerous occasions when the police had been called but very few on which intervention had resulted in any real action against the abuser.

> I called the police but they only let him back out.
>
> (13-year-old white boy)

Also, children felt that they tended to be ignored by police officers, who generally did not talk to them, even when they were the ones who had dialled 999.

Children had strong views about contact with perpetrators. These could usefully be fed into current debates in the Family Court and the civil law more widely (Advisory Board on Family Law, Children Act

Sub-Committee, 2001a and 2001b), where there has been a lack of awareness until very recently of the adverse impact on children of living with domestic violence and the dangers of post-separation violence (Hester and Radford, 1996; Radford *et al.*, 1999). There has tended to be a judicial assumption that it is mothers who oppose contact, in pursuance of their own hostile agendas against former partners (cf. Humphreys, 1999). Yet, for a number of children in the in-depth interviews, it was clear that they had no wish for contact with their fathers, sometimes literally fearing for their own or their mother's lives, and that most who were not in direct contact had no wish to be:

> I don't want to see him because he makes me upset.
>
> > (9-year-old South Asian boy)

> No. What he did to my mum – I don't really want to see him. I don't forgive him.
>
> > (9-year-old white boy)

Beyond this, mothers were often managing quite complex situations of either direct or indirect contact, only occasionally because it was a legal requirement and far more often because they felt it was important the children should not lose touch with their fathers:

> I just don't like to deprive him of seeing them, you know. I suppose I want everything to be friendly.
>
> > (White mother)

In the less-threatening situations, informal contact could occur casually and, especially in the case of South Asian children, in the course of visits to other family members. Most children managed this well, having quite mixed feelings for fathers who were more tolerable now they were not in the same household. There were cases, though, in which children had not wanted contact and felt forced into it by the courts:

> I don't want to go always, but I have to go because the law people said we had to.
>
> > (8-year-old white boy)

There were certainly situations, too, where the contact had led to renewed abuse or violence (in one case, a woman held at knife-point, with her daughter in the house) or was being used by the perpetrator of the violence to try and reassert his control over the family:

> I get upset if he pumps me for information . . . It worries me if he keeps on at me about Mum.
>
> > (12-year-old white girl)

In a number of instances, the abuser was flouting informal agreements. For example, one white mother had, during her marriage, been kicked unconscious in front of her two daughters by a group of women her husband had paid to kill her. After an unsuccessful attempt at reinstating contact at the request of one of the girls, their mother had limited them to regular Sunday phone calls to their father from a number he could not trace and was going back to court. It is to be hoped that the court will take this woman's concerns seriously. However, the current policy situation makes managing contact far more difficult than it should be for women and dangerous both for them and for children (Saunders, 2001).

Other agencies in the statutory sector

Children often could not remember which professionals they had met, and there seemed, in any case, to be only isolated examples of encounters with social workers, court welfare officers, doctors, a child psychologist. Most accounts of the interviews these practitioners had conducted made it clear that they lacked awareness of domestic violence and, consequently, had had only superficial discussions with the children they should have been helping.

> I used to not know what to say. I used to think I was saying the wrong thing.
>
> (15-year-old dual heritage boy)

They were unable to get behind children's health or developmental problems to find out what was actually wrong in their home lives. Nor did teachers ask why children were yawning at school or always believe what children told them. If children sense that adults do not understand about domestic violence, then they will not fully confide in them. Although there is no one syndrome, there is a range of things that practitioners can look out for. Changes in behavioural patterns can indicate underlying distress, for example. Contrary to early accounts in the research literature (see summary in Morley and Mullender, 1994), there is not a gendered pattern with boys copying their violent fathers and girls their supposedly passive mothers (a misrepresentation in any case since we now recognise that women use myriad coping strategies to survive the violence; see summary in Mullender, 1996). In our study we heard about clingy behaviour in a boy:

> B [is] really quiet and he has to stay near A – he won't leave A. If A goes out, he'll sit in here and wait until he comes back. He has to be near him . . . He's like a shadow.
>
> (17-year-old dual heritage girl talking about how her 12-year-old brother relates to her 15-year-old brother)

while his sister had become aggressive:

> If someone annoys me now, I just shout at them whereas, before,
> I wasn't violent when I was little . . . my temper, I lose it quick.
> If someone was joking, I would't take it as a joke . . . I lose my
> temper.
>
> (17-year-old dual heritage girl)

These two young people also illustrate how children in the same family
can react quite differently, despite living through identical events.

Physical effects that children talked about included sickness and dia-
rrhoea, wetting the bed, and particularly problems with sleeping and
headaches:

> Sometimes I do get bad headaches.
>
> (13-year-old dual heritage boy)

Although these problems often receded or disappeared once children
felt safe, they are a reminder to health professionals that what presents
in the form of physical symptoms can turn out to have causes rooted
in home life. Having a routine procedure for asking about this, in
confidence, is essential. Anti-racist awareness is also crucial to avoid
jumping to another set of wrong conclusions – for example, that
minority ethnic children have generalised learning difficulties when
they experience speech or language problems as a reaction to living
with abuse (Culp *et al.*, 1991; McGregor *et al.*, 1994). The message to
medical, psychological, therapeutic and welfare services is that children
are well able to tell us what is really wrong if they trust us to listen and
understand.

Tertiary prevention

Tertiary prevention aims to lessen the damage caused by domestic
violence. In its more elaborate version, it typically takes the form of direct
work, either one to one or in groups. In refuge and other specialist
domestic violence services, including outreach and aftercare, children's
workers in fact undertake a great deal of support of confused and dis-
tressed children in relatively informal ways. In children's minds, in the
in-depth interviews, these workers came second only to friends as people
to whom they had talked and who had supported them:

> There was P [children's worker], she was great. I talked to her at
> the refuge and she made me feel better because, in the past, I was
> unhappy. Now I'm happy.
>
> (9-year-old white boy)

Children are especially sensitive to professionals' genuine interest in them, as opposed to merely being made to feel like an appendage of their mothers. They also appreciate the mutual support offered by other children in the refuge. It is only fairly recently that Women's Aid and other women's organisations have come to celebrate the work that they do with children (Hague and Wilson, 1996; Hague *et al.*, 1996), but this really does represent a key national resource (Humphreys *et al.*, 2000) from which the statutory childcare sector could take a lead.

Only one child mentioned attending a more formalised, weekly children's group, to which she had been referred by the refuge where she lived. The group process and content were helping her come to understand and come to terms with the violence she had experienced:

> there's all other kids who've been through the same thing . . . we all do . . . drawings about – we do about abuse and stuff like that . . . I can talk to them about . . . how it happened and that . . . We talk about abusing and we have a theme each week. Like, say we were happy, what we'd like to draw if we were happy. When we're sad – like when it happens – and sometimes they do puppet shows to show us, like, how it happened.
>
> (9-year-old white girl)

She was also doing weekly one-to-one work with one of the refuge workers. Two other children had also had some counselling – one through school and the other through a specialist domestic violence project.

Children's groups have been only patchily developed in the UK (Humphreys *et al.*, 2000), but are widespread in parts of the USA and Canada (Mullender, 1994; Hague *et al.*, 2001) where they have been positively evaluated (Peled and Edleson, 1995; Loosley *et al.*, 1997). Children's accounts from the study may cast new light on the typical areas dealt with in groupwork manuals (Peled and Davis, 1995; Loosley *et al.*, 1997). Children are taught to recognise and name their feelings (as the girl quoted above had been doing) as a basis for emotional healing, problem-solving and help-seeking. They work on making sense of the violence and whose responsibility it is and on safety planning. As far as feelings were concerned, children in interview were able to name a great range of these, often in respect of events and outcomes rather than people. The talked about sadness more often than adults might have anticipated, as well as fear. They did not appear to be scared of their own anger but felt it was justified by the perpetrator's behaviour. Children in our study generally had less difficulty than groupwork programmes suppose in seeing the abuser as responsible for his own violence. This had taken a few years to dawn fully on some children, but others had held the abuser responsible from the start for doing something that struck them as clearly unfair. Mothers were generally blamed only for not leaving sooner, not for contributing to the violence, and children only rarely (and partially) blamed themselves – notably where the perpetrator had made them the subject of violent rows. While those who work with children might see children who intervene in violent assaults as putting their own safety at risk, and we would obviously share their concern about dangers to children, the most common way of doing this that we came across was by shouting at the abuser, not by getting physically involved. Children did not react unthinkingly to the violence. They were aware of the context and severity of attacks and they made carefully judged decisions, for example when a man was too drunk to listen or where certain actions, such as suddenly appearing in the room, had worked before. Safety planning that recognises children's conscious agency might be the best way to help them work out what to do to help protect both their mothers and themselves.

Conclusion

We undertook this study looking, amongst other things, for messages that could be offered to policy and practice on the basis of children's own perceptions and understandings of living with domestic violence. Overall, children make greatest use of informal support networks, but most of these can be damaged or lost if the family has to move to escape the violence. Children's one consistent link tends to be with their mother, their most important support of all they tell us, and it is vital that professionals nurture this crucial bond if at all possible. Mothers themselves can be encouraged to have more confidence in talking to their children about a painful past that most already know about. Siblings, friends and peers in refuges can be as important to children as adults are. From formal agencies, children tell us they want safety and someone to talk to. Unfortunately, professionals are often guilty of overlooking or ignoring children, of failing to provide a listening ear, or of pursuing their own agendas (child protection, child contact, child health and development) without assisting children to divulge what has been happening at home, let alone talking to them about this in any sensitive or helpful way. Yet there are models available of policy and practice that work for children, both in the UK and beyond, such as educational programmes in schools, children's work in refuges and direct work in groups, all of which are grounded in a full awareness of what domestic violence involves for women and children. Between them, and if they were located in a multi-agency context that functioned better for children, these approaches could meet the need for primary, secondary and tertiary prevention.

Acknowledgement

The researchers were frequently moved by the thoughtfulness and depth of insight, concern and careful reflection given to the research issues by children. Our thanks go to them, and to their mothers, for their willingness to share their experiences so openly and so helpfully with us.

References

Advisory Board on Family Law, Children Act Sub-Committee (2001a) *Guidelines for Good Practice on Parental Contact in Cases where there is Domestic Violence*, London: Family Policy Division, Lord Chancellor's Department.

Advisory Board on Family Law, Children Act Sub-Committee (2001b) *Making Contact Work*, London: Family Policy Division, Lord Chancellor's Department.

AFRCV (Alliance of Five Research Centers on Violence) (1999) *Violence Prevention and the Girl Child*, London, Ontario: AFRCV.

Burton, S. and Kitzinger, J., with Kelly, L. and Regan, L. (1998) *Young People's Attitudes Towards Violence, Sex and Relationships: A Survey and Focus Group Study*, Edinburgh: Zero Tolerance Charitable Trust.

Culp, R., Watkins, R., Lawrence, H., Letts, D., Kelly, H. and Rice, M. (1991) 'Maltreated children's language and speech development: abused, neglected and abused and neglected', *First Language*, 11: 377–89.

Dobash, R.E. and Dobash, R.P. (1979) *Violence Against Wives*, New York: The Free Press.

Farmer, E. and Owen, M. (1995) *Child Protection Practice: Private Risks and Public Remedies*, London: HMSO.

Garmezy, N. and Rutter, M. (1983) *Stress, Coping and Development in Children*, New York: McGraw-Hill.

Gordon, D., Loughran, F. and Parker, R. (2000) *Disabled Children in Britain: A Reanalysis of the OPCS Disability Surveys*, London: The Stationery Office.

Hague, G. and Malos, E. (1998) *Domestic Violence: Action for Change* (2nd edn), Cheltenham: New Clarion Press.

Hague, G. and Wilson, C. (1996) *The Silenced Pain: Domestic Violence, 1945–1970*, Bristol: Policy Press.

Hague, G., Kelly, L. and Mullender, A. (2001) *Challenging Violence Against Women: The Canadian Experience*, Bristol: Policy Press.

Hague, G., Kelly, L., Malos, E. and Mullender, A., with Debonnaire, T. (1996) *Children, Domestic Violence and Refuges: A Study of Needs and Responses*, Bristol: Women's Aid Federation of England.

Hester, M. and Pearson, C. (1998) *From Periphery to Centre: Domestic Violence in Work with Abused Children*, Bristol: The Policy Press.

Hester, M., Pearson, C. and Harwin, N. (2000) *Making an Impact: Children and Domestic Violence – a Reader*, London: Jessica Kingsley.

Hester, M. and Radford, L. (1996) *Domestic Violence and Child Contact in England and Denmark*, Bristol: Policy Press.

Horrocks, C. and Milner, J. (1999) 'The residential home as serial step-family: acknowledging quasi-sibling relationships in local authority residential care', in

A. Mullender (ed.) *We Are Family: Sibling Relationships in Placement and Beyond,* London: British Agencies for Adoption and Fostering.

Humphreys, C. (1999) 'The judicial alienation syndrome: failures to respond to post-separation violence', *Family Law,* 313: 513–15.

Humphreys, C., Hester, M., Hague, G., Mullender, A., Abrahams, H. and Lowe, P. (2000) *From Good Intentions to Good Practice: Working with Families where there is Domestic Violence,* Bristol: Policy Press.

Imam, U.F. (1994) 'Asian children and domestic violence', in A. Mullender and R. Morley (eds) *Children Living with Domestic Violence: Putting Men's Abuse of Women on the Child Care Agenda,* London: Whiting and Birch.

Jaffe, P.G., Wolfe, D.A. and Wilson, S.K. (1990) *Children of Battered Women.* Newbury Park, Calif.: Sage.

Kashani, J. and Allan, W. (1998) *The Impact of Family Violence on Children and Adolescents,* London: Sage.

London Borough of Islington (1995) *STOP: Schools Take on Preventing Domestic Violence,* London: London Borough of Islington, Women's Equality Unit.

Loosley, S., Bentley, L., Lehmann, P., Marshall, L., Rabenstein, S. and Sudermann, M. (1997) *Group Treatment for Children who Witness Woman Abuse: A Manual for Practitioners,* London, Ontario: Community Group Treatment Program for Child Witnesses of Woman Abuse, Children's Aid Society of London and Middlesex.

McGregor, R., Pullar, A. and Cundall, D. (1994) 'Silent at school: selective mutism and abuse', *Archives of Disease in Childhood,* 70: 540–1.

Morley, R. and Mullender, A. (1994) 'Domestic violence and children: what do we know from research?', in A. Mullender and R. Morley (eds) *Children Living with Domestic Violence: Putting Men's Abuse of Women on the Child Care Agenda,* London: Whiting and Birch.

Mullender, A. (1994) 'Groups for child witnesses of woman abuse: learning from North America', in A. Mullender and R. Morley (eds) *Children Living with Domestic Violence: Putting Men's Abuse of Women on the Child Care Agenda,* London: Whiting and Birch.

Mullender, A. (1996) *Rethinking Domestic Violence: The Social Work and Probation Response,* London: Routledge.

Mullender, A. (ed.) (1999) *We Are Family: Sibling Relationships in Placement and Beyond,* London: British Agencies for Adoption and Fostering.

Mullender, A. and Morley, R. (eds) (1994) *Children Living with Domestic Violence: Putting Men's Abuse of Women on the Child Care Agenda,* London: Whiting and Birch.

Mullender, A., Hague, G., Imam, U., Kelly, L., Malos, E. and Regan, L. (forthcoming) *Children's Perspectives on Domestic Violence,* London: Sage.

Peled, E. and Davis, D. (1995) *Groupwork with Children of Battered Women: A Practitioner's Manual,* Thousand Oaks, Calif.: Sage.

Peled, E. and Edleson, J.L. (1995) 'Process and outcome in small groups for children of battered women', in E. Peled, P.G. Jaffe and J.L. Edleson (1995) *Ending the Cycle of Violence: Community Responses to Children of Battered Women,* Thousand Oaks, Calif.: Sage.

Pence, E. and Paymar, M. (1990) *Power and Control: Tactics of Men who Batter. An Educational Curriculum* (revised edn), Duluth, Minn.: Minnesota Program Development Inc. (206 West Fourth Street, Duluth, MN 55806, USA).

Pence, E. and Paymar, M. (1996) *Education Groups for Men who Batter: The Duluth Model* (2nd edn), New York: Springer (1st edn 1993).

Radford, L., Sayer, S. and AMICA (1999) *Unreasonable Fears? Child Contact in the Context of Domestic Violence: A Survey of Mothers' Perceptions of Harm*, Bristol: Women's Aid Publications.

Regan, L. and Kelly, L. (2001) *Teenage Tolerance: Exploring Young People's Experience and Responses to Violence and Abuse*, Dublin: Dublin Women's Aid.

Saunders, H. (2001) *Making Contact Worse? Report of a National Survey of Domestic Violence Refuge Services into the Enforcement of Contact Orders*, Bristol: Women's Aid Federation of England.

10 Children's participation in family law matters

Judy Cashmore

There has been considerable debate in the psychological and legal literature over several decades about the role that children's preferences or wishes should play in the determination of residence and contact arrangements following their parents' separation and divorce. More recently, that debate has included recognition of children's right to be heard in matters that affect them, outlined in Article 12 of the UN Convention on the Rights of the Child. This recognition is also reflected in both the language and focus of legislation in Australia and in other common law countries (see e.g. the Children Act 1989 in England and Wales, and the Family Law Reform Act 1995 in Australia). It has also been the subject of significant discussion and recommendations of various government reports in Australia, Canada and the UK (Australian Law Reform Commission and Human Rights and Equal Opportunity Commission, 1997; Family Law Council, 1996; Family Law Pathways Advisory Group, 2001; Thorpe and Clarke, 2000), and a view expressed by eminent judges. For example, in Re P (A Minor) (Education) (1992), Butler-Sloss LJ said:

> The courts, over the last few years, have become increasingly aware of the importance of listening to the views of older children and taking into account what children say, not necessarily agreeing with what they want nor, indeed, doing what they want, but paying proper respect to older children who are of an age and the maturity to make their minds up as to what they think is best for them . . .
> (Re P (A Minor) (Education), 1992: 321)

At the same time, there are still marked concerns about the way the family law system 'constructs' and excludes children (Family Law Pathways Advisory Group, 2001; L'Heureux-Dubé, 1998; Sawyer, 1999; Smart *et al.*, 1999) and there are questions about the extent to which there has been any real shift in family law practice to accommodate children's views. The aim of this chapter therefore is to outline the different processes by which children may participate in the process, and to review the research on the extent to which children want to be involved and are involved.

First, why is it important to take into account what children want? Then, what do children say they want in relation to their involvement in the decision-making concerning their residence and contact arrangements? With the exception of a small number of studies in the early 1980s and in the past five years or so, there has been little attention given to children's own views about the way decisions are made about them and their own involvement in the decision-making process. As Trinder (1997: 292) pointed out, 'What is striking about the often-heated adult professional debates over children's participation in divorce decision-making is the very limited extent to which children themselves have been players in this ontological game.'

Why is it important to take into account what children want in family law matters?

The general case for involving children in decisions that affect them and taking their views seriously has been clearly outlined by Lansdown (1995a, 2001). Briefly, those reasons include the likelihood of better decisions and outcomes, and of greater acceptance and compliance by children, the basic right of children as people with opinions and feelings of their own to be treated with respect, and the demonstrable fact that adults and even parents do not always act in the best interests of children. In discussing the particular advantages and disadvantages in relation to children's participation in family law matters, Chisholm (2000) suggests that there has generally been undue focus on the potential disadvantages and inadequate consideration of the particular ways in which children might usefully participate. As Justice Chisholm points out, there are a number of ways in which children can be involved without being the decision-maker, especially in the relatively unexplored primary dispute resolution stage. These include being told what is happening, having the opportunity to express their feelings and say what they would like to happen, contributing to the consideration of options and perhaps providing creative and useful solutions not considered by the adults. What the research makes clear is that children are likely to feel happier and the arrangements are more likely to 'work' if the children know what is going on and feel that they have been consulted about the arrangements. Dunn and Deater-Deckard (2001), for example, found that children who had an active role in decisions about shared household living arrangements and those who said they were able to talk to their parents about any problems this caused were more likely to be positive about moving between households. In contrast, the children who were reportedly the least happy and most resentful in several other studies, especially as they got older, were those who felt they could not influence the arrangements for contact, and who could not talk to one or both of their parents (Gollop *et al.*, 2000; Smart *et al.*, 2001). Some felt trapped by court orders that parents could not or would not change, but the long-term effect once children were old enough was that they 'voted with their feet' or refused to comply. As Wallerstein and Lewis (1998) found in their 25-year follow-up study, the children and teenagers who had a rigidly fixed schedule of court-ordered contact visits rejected further contact with that parent when they reached adulthood.

What do children say they want?

There seem to be three main messages that come through from the research on children's views: that is, that children want to know what is going on; they generally want to be consulted and have their views taken into account, and they would like to have flexible, workable arrangements that they can change to meet their changing needs and circumstances.

Children's wish to know what is happening is very understandable and a basic requirement for being able to participate in decisions. It includes having some information about what changes are likely, when they may occur, what the options are, and how the decisions about any changes will be made. In their review of the research on the effects of separation and divorce on children, Rodgers and Pryor (1998) commented on the importance of appropriate information and explanations to children in mitigating their distress at the time of the separation and assisting them to prepare for and adjust to the changes and overcome any fears of abandonment. What the research shows, however, is that parents are often reluctant to tell children what is happening because they are concerned about upsetting them and children often do not know what to ask or how to do so (Douglas *et al.*, 2001; Dunn and Deater-Deckard, 2001; Gollop *et al.*, 2000; Mitchell, 1985; Walczak and Burns, 1984; Wallerstein and Kelly, 1980).

The second message from the research is that many children also want to be consulted about the arrangements that are made and to have their own views taken into account (Douglas *et al.*, 2001; Gollop *et al.*, 2000; Neale and Smart, 1998). For some, this is seen as only fair – after all, they are the ones who have to live with the arrangements (Douglas *et al.*, 2001). In the words of an 11-year-old, unhappy about not being consulted, cited in an Australian study:

> Why is it that everyone is talking about my future and what's going to happen to me and I'm the only one who doesn't get a say in it?

> (Cashmore *et al.*, 1994: 68)

While many children and young people said they believe they should have a greater say in family law decisions that affect them, this does not generally mean that they want to make the decision themselves. Indeed, Gollop *et al.* (2000) and Neale and Smart (1998) indicate that children are clearly able to distinguish between making the decision and participating in the process and having their views considered. For example, as 15-year-old 'Mark' said in relation to a hypothetical situation, not his own:

> I don't think he should necessarily decide, he should get a say in it, he shouldn't just be left out. I mean it's his life as well, he shouldn't be stuck with someone he didn't want to be with.
>
> (Smart and Neale, 2001: 4)

There was, however, marked variation in children's and young people's views, both in terms of their willingness to be involved and in what they actually wanted to happen (Gollop *et al.*, 2000; Neale and Smart, 1998). Some clearly expressed their right to be asked and to say what they wanted, and to influence or even determine the outcome, some wanted to be heard but not to decide, and others did not want to be involved at all, mainly because they were concerned about upsetting or alienating one of their parents. For example, as one 12-year-old girl said:

> She should be involved in sorting it out but I don't think her parents should actually make her choose or anything, because she's going to feel awful is [*sic*] she says one parent and lets the other one down.
>
> (Neale and Smart, 1998: 28)

This variation, and the sometimes unexpected responses of children, point to the danger of simple generalisations or assumptions about children's views, in stark contrast to the legal construction or abstract view of 'the child' which 'assumes a commonality of children's experiences and glosses over their differences' (Neale and Smart, 1998: 7).

The third message from the research on children's perspectives is that they want to have workable and flexible arrangements. A number of studies have indicated that children often want more frequent contact and more flexibility in the contact arrangements than they have, with flexibility becoming increasingly important as children get older and their needs and interests change (McDonald, 1990; Neugebauer, 1989; Walczak and Burns, 1984; Wallerstein and Kelly, 1980). In results reported by Smart *et al.* (2001), just over half the families changed their contact and residence arrangements over a four- to five-year period, often because the parents' views or the circumstances changed. What is less clear is the extent to which children were able to initiate changes or make the arrangements more flexible to meet their needs.

To what extent and in what ways are children involved? What is their experience?

Children's experiences in relation to being informed, consulted and involved in making the arrangements generally seem to fall short of what they would like to happen. This appears to be the case across the continuum from uncontentious matters where parents agree (without the assistance of outside agencies) to those which proceed to formal court hearings involving lawyers, counsellors, court welfare officers and judges. The findings are quite consistent over time and across jurisdictions, taking into account the age of the children involved.

In an Australian study of families with different levels of conflict, McDonald (1990) found that only 25 per cent of the children, aged 8 to 12, reported that they had been consulted about the initial contact arrangements and only 38 per cent about any changes to those arrangements. Similarly, in a more recent study in New Zealand, Gollop *et al.* (2000) found that 37 per cent of the children, ranging in age from 6 to 15 at the time of separation, were consulted about the initial contact arrangements and only 19 per cent about initial residence orders. Teenagers were more likely than younger children to be consulted about both residence and contact, with the curious exception of children under five who were just as likely to be consulted about contact as the teenagers. The current contact arrangements for just over half were either fully determined (28 per cent) or mostly determined by the parents (24 per cent); 16 per cent were determined by the court. In another recent study in England and Wales, Douglas *et al.* (2001) reported that fewer than half the children (45 per cent), aged 7 to 15, said they had been asked about their residence preference but that more (55 per cent) said they wished they had been asked. In a related study, based on parents' reports, only 34 per cent of parents involved in uncontentious divorces said they had discussed the arrangements with their children when making them; 20 per cent said the children were too young, but even when the children were aged 11 to 15, only 51 per cent had done so (Murch *et al.*, 1999).

These studies relied on the reports from children and their parents, and were mostly concerned with the communication between parents and their children. When parents agree on the arrangements for the children, there are generally no legal or administrative requirements in common law jurisdictions that parents consult with their children about those arrangements.[1] In practice, this means that in many cases where parents are concerned about upsetting the children or are unsure how to discuss such matters with them, children's wishes may not be considered at all.

The extent to which children are consulted or involved in the decision-making process tends to be even lower when outside agencies and professionals are involved. In the more formal processes, the main avenues for children's views to be included are via mediators, court counsellors or via a report to the court from a court welfare officer. In some highly contested or difficult matters, children may also have their own legal representation. An even rarer practice is for judges to speak directly with children.

Mediation and conciliation

There is a fair degree of similarity of practice across jurisdictions in that most family mediators and conciliators in Australia, New Zealand, Canada, the US and the UK do not directly seek the views of children in the mediation or conciliation process (Austin *et al.*, 1992–3; Bagshaw, 1992; Pryor and Seymour, 1996). Two studies that have tried to measure this practice have found a low level of direct involvement. An audit of mediation services in the UK by Murch *et al.* (1999) found that although more than half the mediators in the not-for-profit sector said they were willing to work directly with children, the extent to which they actually did so was 'very limited' (p. 233). Private sector mediators were much less willing to do so (fewer than 20 per cent), but nearly all the mediators surveyed (89 per cent) indicated that they 'always' or 'very often' encourage parents to consider the views of their children.

Similarly, an Australian audit evaluation found that counselling and mediation services directly involved children in only about 6 per cent of cases (Attorney-General's Department, 1998; McIntosh, 2000). When children were involved, however, the same study found that both children and parents found it helpful: children because it allowed them to say how they were feeling and to discuss it with someone outside the family without hurting their parents' feelings, and parents because it made them more aware of what their children were worried about and helped them to focus more on their needs (McIntosh, 2000). These findings may encourage those mediators and conciliators across a number of jurisdictions who are increasingly advocating the involvement of children, provided this is done skilfully and with various safeguards (Brown, 1995; Garwood, 1992; Leach, 2000; Pryor and Seymour, 1996).

Court counsellors and court reports

Reports by court counsellors or court welfare officers are probably the most common method by which children's views are brought before the court in contested matters in the UK, Canada, Australia and New Zealand (Australian Law Reform Commission and Human Rights and Equal Opportunity Commission, 1997; Bagshaw, 1992; Huddart and Ensminger, 1992–3). In Australia, for example, they are ordered in almost 60 per cent of contested cases (Australian Law Reform Commission and Human Rights and Equal Opportunity Commission, 1997:

401; Family Court data, 2002[2]). One of the key issues they are usually required to address are the 'ascertainable wishes and feelings of the children' (taking into account their 'age and understanding'). Even if these views are not always explicitly outlined in the report, the reports generally contain recommendations to the court based on an assessment by the court counsellor or court welfare officer. These reports are generally 'highly influential', with the court's final disposition often shaped by their recommendations (Huddart and Ensminger, 1992–3). In Australia, for example, it is estimated that the court's determination is in accord with the reports' recommendations in about 75 per cent of cases (Australian Law Reform Commission and Human Rights and Equal Opportunity Commission, 1997).

Children's involvement in this process is generally restricted to being the subject of an assessment of their needs, attachments and wishes, based on interviews and observations of their interactions with other family members. While parents as parties to the proceedings are given copies of the report and are able to cross-examine the report writer, it appears that children often do not see the report or have any opportunity to challenge the recommendations it makes about them. Despite a lack of systematic follow-up on the outcomes of these recommendations, there is increasing evidence that some children are unhappy about this process. In particular, children have said they do not feel comfortable with the techniques used, the lack of privacy and confidentiality, and the filtering or reinterpretation of what they said. Several young people quoted by Neale and Smart (1998) said, for example:

> There was about seven of them [behind the mirror] it felt weird you know, because you don't know what they're doing . . . I just didn't really talk much because, I mean the other people around me, it's just like including my mum and step dad, it's just, you know . . .
>
> (Neale and Smart, 1998: 34–5)

> The court welfare officer [CWO] and that, they don't really know the family . . . I don't think it helped (talking to the CWO). I didn't see why someone should ask all these questions and then when you do tell them certain things it doesn't go in the report . . . I really had no one to talk to. [You need] someone who isn't going to go straight back and say 'well this and this' [to the court] but just get them sat down and sort of talk between them. [Q: In confidence?] Yes, and then if you do want them to pass it on, they would.
>
> (Neale and Smart, 1998: 35)

Similarly, an 11-year-old in a small Australian pilot study (Cashmore, 2001)[3] who indicated that he wanted to live with his father said he was not happy that his mother was able to hear what he said to the counsellor. When asked what he thought was the best way for the court to find out what hypothetical Daniel wants, he said:

> Like somebody from the court should come to his house and he goes somewhere in private and he tells them.
> *Q: Do you think the counsellor should say what you want or what she thinks is best for you?*
> I think they should say what we want, like they should listen.
> *Q: Were you glad your mum wasn't there?*
> No, not really, 'cos she was behind, she was outside of the door but behind the glass. Afterwards, she said, I know what you said so I think she could hear.[4]

An early study by Meehan (cited by Trinder, 1997) involving children aged 8 to 12 also indicated that the children were unhappy about the indirect questioning technique used by the court assessors. Some of the children wanted to influence the outcome and 'felt misrepresented and angry about being treated "merely" as children'; others who did not want to be involved at all 'were angry about being manipulated by "trick" questions' (Trinder, 1997: 300). In both cases, these children were unhappy about their lack of control over the filtering or reinterpretation of what they said.

Legal representation

The direct involvement of children with lawyers is also low, with children having little input into matters where their parents were legally represented and few children having their own legal representation. Murch *et al.* (1999), for example, found that most parents' solicitors (nearly 75 per cent) said they do not talk to children; 45 per cent said they would never talk to a child, but 28 per cent said they might consider doing so. While they were somewhat more positive about the need to ascertain children's views, they were concerned about burdening children with this responsibility and apprehensive about their role as the parent's representative. According to the accounts given by some children, these concerns are justified. For example:

> Dad got a guy to talk to both me and my sister and find out what we wanted to do, what we should do to make Dad happy and stuff . . . He was pretty arrogant 'cos he didn't really take our views into consideration. He mainly focused on what Dad had said and what Dad wanted.
>
> (Gollop *et al.*, 2000: 395)

> Mum's solicitor talked to me sometimes but he wasn't very nice. He had a scary face. And sometimes he'd asked me where I'd want to live and I'd say with my dad, and he'd say 'Look if you get any say, you've got to tell the court that you want to live with your mum', and stuff like that. But I didn't want to.
>
> (Cashmore, 2001)

The appointment of a separate legal representative for children, which generally occurs in only a small percentage of fully contested cases,[5] did not necessarily mean that children's experiences were much improved. While some jurisdictions have guidelines for the role of the child's representative[6] or allow for guardians *ad litem* to instruct the lawyer concerning the child's best interests, there is still continuing tension in practice between the 'best interests model' and the 'lawyer–client model' (Bagshaw, 1992; Chisholm, 2000).[7] There is evidence, however, that children expect 'their lawyer' in family law and child welfare matters to say what they want them to say, not what the lawyer thinks is in their 'best interests' (Cashmore and Bussey, 1994). In the pilot study, for example, when asked what he thought the lawyer should say to the court, one of the few children who was separately represented said very clearly:

> I think he should say what we want, like they should listen.
>
> (Cashmore, 2001)

The other issues that have emerged from the little data in this area are again, as with court counsellors, the transparency of the professional's purpose, their lack of communication skills, and concerns about breaches of confidentiality. In one case, for example, an 11-year-old said he was upset that his lawyer had taken notes during their meeting and 'given them to his parents, without checking that this was alright with him' (Gollop *et al.*, 2000: 395). Other comments focused on their poor communication skills:

> He was pretty silly, he kept going 'Uh, uh er, er . . .' like that 'cos he really only asked about one question . . .
> *Q: Do you think he really listened to you?*
> No, not really.
>
> (Cashmore, 2001)

> He only spoke to me for about ten minutes. He just asked me who I wanted to live with and why. That was it . . . No, he didn't go in depth, he didn't ask me anything, like any reason for it. No nothing.
>
> (Gollop *et al.*, 2000: 395)

They just got things muddled up. Like the way that I worded it and they [wrote] it a different way. Sort of the real high sort of way, that I can't understand, and it sounded different. It meant the opposite thing to what I meant.

(Gollop *et al.*, 2000: 396)

Judicial interviewing of children

The law and practice whereby judges interview children (often in chambers) varies across jurisdictions and evokes some very different reactions. While rarely used in the UK and Australia (Australian Law Reform Commission and Human Rights and Equal Opportunity Commission, 1997; Chisholm, 1998; Lowe and Douglas, 1998), it is much more common in the US, although there are variations across the states as to use and to requirements for the interview to be recorded and for the child's attorney or guardian *ad litem* to be present (Crosby-Currie, 1996).

Those opposed to the practice generally refer to three areas of concern relating to due process, the effect on the child, and the consequent validity of the process. In relation to due process, Chisholm (1998) outlined what many commentators see as the 'decisive matter':[8]

> if the interview is to be confidential, as the rules provide, the result would be hard to reconcile with natural justice, for the judge would act on material unknown to and untestable by the parties.
>
> (Chisholm, 1998: 5)

If the interview is not confidential or if it is recorded, this is less of a concern (Lyon, 2000) although arguably this may make it more difficult for children to say what they want.

The other concerns about the validity of the process and the effect on the child focus on the fact that judges are not trained and may not have the skills to elicit and interpret the child's views, especially in the short time available to them and in an environment which may be intimidating (Australian Law Reform Commission and Human Rights and Equal Opportunity Commission, 1997; Huddart and Ensminger, 1992–3). Others, however, see this as less difficult for children than testifying in open court in front of their parents (L'Heureux-Dubé, 1998; Lyon, 2000), another option but one which is rarely used in family law matters.

Interestingly, while children vary in their views, some children are very keen to talk to the judge. Some clearly feel frustrated about not being heard or having their views 'filtered' and want to go straight to the decision-maker. Others are keen to get their views across without having their parents involved in the process. For example, children in the Australian pilot study (Cashmore, 2001) said they thought the best way for the court to hear what they wanted was to tell the judge directly:

> Because he's the one that has the overall say and it's straight to him, instead of, like, it might change a bit, through all the people to him. Like the counsellors when they send it, the judge might not get the proper message. But direct, he'd get the proper message.
>
> (11-year-old boy)

> Because then he just knows exactly what you want, and your parents don't have to listen to you saying it. And no-one else has to know.
>
> (13-year-old girl)

Similarly, Lyon (2000) quotes one child as saying:

> It would have been better if I had been able to see the person making all the decisions but all I saw was this person who, I know as a result of today, was called a Court Welfare Officer but she didn't really feel interested in my plan and I think, as it has turned out, my plan would have worked out the best for everyone. Why can't kids see the person who is making these decisions? I think it's wrong that they can decide what should happen in your life without seeing you.
>
> (Lyon, 2000: 68–9)

Do the available processes ensure children's voices are heard?

There appears to be increasing evidence and opinion that the currently available family law processes are not adequate to ensure that children feel they have been heard when decisions affecting them are made (Australian Law Reform Commission and Human Rights and Equal Opportunity Commission, 1997; Family Law Pathways Advisory Group, 2001;[9] Lyon, 2000; Neale and Smart, 1998; O'Quigley, 1999; Piper, 1999).[10] The view of an eminent Canadian judge is, for example, that 'despite our repeated assurances of great interest in their welfare, their voices have gone unheard in the law, or, at best have been misheard or re-interpreted' (L'Heureux-Dubé, 1998: 385).

At all stages, the ways in which children can participate in the process rely on the interpretation and presentation of their views by adults – their parents, counsellors, lawyers or other professionals. Clearly, the extent to which children's views are listened to and taken into account is likely to depend to a great degree on whether the adults evaluating those wishes believe that the children concerned are capable of expressing wishes which are well-reasoned and whether they think it is appropriate for them to be involved.[11]

Not all children wish to be involved but when they do, a common experience is that the adults get it wrong – by not communicating effectively or sometimes not at all with them, by misinterpreting or filtering what they say, and by believing that, as children, they do not have the capacity to know what they want or what is in their own best interests. As Neale and Smart (1998: 36) point out, listening to children is 'not a simple or straightforward activity' especially when 'dogged by the dependency paradigm and its welfare constructions which deny children their personhood and place additional burdens of responsibility on professionals to interpret, re-interpret or override children's views'.

The need for feedback processes

Perhaps the biggest barrier is the lack of follow-up mechanisms, both at the individual and the systemic level, to correct misinterpretations and provide accountability of adults to children. At an individual level, adults – parents and professionals – often assume they know what children want or need and do not think it is appropriate or necessary to check those assumptions with children. The feedback from a number of children indicating that parents are not accurate in their assessment of the children's level of distress or what they want suggests otherwise (Mitchell, 1985; Douglas *et al.*, 2001). Even when adults say they want to facilitate children's participation, and think they are doing so, the evidence is that children often do not think they are doing so (Spall *et al.*, 1998). As one young person said:

> I don't think parents should always assume that they know what their kids are thinking 'cos half the time they don't.
>
> (Gollop *et al.*, 2000: 396)

Similarly, an 11-year-old in the Australian pilot study said, when asked what advice he would give to hypothetical Daniel's parents:

> Like, listen to Daniel, what he wants and who he wants to live with and not just think who *they* think he wants to live with.
>
> (Cashmore, 2001)

At a systemic level, there are few provisions for follow-up or for any feed-back loops to check on the accuracy of professional judgements or decisions and to maximise the likelihood of positive outcomes for children. There are, however, possibilities for building in feedback loops at various stages in the process. For example:

1   In primary dispute resolution, mediators and conciliators could routinely ask parents whether they have talked with their children

about various options and possible arrangements for contact and residence. It is worth noting, for example, that Murch *et al.* (1999) reported that mediators say they often do this. They also found that parents in uncontentious divorces were more likely to discuss the arrangements with their children if they had been advised to do so by their lawyer.

2   The preparation and presentation of a family report would be a more transparent process and one that was respectful of children's right to be informed about the way information they provide may be used if the report writer is very clear with children about the limits of confidentiality.

3   Some consideration may need to be given to children being told what is said about them in a family report if they wish to know. Whereas parents can challenge the contents and recommendations of a court report, children rarely see them or know what is in them (see Masson, 2000, for similar issues in relation to public law matters).

4   Similarly, separate legal representatives for children should explain to their clients what they will say in court, how they will say it, and ask whether that is what they expect them to say. After the hearing, they should be under an obligation to explain to the child what they had said, and if that was any different from what the child had expected, what their reasons were.

5   Adult clients generally have avenues of complaint if they are unhappy about the way they are treated. This is more difficult for children, but quality assurance processes could involve some follow-up with children after a matter is finalised, asking them how satisfied they were with the way their legal representative treated them and took account of their views.

6   One means of making the process more transparent has been suggested in a recent Australian case, R and R (Children's Wishes) (2000). In this case, the Full Court of the Family Court of Australia held that while a judge might reach a conclusion contrary to children's validly held wishes, he or she needs to provide good reasons for doing so. The Court indicated that where children have expressed a preference about a residence or contact issue, they should also be asked by counsellors or child representatives how they would feel if the judge reached a different conclusion. As Sandor (2000: 16) points out, not only does this add to the information which the Court can use in making its decisions, such a practice may also reduce the risk that asking children about their wishes will leave them with the 'false impression . . . that their wishes will decide the outcome of a family dispute'.

7   There are good reasons why the court's decision might not be in accord with the child's wishes in some cases (Jones and Parkinson, 1995) and children should be made aware of this both before and

after the determination. It would also be valuable for them to be told why this was the case, in the same way that local authorities are required to do so in relation to care plans for children in public law matters in the UK (Department of Health, 1991; Schofield, 1998).

8   Court orders could be more child-centred if they were crafted to contain some flexibility and a possibility of variation with the age and wishes of the child, especially if these changed or were more directly expressed (L'Heureux-Dubé, 1998).

9   Finally, research could provide one of the best means of monitoring and reviewing the operation of the system and the outcomes for children. Yet, to the best of my knowledge there are no established procedures to routinely collect information on:

*   the outcomes of cases 'down the track'
*   the number of cases in which further proceedings changed the outcome relative to the recommendations of the court report
*   the views of family members about the family report at the time and whether those views changed over time
*   whether children will censor what they say to court professionals in a way that is detrimental to their 'best interests' if they are clearly informed about the limits of confidentiality
*   the extent to which children are involved in various ways in the decision-making process.

The value of judges and other professionals involved in the decision-making process receiving feed-back on the outcomes and on the views of those affected is that it provides important information on the effects of their decisions and may challenge some of their assumptions. As Smart *et al.* (2001) proposed, research is needed 'to track the impact of court orders on all family members, not least because judges operate in a vacuum and have little idea whether their orders do more harm than good'.

The feedback from Matthew, one of the children in the pilot study, provides a good illustration of the need for this feedback (Cashmore, 2001) and perhaps it is appropriate to give a child the last say in this chapter. In this case, Matthew had consistently said that he wanted to live with his father who persisted in trying to secure this arrangement in a series of contested hearings over five years. At the first hearing, when Matthew was six years old (and had been at school for only a short time), the judge rejected the application, stating:

I am satisfied that if there were any problems of a severe nature in the mother's household they would come out in the school reports. Mr X [Family Court Counsellor] was not prepared to concede that, but I am not prepared to accept his evidence in that regard because my long experience of hearing custody matters over many years, and of school reports and their relationship to children's behaviour, convinces me that if there are any real problems in a household of a custodial parent, one way or the other, they will seep through into the school reports, and that close examination of the school reports in this case reveal that they have not.

(Cashmore, 2001)

Five years later after the final hearing which allowed him to live with his father, Matthew (then 11) said:

It's much better now. It wasn't good at all when I was living with my mum. It was all right when I was living with my dad and my mum, but the main thing I liked about it was that I had time with my dad and he looked after me. And then when I got to this house, it was a lot better, 'cos I could always spend time with my dad, and my new mum was here, and she's nice. I'm getting better school marks now. I used to get Cs and Ds and now it's all 'good' or 'very good'. I think the only one I don't get good marks for is my writing.

(Cashmore, 2001)

Such feedback may help those involved in making decisions such as these to approach 'each case as in a position of uncertainty, respecting the complexity and ambiguity' of each child's life and circumstances (Trinder, 1997: 302).

Notes

1 In the UK, for example, the obligation under the Children Act 1989 to consider the 'ascertainable wishes and feelings of the child' applies to public law or child welfare matters and to contested private law proceedings, but not to private law matters which are uncontested. This was quite clearly intended to protect family autonomy and to encourage parents to continue to exercise parental responsibility after the separation and divorce. This approach is, however, criticised by some who see it as 'obscuring the voice of the child beneath a near-irrebuttable assumption that parents would behave appropriately towards children' (Sawyer, 1999).

  In contrast, the law in several Scandinavian countries is very broad-ranging, extending to decision-making by parents as well as other custodians. For example, the Finnish Child Custody and Rights of Access Act 1983 states that: 'Before a custodian makes a decision on a matter relating to the person of a child he shall, where possible, discuss the matter with the child taking into account the child's age and maturity and the nature of the matter. In making the decision the custodian shall give due consideration to the child's feelings, opinions and wishes' (Lansdown, 1995b: 22).

2 The Family Court of Australia has kindly provided data for 2000/2001 that confirms that the 60 per cent figure is a reasonable estimate of the cases in which family reports or expert reports are ordered and play some role involved in defended matters which go to hearings or result in settlements before or without a hearing.

3 This pilot study, funded by the University of Sydney, was conducted by Cashmore and Parkinson in Sydney and is the basis of a larger study, funded by the Australian Research Council, now underway.

4 Interestingly, parents were also uncomfortable with the one-way glass observation technique. As one parent in the Australian pilot study commented: 'It stank! You're taken into this room and told you're being watched through this one-way glass, and they say "Play, be natural".'

5 While the court may see the need and make an order requesting separate legal representation for a child, the appointment and funding of a child's representative may not be under the control of the court. In Australia, for example, Legal Aid controls this process.

6 The Chief Justice of the Family Court in Australia is currently seeking advice on the development of a practice direction which will set out the court's expectations of child representatives in that court.

7 On one view, lawyers have no special training or capacity to 'determine' the best interests of the child and it is in fact the function of the court to make this determination. On the other hand, it is argued that lawyers should advocate the child's views only when the children have the capacity to give instructions, and this of course raises the question of when children have this capacity.

8 Huddart and Ensminger (1992–3: 103) also cite Abella and L'Heureux-Dubé's (1983) concerns about the interview being 'a violation of the judge's function as an impartial trier of fact' because of the need to assume an inquisitor role when questioning children.

9 For example, the Family Law Pathways Advisory Group (2001) 'found that the system's current focus on children is limited, and concluded that children need to be heard and have their needs included at all levels of their families' involvement in the family law system . . . Court processes include opportunities for a child's wishes to be made known but rarely is the child able to express these views directly. The result is that children often feel powerless in a system that purports to put their interests first' (pp. xxii, 11).

10 Similar conclusions are drawn in relation to public law welfare matters (for example, Masson, 2000).

11 Douglas *et al.* (2000) found, for example, that 75 per cent of judges in their UK survey said that children's views should not be ascertained because of concern about the burden of responsibility or the possibility of them being pressured to give a certain view. Felner *et al.* (1985), however, found that professionals indicated that they were suspicious about children's motives in expressing a particular view, a suspicion that was not warranted by the actual reasoning that children used in coming to their view.

References

Attorney-General's Department (1998). *Child inclusive practice in family and child counselling and family and child mediation*, Report by Strategic Partners to Legal Aid and Family Services Branch, Attorney-General's Department, Canberra.

Austin, G.W., Jaffe, P.G. and Hurley, P.M. (1992–3). Incorporating children's needs and views in alternative dispute resolution approaches. *Canadian Family Law Quarterly*, 8, 69–79.

Australian Law Reform Commission and Human Rights and Equal Opportunity Commission (1997). *Seen and heard: Priority for children in the legal process*. Canberra: Commonwealth of Australia.

Bagshaw, D. (1992). Children of divorce in Britain and the United States: Issues in relation to child custody and access. *Australian Journal of Family Law*, 6, 32–56.

Brown, C. (1995). Involving children in decision making without making them the decision makers. Paper presented to the Association of Family and Conciliation Courts Northwest Regional Conference, Skamania Lodge, 2–5 November 1995.

Cashmore, J. (2001). Children's participation in family law matters. Paper presented at 2001 World Congress on Family Law and the Rights of Children and Youth, Bath, England, September, 2001.

Cashmore, J. and Bussey, K. (1994). Perceptions of children and lawyers in care and protection proceedings. *International Journal of Law and the Family*, 8, 319–36.

Cashmore, J., Dolby, R. and Brennan, D. (1994). *Systems abuse: Problems and solutions*. Sydney: New South Wales Child Protection Council.

Chisholm, R. (1998). Children's participation in litigation. Paper presented at the Third National Family Court Conference, October 1998, Melbourne. http://www.familycourt.gov.au/papers/fca3/chisholm.pdf

Chisholm, R. (2000). Children's participation in Family Court litigation. Paper presented at the International Society of Family Law 10th World Conference, 9–13 July 2000, Brisbane.

Crosby-Currie, C.A. (1996). Children's involvement in contested custody cases: Practices and experiences of legal and mental health professionals. *Law and Human Behavior*, 20, 289–311.

Department of Health (1991). The Children Act 1989, Volume 3: *Guidance and Regulations*. London: Her Majesty's Stationery Office.

Douglas, G., Murch, M., Scanlan, L., and Perry, A., (2000). Safeguarding children's welfare in non-contentious divorce: towards a new conception of the legal process? *Modern Law Review*, 63, 177–96.

Douglas, G., Murch, M., Robinson, M., Scanlan, L. and Butler, I. (2001). Children's perspectives and experience of the divorce process. *Family Law*, 31, 373–7.

Dunn, J. and Deater-Deckard, K. (2001). *Children's views of their changing families*. York: Joseph Rowntree Foundation.

Family Law Council (1996). *Involving and representing children in family law: A Report to the Attorney-General prepared by the Family Law Council*. Canberra: Commonwealth of Australia.

Family Law Pathways Advisory Group (2001). *Out of the maze: Pathways to the future for families experiencing separation*. Report of the Family Law Pathways Advisory Group. Canberra: Commonwealth of Australia.

Felner, R.D., Terre, L., Farber, S., Primavera, J. and Bishop, T.A. (1985). Child custody: Practices and perspectives of legal professionals. *Journal of Clinical Child Psychology*, 14, 27–34.

Garwood, F. (1992). Conciliation: A forum for children's views? *Children and Society*, 6, 353–63.

Gollop, M.M., Smith, A.B. and Taylor, N.J. (2000). Children's involvement in custody and access arrangements after parental separation. *Child and Family Law Quarterly*, 12, 383–99.

Huddart, C.M. and Ensminger, J.C. (1992–3). Hearing the voice of children. *Canadian Family Law Quarterly*, 8, 95–120.

Jones, E. and Parkinson, P. (1995). Child sexual abuse, access and the wishes of children. *International Journal of Law and the Family*, 9, 54–85.

Lansdown, G. (1995a). Children's rights to participation and protection: A critique. In C. Cloke and M. Davies (eds), *Participation and empowerment in child protection* (pp. 19–38). Chichester, England: John Wiley & Sons.

Lansdown, G. (1995b). *Taking part: Children's participation in decision making.* London: Institute for Public Policy Research.

Lansdown, G. (2001). *Promoting children's participation in democratic decision-making.* Florence: UNICEF Innocenti Research Centre. Available: www.unicef-icdc.org

Leach, V. (2000). Children unseen and unheard – A challenge to the practice of family mediation. Paper presented at the International Society of Family Law 10th World Conference, 9–13 July 2000, Brisbane.

L'Heureux-Dubé (1998). A response to remarks by Dr. Judith Wallerstein on the long-term impact of divorce on children. *Family and Conciliation Courts Review,* 36, 384–91.

Lowe, N. and Douglas, G. (1998). *Bromley's Family Law.* (9th edn). London: Butterworths.

Lowe, N. and Murch, M. (2001). Children's participation in the family justice system – translating principles into practice. *Child and Family Law Quarterly,* 13, 137–58.

Lyon, C. (2000). Children's participation in private law proceedings with particular emphasis on the question of meetings between the judge and the child in family proceedings. In M. Thorpe and E. Clarke (eds) *No fault of flaw: The future of the Family Law Act 1996.* Papers presented at the President's Third Inter-disciplinary Conference on Family Law, Dartington Hall, Totnes, 24–26 September, 1999 (published by Family Law in 2000).

McDonald, M. (1990). *Children's perceptions of access and their adjustment in the post-separation period.* Family Court of Australia, Research Report No. 9.

McIntosh, J. (2000). Child-inclusive divorce mediation: Report on a qualitative research study. *Mediation Quarterly,* 18, 55–70.

Masson, J. (2000). Participation, placation and paternalism: young people's experiences of representation in child protection proceedings in England and Wales. Paper presented at the International Society of Family Law 10th World Conference, 9–13 July 2000, Brisbane. Available: www.gu.edu.au/centre/flru/masson.doc

Mitchell, A. (1985). *Children in the middle – living through divorce.* London: Tavistock.

Murch, M., Douglas, G., Scanlan, L., Perry, A., Lisles, C., Bader, K. and Borkowski, M. (1999). *Safeguarding children's welfare in uncontentious divorce.* Report to the Lord Chancellor's Department: Research Series 7/99. London: Lord Chancellor's Department.

Neale, B. and Smart, C. (1998). *Agents or dependants?: Struggling to listen to children in family law and family research.* Centre for Research on Family, Kinship and Childhood, University of Leeds, Working Paper 3.

Neugebauer, R. (1989). Divorce, custody and visitation: The child's point of view. In R. Neugebauer (ed.) *Children of divorce: developmental and clinical issues.* New York: Haworth.

O'Quigley, A. (1999). *Listening to children's views: The findings and recommendations of recent research.* York: Joseph Rowntree Foundation.

Piper, C. (1999). Ascertaining the wishes and feeling of the child. *Family Law,* 27, 796–800.

Pryor, J. and Seymour, F. (1996). Making decisions about children after parental separation. *Child and Family Law Quarterly,* 8, 229–42.

R and R (Children's Wishes) (2000) FamCA 43. Available: www.familycourt.gov.au/html/2000.html

Re P (A Minor) (Education) (1992) 1 FLR 316 at 321.

Rodgers, B. and Pryor, J. (1998). *Divorce and separation: The outcomes for children.* York: Joseph Rowntree Foundation.

Sandor, D. (2000). Children's wishes under the Family Law Act. *Australian Children's Rights News*, 25, 15–16.

Sawyer, C. (1999). *Rules, roles and relationships.* Oxford: Centre for Socio-legal Studies.

Schofield, G. (1998). Making sense of the ascertainable wishes and feelings of insecurely attached children. *Child and Family Law Quarterly*, 10, 363–75.

Smart, C. and Neale, B. (2001). Post-divorce childhoods: Perspectives from children. Available: http://www.leeds.ac.uk/family/research/findings-post.htm

Smart, C., Neale, B. and Wade, A. (2001). Making Contact Work: A Response to Consultation paper by the Children Act Subcommittee of the Advisory Board on Family Law. Available: http://www.leeds.ac.uk/family/research/making.htm

Smart, C., Wade, A. and Neale, B. (1999). Objects of concern? – children and divorce. *Child and Family Law Quarterly*, 11, 365–76.

Spall, P., Testro, P. and Matchett, P. (1998). *Having a say.* Sydney: New South Wales Child Protection Council.

Thorpe, M. and Clarke, E. (eds) (2000). *No fault of flaw: The future of the Family Law Act 1996.* Papers presented at the President's Third Inter-disciplinary Conference on Family Law, Dartington Hall, Totnes, 24–26 September, 1999 (published by Family Law in 2000).

Trinder, L. (1997). Competing constructions of childhood: children's rights and children's wishes in divorce. *Journal of Social Welfare and Family Law*, 19, 291–305.

Walczak, Y. and Burns, S. (1984). *Divorce: The child's point of view.* London: Harper & Row.

Wallerstein, J. and Kelly, J. (1980). *Surviving the breakup: How children and parents cope with divorce.* New York: Basic Books.

Wallerstein, J. and Lewis, J. (1998). The long-term impact of divorce on children: A first report from a 25-year study. *Family and Conciliation Courts Review*, 36, 368–83.

Weithorn, L.A. and Campbell, S. (1982). The competency of children and adolescents to make informed treatment decisions. *Child Development*, 53, 1589–98.

11 The social construction of competence and problem behaviour among children

Elisabeth Backe-Hansen[1]

Introduction

Research about children should, in Berry Mayall's words, 'increase knowledge about children's experiences, knowledge and views; these data can then contribute to policy-oriented work towards improving the social condition of childhood' (1999: 13). As Allison James, Chris Jenks and Alan Prout (1988) point out, childhood has moved to the forefront of personal, political and academic agendas over the last two or three decades. We can conceptualise the structuring of childhood experience in terms of the 'stages and scripts' in which space and time are closely interwoven. These stages and scripts, or what is often called arenas – primarily the family, the school and peer group – generate the essential questions concerning children's environments. Answers to such questions can be sought from children themselves, and from grown-ups who interact closely with children as part of the latter's daily lives. In this chapter, the questions asked concern social competence and problem behaviour among children.

From this perspective a useful assumption in our understanding of social competence as well as problem behaviour among children is that they are relational and contextualised phenomena. Social competence can be seen as relational because acts that are construed as competent or not competent take place in relation to others. It can be seen as contextualised because what acting competently means differs between social arenas like the home and school settings, or in relation to friends in contrast to parents (Ogden *et al.*, 1998; Petersen, 1988; Steinberg, 1995). Indeed, children may well choose different strategies on different arenas although the goals they want to achieve on these arenas are similar. For instance, different types of arguments might justify not having done one's homework when talking to parents and teachers, or aggressive or assertive behaviour might be seen as functional in relation to peers but not siblings (Griffith *et al.*, 2000). Even more strongly, it may be argued that competence cannot be separated from the structural contexts in which it is displayed or negotiated (Hutchby and Moran-Ellis, 1998). The same arguments easily pertain to our understanding of children's problem behaviour.

This way of understanding social competence as well as problem behaviour presupposes at least some kind of common definition, perception, or understanding between a child and the different persons relating to him or her. As a consequence of this, studies of children's social competence and problem behaviour cannot rely on a single informant, but need to combine data from different informant groups, like the children themselves, their parents, teachers, and peers. Thus it is relevant to understand both social competence and problem behaviour as socially constructed in Berger and Luckmann's (1967) terms. According to their way of thinking an individual will expect that orderly and patterned realities of daily life exist independently of him or herself. At the same time this is a shared world, and we presuppose a sufficient and lasting agreement between 'their' and our own experience of this world. When individuals interact they will relate to 'the other' according to categories like 'parent', 'friend', or 'teacher'. The reciprocal development of how 'the other' is perceived will be a result of ongoing negotiations, and consist of socially created constructions.

In this chapter I will present and discuss some results from a Norwegian study of social competence among children, where questionnaire data was collected when the participants were 10 and 12 years old respectively.[2] Social competence was defined as 'relatively stable characteristics in the shape of skills, knowledge and attitudes, making the establishing and maintenance of social relations possible' (Ogden, 1995: 83). The children were in the 5th and 7th grades when data were collected, thus still in primary school. They were in the same class and, for the most part, with the same class teacher.[3] The children themselves, their parents and teachers answered questions about the children's social competence. In addition the parents and teachers answered questions about externalising and internalising problem behaviour, while the children were asked how often they engaged in different types of antisocial and oppositional acts. This has created a fruitful analytical contrast as all the children were construed as competent at least to a certain degree, while just a few children were construed as problematic. Information was given from two different but significant contexts in the children's lives, namely the home and school arenas, and from different actors on these arenas. That data were collected at two points in time has made it possible to analyse stability and change within and between informant groups as well.

The issues to be discussed in this chapter arise from the relatively moderate agreement or concordance that was found between the informant groups about the children's social competence, as well as their problem behaviour. This is incidentally a quite common result in research utilising what is often called a multi-informant design (Achenbach *et al.*, 1987;

Fagan and Fantuzzo, 1999; Steele *et al.*, 1996; Sweeting, 2001), and gives rise to the conclusion that no informant can substitute for another (Stanger and Lewis, 1993). Consequently children and young people are indispensable informants about their own situation (Verhulst and van der Ende, 1992; van der Ende, 1999). It is also necessary to reflect on how best to understand agreement or lack thereof between children and grown-ups, or between grown-ups with different positions in relation to children. Above all it is necessary not to dismiss any informant group as 'wrong', or focus too much on which informant group supplies the 'better' or more 'correct' perceptions (Sweeting, 2001; Sweeting and West, 1998; Tein *et al.*, 1994).

In the rest of this chapter I will first elaborate on the question of stability and variation in the perception of the same phenomenon by different informant groups. This will be done through a presentation of results from pertinent research and a discussion of how other authors have tried to resolve dilemmas associated with the interpretation of results from this way of doing research with and about children. Then I describe how the study mentioned above was conducted and present some relevant results. Finally the results are discussed.

Different positions but not irreconcilable perceptions?

As mentioned above, one conclusion from studies utilising a multi-informant design is that one cannot rely on a single informant to draw a comprehensive picture. There may be different perceptions between generations – for instance, if mothers and fathers or parents and teachers perceive the same phenomenon more similarly than children do. There may be sex differences – for instance, if girls and parents have more similar perceptions than boys and parents.

Where the perception of patterns within the family like child-rearing, cohesion or conflict level is concerned the extent of child–parent agreement amongst other things varies according to age and sex of the child (Sweeting, 2001). For instance, younger adolescents and children seem to have more positive and similar perceptions of the family to those of their parents than do older adolescents, and girls may be more in accordance with their parents about child-rearing practices than boys are. Girls may also perceive both parents as more loving and less rejecting, while boys may perceive both parents as more dominant and controlling than girls do (Ohanessian *et al.*, 1995). Perceptions of parenting behaviours have also been found to be related to demographic factors. The lower the socio-economic status or parental education, the less male adolescents may perceive their parents as being supportive, controlling, and consistent. In addition, delinquent and maladjusted children or children from families with high levels of conflict seem to have a less favourable picture of their parents (Tein *et al.*, 1994).

In general it may be argued that parents are probably more biased (or less objective) because of the high levels of investment they have in their families, while in particular older adolescents tend to have lower levels of investment and thus be more likely to be objective. Adolescents who are in the process of establishing themselves as individuals and separating from their families may take a more negative view than younger adolescents and children, who still perceive themselves as being integral parts of their birth family. On the other hand parents, looking for validation of their efforts on behalf of their families, are likely to take a more positive view (Noller *et al.*, 1992). Perhaps each generation views family life in terms of its own bias or stake, which may also vary according to the children's ages. Thus the question of objectivity or who has the most 'correct' perception becomes insufficient, and has to be supplemented with a discussion of what is at stake for whom. This may also be the case when different informant groups judge children's adjustment and health, which is a second area where researchers utilise a multi-informant approach.

In one study mothers, fathers and teachers rated preschool children's social skills. While the mothers and fathers perceived the children fairly similarly, particularly in the families where the fathers had shared the responsibility for child-rearing, the parents and teachers differed quite a lot in their judgements. These differences were tentatively explained by differences between teachers and parents in terms of class and ethnicity, by the fact that parents and teachers observe children in different contexts, and that expressions of social competence or social skills are less visible than for instance aggressive behaviour. However, such differences may impede communications between home and school both for children with and without behaviour problems (Fagan and Fantuzzo, 1999). In another study the social competence of foster children was the issue, as perceived by the children's foster carers and their teachers. Here again there was quite strong agreement between the foster parents, but not between them and the teachers. This again underlines the importance of context when rating children's behaviour (McAuley and Trew, 2000).

In a third study both parents and 11-year-olds rated the children's health status. Although the two informant groups were in agreement about on the prevalence of long-standing illnesses, they differed where the general judgement of the children's health the previous year was concerned. The children actually assessed their health as less good than their parents did. The parents' rates of different conditions and symptoms were lower than that reported by their children as well. Parents and children were least likely to agree on a child's emotional state, which may fluctuate and is less visible than other states or symptoms. Parent–child agreement was highest for conditions that are common, visible, or diagnosed (Sweeting and West, 1998). In this way the relational aspects of the phenomenon under study were highlighted in addition to the contextual, particularly through the focus on visibility.

The final area to be discussed here where inter-informant stability and variation has been studied is behaviour problems among children. Behaviour rating scales completed by parents, teachers, and often young people themselves are amongst the most important measures used in assessing the extent of children's and adolescents' behaviour problems. In one such study teacher and parent ratings of children were used to measure the similarity and difference between these two groups of informants concerning symptoms of hyperactivity (AD/HD). While both teachers and parents made consistent assessments at two points in time, the concordance between them was moderate. This suggests that parents and teachers contribute unique information to the understanding of children's inattentive and hyperactive-impulsive behaviour (DuPaul *et al.*, 1998), which is another way of saying that context matters.

In the final study to be presented here it is taken as a point of departure that parents and adolescents often disagree in their reports on the presence and severity of problem behaviour, and that each informant represents a different perspective of an individual's functioning that may be valid in its own right (Verhulst and van der Ende, 1992). Here, the aim was to investigate the degree of agreement and the direction of discrepancies in reports of problem behaviour from 11- to 19-year-olds and their parents. In contrast with many other studies, moderate or fairly high concordance was found between the two informant groups concerning scores for symptoms of common diagnostic categories. Another result, which is quite common and is reflected in the study of children's health mentioned above, was that the young people reported many more problems than their parents did. This was true for symptoms of anxiety and depression as well as delinquent behaviours. It seemed, however, that girls agreed more than boys with their parents in their reports of inner feelings and thoughts. Older girls also agreed less well with their parents on aggressive behaviours than younger girls.

The authors discuss several possible reasons for these results. First, young people will increasingly enter their own environments separate from their parents, preventing them from observing their behaviour. Second, self-reports of an individual's problems reflect her or his perceptions, judgements, and tolerance of her or his own behaviour, feelings, thoughts, and fantasies across different situations, whereas parents' reports are based on the observable behaviour of their child in the home, plus verbal reports from the child and others concerning the child's problems. Third, children may increasingly keep inner feelings to themselves as they grow older (Verhulst and van der Ende, 1992). This again highlights both the contextual and relational aspects of the phenomenon under study. Contextualisation becomes important because it is supposed that different contexts give rise to different behaviours. The relational aspect becomes evident through the focus on self-awareness in contrast with others' awareness of the self.

In this part of the chapter I have presented some examples from the quite extensive research utilising a multi-informant design in the areas of family functioning, child adjustment, and health and problem behaviour among children and young people. As I have already argued, the results as well as the various authors' discussions of these results show that the phenomena under study are better understood as contextual and relational. The results also indicate how different informant groups live both in the same and in different worlds when they reflect on these phenomena, making further reflection both important and challenging. I will return to a more thorough discussion of these issues after the presentation of results from my own newly completed study of social competence and problem behaviour among children.

Method

Several large-scale and cohort-based Norwegian studies and one Nordic study have addressed the phenomenon of social competence among children and youth since the beginning of the 1990s. All have used multi-informant questionnaire designs, with data collected from children and youths, their parents and teachers. Some of the studies have been cross-sectional while others have collected data twice in two to three years. The research has broadly addressed the two following issues: how to understand the phenomenon of social competence, and how to study the interplay between individuals and their various social arenas in meaningful ways (Andersson, 1998; Backe-Hansen and Ogden, 1998; Ogden, 1995; Sørlie and Nordahl, 1998). All studies have included questions about problem behaviour as well. The study reported here builds on the previous ones, focusing even more specifically on different arenas in children's lives and links between them.

Procedures and instruments that were used at both points in time and results from the first data collection are presented more comprehensively in Backe-Hansen (1999). Here I will just give a short overview. The measure of social competence used by the children was Harter's 'self-perceived competence scale' (1982). This scale consists of 28 items which can be divided into one global scale and four sub-scales: athletic competence, social competence, self-esteem and academic competence. The items come in the form of opposite statements, and the children are asked to choose the most appropriate statement and to what extent this describes them. Nine hundred and seventy-two 10-year-olds participated in the first data collection, 714 in the second.[4] All comparisons over time are of course based on those who participated both times. The children's social skills were also judged by their parents and teachers, who filled in Gresham and Elliot's 'social skills rating scale' (1990). This scale consists of a series of items in the shape of descriptions of various social skills, and the parents and teacher are asked to judge how well a child masters these. Most of the questions asked are identical, but some are formulated to fit the school and home settings respectively. Analytically the scale consists of one global score and scores on three sub-scales: cooperation, self-assertion and self-control. The scores on both scales range from 1 to 4, with 4 as the most positive. In addition the 'social skills rating scale' contains a series of questions about different types of problem behaviour, which can be construed as externalising and internalising behaviours respectively. Examples are 'Seems lonely', 'Often seems anxious in groups', 'Becomes angry easily', 'Threatens or bullies others'. For the 10-year-olds a dimension of restlessness was included as well. These questions are identical in the teacher and parent versions, and the alternative responses are 'Never', 'Sometimes', 'Often', or 'Very often'. Eight hundred and four parents filled in their questionnaire at the time of the first data collection, 624 at the time of the second. Correspondingly, teachers of 912 and 709 children did the same.

Most of the children were perceived as competent by all informant groups

The main results from the study were that the majority of the children in both age groups seemed to be doing well and were competent socially as well as academically, whether they themselves, their parents or teachers were judging them. Not more than 15–16 per cent of the 10-year-olds showed obvious problems in different areas. Nor was social competence significantly correlated with socio-demographic indicators, type of school the children attended or the municipality they lived in (Backe-Hansen, 1999). These results are all in accordance with results from previous studies (Ogden, 1995; Backe-Hansen and Ogden, 1998; Sørlie and Nordahl, 1998). Two years later the picture was equally positive, and the children themselves, their parents and teachers still found the children generally competent.

The children's perceptions of themselves were fairly stable over time.[5] However, there were changes that seemed to depend on how they perceived themselves initially, particularly if they judged themselves to be incompetent or very competent as 10-year-olds. This became apparent when the sample participating in both data collections was divided into three groups: the 15 per cent (101 children) with lowest self-perceived competence, the 15 per cent (103 children) with highest self-perceived competence, and a large middle group (461 children). Over time there was a slight increase in the middle group, as more children moved from the extreme groups to the middle group than in the opposite direction. However, as many as 44 per cent (45) of the children who perceived themselves most negatively as 10-year-olds still did so two

years later, while not more than 32 per cent (33) still perceived themselves as very competent.

The parents' assessment of their children was slightly more stable
over time than the children's assessment of themselves,[6] and overall
the parents perceived their children as even more socially skilled as 12-
year-olds than they had done two years previously. The same general
pattern appeared as when the children assessed themselves: there were
movements between the extreme groups and the middle group, but
more from the extremes to the middle than vice versa. More, however,
moved to the most than the least socially skilled sub-group as the
parents perceived them. Still slightly above half of the 15 per cent (98)
judged as least socially skilled as 10-year-olds were perceived in the same
way two years later (51 children). The same pertained to the 15 per cent
(88) that were perceived as most socially skilled initially, where just
about half (45) remained over time.

The teachers' perception of the children over time was even more
stable than that of the parents.[7] However, the teachers did not, as the
parents did, judge the children as significantly more socially skilled
after two years. The same pattern appeared as for the other two informant groups, in that changes were more common towards the middle
than towards the extremes. However, and contrary to the changes in
the parents' assessment, more of the children had moved to the least
competent sub-group as the teachers perceived them. In addition slightly
above half of the 15 per cent (80 children) judged as least competent as
10-year-olds were in the same sub-group two years later (42 children),
while the same pertained to 45 per cent (52) of those perceived as most
competent.

As stated above, the three informant groups were in agreement about
the general level of competence among the children, with a fairly high
stability over time particularly through the eyes of the teachers. Fortunately this stability was not absolute, as it was still possible for those
who either perceived themselves or were perceived as least competent
to improve their relative position over time. Still it can give cause for
concern that about 7–8 per cent of the children remained in the least
favourable position relatively speaking.

This picture of stability within informant groups becomes more
complex when the judgment of all three informant groups are analysed
in relation to each other. When the children were 10 years old the correspondence between them was moderate to low, particularly between
the children and their parents. The correspondence was greater between
the children and the teachers, and the parents and teachers.[8] There was
of course some agreement, which here primarily means that positive
self-perceptions were mirrored by positive assessments by teachers and
parents to a certain degree. On the other hand the differences were
sufficiently great that some of the children who perceived themselves

less positively might be judged as socially competent by their parents or teachers, and vice versa. It must also be kept in mind that this variation took place within a general context of evaluations that were positive overall. Still, the fact that lack of agreement or concordance may be expected is important to keep in mind when discussing for instance collaboration between home and school.

The dilemmas and tensions that may well be inherent in lack of agreement between informant groups can be illustrated by the phenomenon of sex differences among the 10-year-olds. With one exception, the girls and boys did not answer the questions about self-perceived competence in significantly different ways. The exception was the area of physical competence, where the boys as a group perceived themselves as more competent than the girls. In the area of sex differences there was, thus, a generation divide between the informants, in the sense that both parents and teachers found the girls more socially competent than the boys.

There was also a divide according to the grown-ups' position, however. First, the sex differences as assessed by the parents were much smaller than that of the teachers. It was through the eyes of the teachers that the girls were deemed to have high levels of competence. Second, the parents and teachers did not weigh different aspects of the children's social skills in the same way. As mentioned above the rating scale used by the grown-up informants is divided into three sub-scales; cooperation, self-control and self-assertion. Both teachers and parents judged the sex differences as smallest in the area of self-assertion although the existing difference was significant. On their part the parents judged the sex differences to be biggest in favour of the girls in the area of self-control, while the teachers found the sex differences really great in the area of cooperation.

It might be that many of the expectations that are associated with the female sex role, even in the Nordic countries, are more suited to implicit and explicit expectations of the role as pupil. It might also be that the school creates different roles for boys and girls, which increases the probability of girls being perceived as more competent as long as they conform to the role as 'the good pupil'. Girls seem oriented towards adaptation and empathy to a larger degree than boys, while boys seem to prefer interaction and confrontation. Because of this, girls more easily get praised while the boys more easily get sanctioned. Matched with what may well be a qualitatively different way of perceiving themselves as girls and boys where social competence is concerned, this 'generation gap' makes for tension and conflict which are important to be aware of.

As discussed above, the combination of inter-group stability and between-group differences is common in the kind of research I have conducted, about adaptive as well as problematic behaviour. The results I have just presented and discussed show that context matters where perception of social competence is concerned. Children behave differently at school and at home, and the role as pupil has different connotations from the role as 'child at home'. As I will now show, there was fairly moderate agreement between the teachers and the parents in their assessment of the children's problem behaviours as well.

Externalising or internalising problems, according to teachers or parents?

The children who participated in the study came from so-called non-clinic samples, in that they were recruited as belonging to two specific age cohorts in a number of Norwegian municipalities. Whether they were in contact with any of the helping services or not was not an issue. As a consequence of this we were not specifically focused on diagnosing different types of psychopathology, and the questions asked of the parents and teachers were few and fairly general. Two dimensions were present in the questions at both points in time: externalising and internalising behaviour. In addition questions were asked about restlessness and over-activity (not hyper-activity) on the part of the 10-year-olds.[9]

Again, the parents' assessments showed fairly high stability over time,[10] which means that most of the parents did not find that their children showed much problematic behaviour at all. Of the participating children, 15.6 per cent (152) were judged as belonging to the most extreme group as 10-year-olds. Two years later this group still encompassed 15.6 per cent (112 children), consisting of 43 children who had been assessed as quite problematic two years previously and 69 'new' children.

The five types of problem behaviour that concerned the parents most when the children were 10 years old were the following: acts impulsively, easily angry, easily distracted, easily embarrassed, and quarrels with others. Two of these behaviours can be classified as examples of over-activity, two as examples of externalising behaviour and one as an example of internalising behaviour. Two years later there were no questions about over-activity, only about externalising and internalising behaviour. When the children were 12 years old, the five types of problem behaviour most frequently mentioned by the parents were: easily sad, easily embarrassed, quarrels with others, angry outbursts, easily angry. In other words the parents mention both externalising and internalising behaviours as frequent when the 12-year-olds showed some kind of problem behaviour.

The teachers showed about the same pattern in their judgements as the parents did. Altogether 13.4 per cent (131) of the participating children were assessed to be amongst the most problematic sub-group of children as 10-year-olds. After two years this number had decreased slightly to 12.7 per cent (91 children), of whom 34 were in the same group as 10-year-olds with 57 'new' children being included. Thus, the teachers' assessments were about as stable as the parents'.[11]

Whereas the parents seemed to focus on problem behaviours among the 10-year-olds that illustrate externalising or over-active behaviours, the teachers seemed to focus more on internalising behaviours. The five types of problem behaviour of most concern to the teachers at that point in time were: seems sad and depressed, isolates himself or herself, is anxious about participating in a group of pupils, threatens or bullies others, and seems lonely. When the children were 12 years old, the agreement was slightly larger concerning the type of behaviour if not the examples, as the five types of problem behaviour of most concern at this point in time were: easily embarrassed, quarrels with others, low self-confidence, becomes angry easily, and has difficulties controlling his or her anger.

In conclusion, then, the parents and teachers were in agreement about the children's problem behaviour in the sense that they judged about the same amount of children to be among the most problematic as this was defined. On the other hand, they differed slightly with regard to the types of problem behaviour that concerned them the most. Finally, parents and teachers differed quite a lot with regard to who the problematic children actually were.[12] They did not agree about more than 14 children, or about 16 per cent of those included by the parents and about 13 per cent of those included by the teachers (see Backe-Hansen, 2002 for a more thorough discussion of the results about problem behaviour).

Discussion: constructing social competence and problem behaviour

The substance of the results presented here is that most of the children included in the study seemed to do well and were part of environments that foster positive development. This is in accordance with results from similar studies (see Backe-Hansen and Ogden, 1998), and may be expected in Nordic welfare states where, for instance, redistribution and taxation policies favour families with children and contribute to low rates of child poverty (Bradshaw, 2001). The main issue in this chapter has not been to discuss the extent of competence and problems among Norwegian children, however. My focus has rather been on the necessity of adopting a contextualised and relational approach to the understanding of children as actors in different arenas in their daily lives, and how this approach can create constructive opportunities for better collaboration and understanding across arenas as well as generations.

Children, parents and teachers showed higher agreement with themselves over time than with each other at the same time, with slightly lower agreement on the part of the children than on the part of the grown-ups. The children included in this study were 10 to 11 years old at the time of the first data collection and two years older the next time. Thus, many of them had become young adolescents in the meantime, and it is not surprising if they perceived themselves differently as social beings on account of that. Parents and teachers will probably perceive the same children as more like themselves over time and see changes in behaviour and reactions more as expressions due to puberty and thus more apt to be transitional.

As expected, agreement was moderate between informant groups. As an illustration of the contextualised nature of children's behaviour as well as the way their behaviour is judged by others, it is important to study the nature of these differences in more detail. One example of this was given earlier through the example of the different perceptions of the social competence of girls and boys across generations and positions. Another example is the differing movements to and from what I called the extreme groups over time. It was shown that where social competence was concerned, fewer children placed themselves in the extremely competent group than at the other extreme at both points in time. On the other hand, the parents as a group saw a development towards more competence over time, while the teachers' judgement was more in accordance with the children's. These differences may be explained in several ways, and it is outside the scope of this study to find exact explanations. But it is, for instance, reasonable that children approaching or just having entered adolescence may become increasingly unsure of themselves, not in the least because their social relationships and the social expectations they encounter become more fluid. It is also reasonable that as a group, parents to a larger degree than teachers see their own children in a developmental perspective, and prefer to perceive this development along a positive trajectory unless forced to think otherwise. On their part teachers see children as part of a group, and will to a greater extent than parents use group norms in their assessments of individual children, including what can be construed as age-typical, undesirable behaviour.

These results also indicate that children do indeed behave differently across settings, which underlines the issue raised earlier about the importance to avoid too much focus on finding the 'correct' assessment or the 'best' informant. Rather it is important to presuppose that each informant contributes with unique knowledge which has to be combined in order to paint a comprehensive picture. For most children there will still be a sufficient amount of agreement between grown-ups in their environment, in the sense that they are met with an appropriate amount of consistency and at the same time can still keep the freedom to behave differently across settings. Issues will concern functionality rather than normative standpoints.

However, if children need better care, or treatment, or opportunities, for instance, agreement between significant grown-ups may be fundamental. Since such situations are often associated with guilt on the part of the grown-ups because a child does not experience a 'normal, happy childhood', normative issues more easily become paramount. In such cases the focus on the inherent value of knowledge from several sources, including the children themselves, will be an important reminder. Then, the richness associated with concrete and specific knowledge from many informants can increase the chances of finding better opportunities for the children involved, not in the least if this leads to more positive socially constructed ways of perceiving them.

Notes

1 I wish to thank licensed psychologist Espen Arnevik for assistance with the data analyses.
2 The study 'Children's development and living conditions in a resource-oriented and holistic perspective', was financed by the Norwegian Research Council from 1996–2002. The first data collection took place in 1997, the second in 1999. Initially the study included 972 10-year-olds and 858 13-year-olds from eleven strategically selected Norwegian municipalities. The discussion in this chapter will be limited to the youngest sample.
3 In Norway, children start school at six years old and stay for seven years in primary school, before changing to secondary school for a further three mandatory years when they are 12 or 13 depending on the time of the year when they are born. The cut-off point deciding which grade children enter is whether they are born before or after 31 December. Data were collected during the spring term before the children changed schools.
4 The participation rate was 78 per cent on the part of the children at the time of the first data collection. At the second data collection 85 per cent of those who had not moved participated. Not all the children have answered all questions properly, so the number of valid responses varies.
5 The correlation between the children's responses as 10-year-olds and 12-year-olds was 0.48 for the sample of children as a whole.
6 The correlation between the parents' assessment of their children as 10-year-olds and 12-year-olds was 0.56 for the sample as a whole.
7 The correlation between the teachers' assessment of the children as 10-year-olds and 12-year-olds was 0.62 for the sample as a whole.
8 The intercorrelation between the children's self-perception and the parents' perception of their social skills was 0.12. Between the children and the teachers the intercorrelation was 0.28, and between the parents and the teachers the intercorrelation was 0.26 – about the same, moderate level.
9 As the questions the children were asked about problem behaviour were quite different from those asked of the parents and teachers, the children's responses are not analysed here.
10 The intercorrelation between the parents' assessments at the two points in time was 0.53.
11 The intercorrelation between the teachers' assessments at the two points in time was 0.60.
12 The intercorrelation between the parents' and the teachers' assessments were 0.42 and 0.37 at the two points in time.

References

Achenbach, T.M., McConnaughy, S.H. and Howell, C.T. (1987). Child/adolescent behavioral and emotional problems: Implications of cross-informant correlations for situational specificity. *Psychological Bulletin*, 101, 213–32.

Andersson, G. (1998). Samband mellan social kompetens, beteende och skolmotivation? In E. Backe-Hansen and T. Ogden (eds) *10-åringer i Norden. Kompetanse, risiko og oppvekstmiljø*. København: Nordisk Ministerråd.

Backe-Hansen, E. (1999). Barn og unge sett med egne og voksnes øyne. In A.-M. Jensen, E. Backe-Hansen, H. Bache-Wiig and K. Heggen (eds) *Oppvekst i barnets århundre. Historier om tvetydighet*. Oslo: Ad Notam Gyldendal.

Backe-Hansen, E. (2002). Foreldres og læreres oppfatning av problematferd blant barn og unge. Submitted to *Tidsskrift for Norsk Psykologforening*.

Backe-Hansen, E. and Ogden, T. (eds) (1998). *10-åringer i Norden. Kompetanse, risiko og oppvekstmiljø*. København: Nordisk Ministerråd.

Berger, P.I. and Luckmann, T. (1967). *The social construction of reality*. New York: Anchor Books, Doubleday and Company.

Bradshaw, J. (2001). Kan sosialpolitikk forhindre fattigdom blant barn? In A.-H. Bay, B. Hvinden and C. Koren (eds) *Virker velferdsstaten?*, Kristiansand: Høyskoleforlaget.

DuPaul, G.J., Power, T.J., McGoey, K.E., Ikeda, M.J. and Anastopoulos, A.D. (1998). Reliability and validity of parent and teacher ratings of Attention-Deficit/Hyperactivity Disorder symptoms. *Journal of Psychoeducational Assessment*, 16, 55–68.

Fagan, J. and Fantuzzo, J.W. (1999). Multirater congruence on the Social Skills Rating System: Mother, father, and teacher assessments of urban Head Start children's social competencies. *Early Childhood Research Quarterly*, 14, 229–42.

Gresham, F.M. and Elliot, S.N. (1990). *Social Skills Rating Scale. Manual*. Circle Pines: American Guidance Service.

Griffith, M.A., Dubow, E.F. and Ippolito, M.F. (2000). Developmental and cross-situational strategies in adolescents' coping strategies. *Journal of Youth and Adolescence*, 29, 183–204.

Harter, S. (1982). The perceived competence scale for children. *Child Development*, 53, 87–97.

Hutchby, I. and Moran-Ellis, J. (1998). Situating children's social competence. In I. Hutchby and J. Moran-Ellis (eds) *Children and social competence. Arenas of action*. London: Falmer Press.

James, A., Jenks, C. and Prout, A. (1998). *Theorising Childhood*, Cambridge: Polity Press.

McAuley, C. and Trew, K. (2000). Children's adjustment over time in foster care: Cross-informant agreement, stability and placement disruption. *British Journal of Social Work*, 30, 91–107.

Mayall, B. (1999). Children and childhood. In S. Hood, B. Mayall and S. Oliver (eds) *Critical issues in social research. Power and prejudice*. Buckingham: Open University Press.

Noller, P., Seth-Smith, M., Bouma, R. and Schweitzer, R. (1992). Parent and adolescent perceptions of family functioning: A comparison of clinic and non-clinic families. *Journal of Adolescence*, 15, 101–14.

Ogden, T. (1995). *Kompetanse i kontekst*. Oslo: Barnevernets Utviklingssenter.

Ogden, T., Schultz Jørgensen, P. and Backe-Hansen, E. (1998). Perspektiver og problemstillinger. In E. Backe-Hansen and T. Ogden (eds) *10-åringer i Norden. Kompetanse, risiko, og oppvekstmiljø.* København: Nordisk Ministerråd.

Ohanessian, C. McCauley, Lerner, R.M., Lerner, J.V. and von Eye, A. (1995). Discrepancies in adolescents' and parents' perceptions of family functioning and adolescent emotional adjustment. *Journal of Early Adolescence*, 15, 490–516.

Petersen, A.C. (1988). Adolescent development. *Annual Review of Psychology*, 39, 583–607.

Stanger, C. and Lewis, M. (1993). Agreement among parents, teachers and children on internalizing and externalizing behaviour problems. *Journal of Clinical Child Psychology*, 22, 583–607.

Steele, R., Forehand, R. and Devine, D. (1996). Adolescent social and cognitive competence: Cross-informant and intra-individual consistency over three years. *Journal of Clinical Child Psychology*, 25, 60–5.

Steinberg, L. (1995). Commentary. On developmental pathways and social contexts in adolescence. In L. Crockett and L. Crouter (eds) *Pathways through adolescence.* Mahwah, N.J.: Lawrence Erlbaum Associates.

Sweeting, H. (2001). Our family, whose perspective? An investigation of children's family life and health. *Journal of Adolescence*, 24, 229–50.

Sweeting, H. and West, P. (1998). Health at age 11: reports from schoolchildren and their parents. *Archives of Disease in Childhood*, 78, 427–34.

Sørlie, M.A. and Nordahl, T. (1998). *Problematferd i skolen. Hovedfunn, forklaringer og pedagogiske implikasjoner.* Report no. 12a/98. Oslo: Norwegian Social Research.

Tein, J.-Y., Roosa, M.W. and Michaels, M. (1994). Agreement between parent and child reports on parental behaviors. *Journal of Marriage and the Family*, 56, 341–55.

van der Ende, J. (1999). Multiple informants: Multiple views. In H.M. Koot, A.A.M. Crijnen and R.F. Ferdinand (eds) *Child psychiatric epidemiology. Accomplishments and future directions.* Assen: Van Gorcum.

Verhulst, F.C. and van der Ende, J. (1992). Agreement between parents' reports and adolescents' self-reports of problem behaviour. *Journal of Child Psychology and Psychiatry*, 6, 1011–23.

12 Reconstructing disability, childhood and social policy in the UK

John Davis, Nick Watson, Mairian Corker and Tom Shakespeare

Abstract

This chapter critically assesses the recent change in the way social policy characterises disabled children and young people. It briefly illustrates that social policy has moved from being dominated by medical assumptions that disabled children are inevitably passive, 'vulnerable' and in 'need'. It suggests that this movement has been guided by 'social model' and 'social inclusion' notions that disabled children have rights, are active citizens and should be fully included in educational and cultural activities. It argues that the social structural discourses that underpinned this change have their failings. Specifically, it argues that 'social model' and 'social inclusion' perspectives on social policy are flawed because they present disabled children as a homogeneous grouping, ironing out the complexity and difference in their lives. It suggests that in order for an effective policy framework for the social and economic inclusion of disabled children to be developed, social policy must take as its point of departure the accounts of disabled children. By employing ethnographic data to demonstrate the complex and fluid nature of disabled children's lives, this chapter proposes a multi-layered approach for social policy. Central to this approach are strategies that help develop dialogue, empowerment and interdependency between children, young people, parents, policy-makers, practitioners and peer group.

Introduction

This chapter examines the medical and social 'models' that have underpinned social policy aimed at disabled children. It suggests that both 'models' are premised on notions of deficit and dependency. By drawing on ethnographic data, this chapter challenges some of the 'taken-for-granted' assumptions that inform policy approaches to disability and childhood. We want to suggest that what pertains is not natural, or obvious, or automatic, but rests on a particular cultural approach to disability as a 'problem'. By showing that there is nothing inevitable about disabled children's lives, we want to suggest that we can change the ways that we understand and deal with disability in social policy. This chapter will demonstrate the 'need' for policy-makers to respond to the complex and fluid nature of disabled children's lives. It will conclude that in order for an effective policy framework to be developed, policy-makers must do more than simply carry out consultation with disabled young people. They should not only develop sustained and ongoing dialogue with disabled children but should also act to enable them to alter the service provision that they encounter.

Medical model and social policy

Social policy during the 1970s to the 1990s was regularly attacked for being dominated by medical notions of disability. Dominant approaches to the issue of disability within social policy and medical sociology individualised the issue of disability. This approach, labelled 'the medical model', was criticised by writers in the disability studies tradition, who located the problem of disability in social relations and structural exclusion, rather than in personal deficits of body or mind (Oliver, 1990).

In her research with disabled children in care, Jenny Morris criticised the 'medical model' for failing to look at the context of children's lives:

> There is no room here for recognising that the inability of a 15 year old, who has speech difficulties as a result of cerebral palsy, to be part of the local teenage sub-culture is created by the prejudicial attitudes and inaccessible environments which restrict his or her activities, rather than cerebral palsy or speech difficulties in themselves.
>
> (Morris, 1997: 243)

She argued that the medical model reduced children's experiences to biological explanations. In so doing, she believed it ignored the possibility that the social or emotional problems of disabled children may result from a lack of stimulation, interaction, security and love that all children need, and to which children in care may not have access. She states:

> To assume that all communication, mobility and behavioural difficulties are solely caused by impairment is further to disable those children by failing to recognise their actual experiences.
>
> (Morris, 1997: 244)

Ideas within disability studies developed by writers such as Morris paralleled work within social gerontology on the structured dependency of old age (Townsend, 1981). For example, Estes argues:

The needs of older persons are reconceptualised as deficiencies by the professionals charged with treating them, regardless of whether the origins of these needs lie in social conditions over which the individual has little or no control, in the failings of the individual, or in some policy-makers decision that a need exists.

(Estes, 1979: 235)

From a disability studies perspective medical model discourses that surround disabled children are based on a number of assumptions: that being a disabled child involves a life of suffering; that disabled children are inevitably dependent on others; and that the state will ultimately have to bear the cost of supporting disabled children. Disability studies writers didn't have to look far for evidence of such assumptions; for example, during the 1988 parliamentary debate about abortion, comments such as the following were common:

The private financial burden of caring for a severely handicapped child has been estimated by the courts as £500,000. If one takes into account the cost to the state of statutory provision, the cost could well be another £500,000 . . . Why should the House consider forcing people to accept such a burden if they do not want it?

(*Hansard*, 22 January 1988, in Bailey, 1996: 162)

Medically influenced discourses tended to pathologise the physical experience of impairment. The problem of disability was defined as that of the person with impairment. Disability was individualised and abstracted from the social context. Consequently, the disabled child or adult was seen as a tragic victim and an unfortunate burden on others (Shakespeare and Watson, 1998). The fact that life involves mutual aid and that everyone is in some measure dependent on others was ignored. In the case of families and relationships, it was assumed that there was a polar dichotomy between families with disabled members, and other, 'normal' families. One set of relationships was perceived to be normal and benign, and the other was viewed as problematic and pathological. It was argued that the problem inhered in the individual with impairment, not in the wider social context in which the whole family found itself (Shakespeare, 2000).

Literature on disabled children was based on a range of normative assumptions about the effects that having a child with impairment had on the parental relationships or family dynamics. For example, having a disabled child meant that family relationships would break down, or that siblings would suffer. The assumption was that typical loving parental relationships were replaced by a relationship of caring and physical support based around the performance of certain tasks (Shakespeare, 2000). Service provision for families with disabled children reflected this assumption. Considerable stress was placed on the need for respite care, for example, on the basis that the intolerable responsibilities of having a child with impairment typically necessitate a break, or a rest (Shakespeare and Watson, 1998). Very little consideration was given as to whether children needed a break from the pressures of being judged as in deficit and of having their bodies and behaviours stereotyped as 'abnormal' and as in need of 'fixing'. By constituting disabled children as passive and 'vulnerable', these discourses failed to explore fully the cultural context within which the experience of social isolation, segregation, and poor self-image are lived. The focus on disabled children's and families' 'service needs' served to perpetuate an image of disabled children as inevitably being in need of 'care' (Robinson and Stalker, 1998). The diverse views of disabled children tended not to be recognised within this focus. They were often presented as a homogeneous grouping; little attempt was made to recognise complexity and difference in their lives. Many policies placed emphasis on the needs and wishes of parents and siblings; it was rare that disabled children themselves were asked for their views (Priestley, 1998).

Medical discourses have not simply disappeared. For example, public health writers such as Nicholas Wald make explicit the ways in which screening programmes are presently evaluated on the basis of cost–benefit analysis regarding the avoidance of the 'burden' of disabled children (Wald, 1992). However, over time alternative constructions of disability emerged that redefined disabled people's life problems as the consequence of the social. These constructions became known as the 'social model of disability' (Oliver, 1990). In the next section we compare this model to recent social policy developments in the area of childhood.

Social model of disability and childhood policy

The changing policy context, with an increased emphasis on rights and inclusion, demanded that academics and policy-makers recognise the social construction of disability and the importance of disabled people's own views (Oliver, 1990). The 'social model' was founded on the assumption that people are disabled by society, not by their bodies. The finger of blame for disabled people's negative life experience was pointed at the social and environmental barriers, prejudicial attitudes and other processes that served to exclude people with impairments from the mainstream.

In terms of social policy, this shift in thinking brought about the concept of independent living, developed by the Independent Living Movement. The ILM has its roots in the USA and the Physically Disabled Students Program (PDSP) at the University of California, Berkeley, in the early 1960s. Four assumptions underlie the practice of the Independent Living Movement:

All human life is of value.
Anyone, whatever their impairment, is capable of exerting choices.
People are disabled by society not by their bodies.
Disabled people have a right to participate fully in society.

(Morris, 1993: 21)

The Independent Living Movement gives prominence to issues such as the right to form personal and sexual relationships (Shakespeare *et al.*, 1996); the right to be a parent (Wates, 1997); the right of equal access to a range of settings (Swain *et al.*, 1993). Whilst the movement endeavours to promote the full range of human and civil rights of disabled people, the promotion of personal assistance as the key strategy in breaking the link between disability and dependency in everyday life has traditionally been its key focus (Morris, 1993).

The provision of personal assistants has been central to the development of ILM in the UK. The cost of this provision is met through direct payments. The Community Care Direct Payments Act (1997) enabled disabled people to manage their own support requirements. This resulted in many disabled people ceasing to be dependent on local service provision. Independent living has mainly been associated with adult services. There is very little recognition of the experiences of disabled children within 'social model' writing on disability. However, moves towards independent living have been mirrored by the emergence of a children's rights agenda within the UK.

Recent political developments in the UK have recognised the lack of children's involvement in service provision. The 1990s saw the development of a rights-based approach to social policy in childhood. For example, the Children (Scotland) Act (1995) enshrined the right of children in Scotland to have their views heard about services they used. Attempts were made to move to a more comunitarian approach to supporting children. MacMurray (1932) argued that a sense of community is reliant on the quality of local personal relationships, economic interdependence and material equality. Central to his work was the perspective that communities are built on mutual relationships established on the basis of trust, respect, reciprocal rights, obligations and support. In the UK this idea has become associated with the concept of integrated services and the 'war' on poverty and injustice (Levitas, 1998). In Scotland, New Community Schools had been one of a number of policy initiatives that have emerged with the aim of challenging the effects of poverty and social exclusion on childhood.

Since devolution in Scotland, New Community Schools have been developed from the concept of Full Service Schools in the USA (Scottish Executive, 1999, 2000). Just as in the USA the New Community Schools vary in size, structure and the new and established initiatives they incorporate. The first phase of 37 projects began in March 1999 and included

150 schools (primary and secondary), nurseries and family centres. Their aim is to work with parents and families to break the destructive cycle of underachievement and address barriers to children's learning to ensure that every child has the fullest possible opportunity to maximise his or her potential (Scottish Executive, 1999). This aim is underpinned by a commitment to integrated services. Children, parents, other community members, teachers, childcare professionals, social workers, and health personnel are expected to work together to adopt strategies that meet each child's developmental, educational, emotional, health and social needs.

New Community Schools aim to make the inclusion of disabled children the 'norm'. Following the passing of the Standards in Schools etc. Act (2000), in Scotland there is a presumption that disabled children will be educated alongside their peers.[1] In England the Children's Fund initiative has similar aims. For example, The Liverpool Children's Fund Plan 'Realising Dreams and Ambitions' (June 2001) sets a number of aims with regards to disabled children. These are to:

- Engage with disabled children to improve participation, inclusion and access to services.
- Empower children as users of services and to increase their participation in service planning.
- Support improved co-ordination of services and access to information.
- Achieve a shift in the culture of play, youth and leisure services towards greater inclusion.

Both the New Community Schools and The Children's Fund initiatives place major importance on the inclusion of disabled children in everyday educational and cultural activities. It appears that there has been a major shift in social policy that aims to influence the social and political context of disabled children's lives. In this chapter we explore the philosophical basis for this change and examine the value of the above objectives in the light of disabled children's experiences.

The study

The data in this chapter is drawn from an ESRC Children 5–16 Programme Project: 'Life as a Disabled Child'. The study used a range of qualitative methods, including participant observation and interviewing. However, particular attention was paid to employing informal techniques to develop good working relationships that enabled us to engage with young people on their own terms. The research was carried out in three 'special' schools and three 'mainstream' schools in Scotland and four 'special' schools and four 'mainstream' schools in England.

After observing more than 300 children and young people aged 12–19 in their schools, we continued to work with around half in a more in-depth way in their homes and neighbourhood. This included informal individual, paired or group interviews, as well as the compilation of written and visual accounts.

The data used here is from both Scotland and England and includes the views of children who had experienced special and mainstream schools. In the interest of confidentiality we do not want to say too much about the specific young people, their ages, the types of schools they attended and their impairments because this information may be enough for others to uncover their identity. The project has resulted in a number of publications concerning research methods, children's rights, inclusive education, theories of disability and geographies of play. In the discussion that accompanies the data we draw from these papers to add further context to the text.

Structural exclusion, parents and independent living

In our study issues of financial resources dominated discussions with parents. Though not all the families presented their child as in 'need' of service provision, some were compelled to plead special cases for material and legal provision from central and local government:

> *Parent:* We are seen as a financial burden and in terms of our needs we have to fight for everything and only really get things from social work and education which are cheap or easy to provide. I once drew a tree of the people Eddie meets and he had over 40 professionals involved in his life.

A lack of resources at local authority level very often meant that services for disabled children were provided on a 'block' basis (e.g. all children with the same impairment were offered similar services until the money ran out). Often parents had to overemphasise their children's impairments in order to access resources such as after-school care. They were forced by social policy agendas to reproduce the very medical discourses that disabled people find disempowering. This finding reinforced that of other studies that suggested services were very rarely tailored to children's individual requirements and that resources are disproportionately allocated to a minority of disabled children (Fairbairn and Fairbairn, 1992). In order to receive support many disabled children had to go through an inordinate amount of testing and their parents had to shuttle them from 'pillar to post' between different service providers. Many of the families were in constant conflict with different directorates within their local authorities. The long-term consequences of this for the health and well-being of family members can only be guessed at.

We do not mean to insinuate that these families were somehow uniquely 'worse off'. As Beresford (1994) points out, many of the experiences of families with disabled children do not differ qualitatively from those of families with non-disabled children, many of which are 'isolated' and 'impoverished'. Many parents argued that the solution to the problems of service provision lay in the development of key workers to liaise between agencies and the provision of direct payments to disabled children and parents. There is no doubt that many families with non-disabled children would benefit from having a 'key worker' who could seek out access to scarce resources but they would also gain from the reorganising of the way material resources are distributed in society.

The benefits of having direct access to financial resources can be seen in the next example. Bruce received a very large award from a lawsuit at the age of 12. It meant that he could afford two personal assistants, his own transport (van and power chair) and a number of changes to his home to make it more accessible. Bruce was in a position to make choices about his life, deciding what he wanted to do with his 'free' time. In this case Bruce's personal assistant tells the story. Bruce did not use spoken words but confirmed his agreement by use of eye movements:

> *PA:* He gets in about quarter to 4. What he'll do is he'll come in and sit and watch his TV and wait for either myself or [the other PA] to come in . . . he's waiting until I come in about quarter past and sit with him for about 10/15 minutes. Have a quick drink of coffee and then when the weather has gone off and what night it is. 'Cause on a Tuesday and Wednesday night he goes for a video, 'cause they're only a pound. So that's something he likes doing on a Tuesday and Wednesday. And obviously if it's raining he'll just give it a skip or we'll take it along in the van. And now with . . . being summer time he's out. But as the dark nights are drawing in. The nights are fairly drawing in. On a Friday and Saturday he's off out on his own either with myself or [the other PA]. We go to the pictures or we go bowling or we go into town.

Bruce's eyes lit up when his assistant talked about the social activities he did. Bruce experienced an element of social freedom because he had access to financial resources. His experiences contrasted with those of children and young people who had to lobby for access to power chairs or rely on voluntary and 'charitable' organisations for the opportunity to attend social events.

This example reinforces social structural characterisations of disability. It emphasises the 'social model' perspective that disability is caused by the unequal distribution of material resources. It also demonstrates the potential importance of direct payments for children and young people. Bruce and his family no longer had to wait for social services to provide him with support, he and his family could directly employ assistants and purchase equipment to meet his requirements. Traditionally in the UK direct payments have not been available to children. Bruce's example suggests that disabled children could benefit from the concept of independent living being applied to them.

Many authors have criticised the 'social model' of disability because it emphasises structural explanations of disabled people's lives at the expense of investigating the cultural context of those lives (Corker and French, 1999). In addition to this criticism, we believe that the implications of social model approaches are that the agency of disabled children is downplayed because their lives can only be analysed in terms of isolation, access to service provision and the acquisition of material support (Davis and Watson, 2002). The problem with this type of characterisation is that it is similar to the medical characterisations of disabled children discussed earlier because it represents these young people as passive victims who require adults to take action to 'fix' their problems.

We also believe that there is a danger that social structural explanations of disability and 'social model' responses to disability enable service providers to ignore deep-seated discrimination that exists in families, schools, hospitals, leisure/community centres, youth clubs and other social settings that children and young people attend. That is, they enable professionals to reduce disabled children's experiences to a technical rational agenda. This results in the concept of social inclusion being reduced to a concept of integration.

Bruce experienced integration because he was able to attend the same social locations as his peers. He did not experience inclusion because he was unable to interact with his peers during this experience. He attended a 'special' school and very rarely interacted with children his own age who were not disabled. His financial status allowed him some form of independence from his family but he spent much of his time with his adult PAs. His PAs had become friends as well as employees. Bruce's financial independence did not mean he had social independence. A more meaningful approach requires the development of an understanding of disability based on a greater examination of its cultural context.

The variability of disability

Many disabled children suggested that their lives varied, depending on the other people they encountered in a specific social context. For example, two Deaf[2] children explained the variability of their family relationships and friendships:

Imran:[3] With my sister, I feel we're the same we can fingerspell and we help each other. We might play football or watch TV and that's OK. With my mum tough, if she is trying to explain about a friend of ours who will visit, she will gesture as best she can and that helps me understand. My dad usually initialised everything and that's OK. My mom initialises too and that's OK and I can't communicate with my brother.

Imran tells us that he gets on well with his sister because she can sign but he can't communicate with his brother. He experiences different forms of inclusion within the same family setting. Zoebia's family did not sign and she does not have any close friends; however, she taught her cousin to sign:

M: Yeah . . .
Z: In terms of friends I don't have any best friends – only people I know.
M: Mm., would you like to have a best friend?
Z: I do have one best friend in . . . [signs name] . . . [to cousin] they live next door.
M: Your cousin seems able to sign very well . . .
M: Your cousin seems very fluent, how did you learn to sign?
C: [indistinct]
M: From Z. [to Z] So you taught her?
Z: [Nods].
M: [to cousin] You are very fluent and when I walked in I wondered if you were deaf.
Z: No, she is hearing.

For many years a discourse existed within social policy circles that suggested that 'Asian' families reject children who have impairments (Ahmad *et al.*, 2000). Zoebia's relationship with her family may be problematic because they do not communicate 'well' with her. But this may be the same for children in other families who are not Muslim and are not Deaf. These examples force us to question the influence of different categories such as family, ethnic group, 'deaf'. They also warn us not to essentialise these categories or privilege one over the other as causes of service 'need' (Corker and Davis, 2000). In the above case, Zoebia's family had not had the opportunity to learn sign in a form that took account of their multilingual culture or that enabled issues of different cultures ('Asian' and 'Deaf') to be discussed. There is a hint of a suggestion that different family members may have been more or less willing to engage in this learning process. It is tempting to reduce this example to a technical rational discussion of the provision of local sign language training. This would only serve to reinforce the 'hearing' vs.

'Deaf' divide. By teaching her cousin to sign Zoebia addresses some of her 'isolation' from peer group and family. She demonstrates the importance of child-centred solutions and establishes her ability to bridge the 'Deaf' v 'hearing' divide. This ability raises issues for how we analyse ethnicity and disability.

A number of authors have argued that ethnicity is overlooked in care and educational settings (Ali *et al.*, 2001; Ahmad *et al.*, 2000), that disabled children from different ethnic backgrounds believe they are discriminated against in educational settings (Bignall and Butt, 2000; Vernon, 1996), and that these children encounter 'eurocentric' service provision (Begum *et al.*, 1994). The stereotyping of 'Asian' families as rejecting disabled children is questioned by a number of authors (Ali *et al.*, 2001; Ahmad *et al.*, 2000; Corker and Davis, 2000). Ahmad *et al.* (2000) argue that South Asian families are generally supportive of deaf children and that it is social services and education departments that more generally fail disabled children from a variety of ethnic backgrounds because they discount issues of ethnicity.

Though we witnessed such failure – for example, in one area children with Down's syndrome were expected to use facilities in a school on an estate with a history of racial violence (Watson *et al.*, 2000) – we would be wary of essentialising the separation between groups who use services and the people who provide them. Indeed, dualisms such as 'good' and 'bad', 'mind' and 'body', 'deafness' and 'blindness', 'black' and 'white' tend to obscure more than they reveal (Corker, 2002; Corker and French, 1999). They tend to iron out the complexity of people's identities, as Zeobia points out:

> *Zoebia:* Well yeah they [the school] wanted me to change into trousers and I didn't want to, I'm Asian [second-generation Pakistani Muslim] and I enjoy wearing Asian clothes like the ones I'm wearing now. Like this, there are a lot of Asian girls who do wear trousers, I don't. All that changing all the time . . . There is a boy in year 9 everyone in his family are Muslim but his Mother chooses to wear trousers sometimes and not Muslim clothes like I'm wearing. It seems strange that she is Muslim but doesn't always wear Muslim clothes. I suppose my Mother compared to his is more [Zoebia begins to sign 'strict' and only executes half of the sign] . . . His parents are Muslim and sometimes his mother will wear clothes like yours and sometimes clothes like mine. My family only wear clothes like this and never like them . . . it's strange . . . I have asked him whether his family are Muslim and he says yes and when I asked why his family wear English clothes he said that he didn't know . . . It's strange . . . because I thought that all Muslims wore similar clothes but Wasim doesn't and that's different and so I thought that he may be Sikh but he's not he is Muslim.

We should not assume that all disabled children from South Asian backgrounds have the same experiences. Children are aware that culture is not fixed and try to make sense of cultural differences within their own cultural groupings (in this example 'Asian' and Muslim). It is important to note here that the difficulty of understanding cultural difference encountered by Zoebia is a difficulty that disability studies has been slow to recognise. Indeed, the social model of disability that emphasises the structural nature of disability has been criticised for ignoring the view of disabled people of different ethnic backgrounds (Begum *et al.*, 1994; Vernon 1996). At the centre of this criticism is the wish that writers on disability take more account of culture.

Overcoming essentialism, understanding our differences

We promote a fluid idea of culture. We believe that processes of social interaction are contingent on the varied identities of social actors and the variety of relationships that people forge on a daily basis – for example, power relations, relations of negotiation, relations of generation (Davis and Corker, 2001). This definition of culture causes problems for service providers. For example, in Zeobia's case how can they know when being Muslim is important and when it is not? The answer surely is to ask the children. However, the institutional and power arrangements of childhood do not lend themselves to promote the speedy facilitation of such cultural exchange.

Policy decisions rarely take account of disabled children's opinions because professional practices can get in the way of asking, and the personal prejudices and vested interests of service providers are promoted before those of children. For example, school rules can be applied in an overprotective way to disabled children because they are also used to protect adults against the fear of litigation:

> *Dibly:* The people here are too protected. I can do a lot more things than they give me credit for. For example, a few months ago I got a pass to go to the back shops and the access person and I agreed that I can go through there, that I've got the confidence to do it. But for the first few times they kept on checking up, following me, and they still check up. But I'm very confident about it. I can do it. I can't understand why they want to check up on me, but they do and they keep on doing it. You get this awful feeling, you're over protected. At home I negotiate my way round the local town OK. I'm capable of doing lots. My mother never had any quibbles about it. I just do what I can do, and I just wish here they wouldn't be so over protective.
>
> (Davis and Watson, 2001: 683)

Many of the professionals that worked with Dibly said that they engaged in defensive practice because they feared that their colleagues or senior staff would not respect them or that they would get into trouble if 'something' happened to the children. This demonstrates another tension within social policy. Adults who make decisions about provision for disabled children very often are influenced by legislation that seeks to protect children and their rights. This legislation – for example, Children (Scotland) Act 1995 – guides adults both to ensure that children have choices and that they are protected from harm. This means that adults have to strike a balance between rights and safety. Some service providers resort to rigid policies that protect adult staff more than they take account of the wishes of children (Davis and Watson, 2001). This especially occurs where adults use 'rules' and 'guidelines' unreflexively to deny children choices (Davis *et al.*, 2000).

As Maria indicates there can often be a separation between adults and children:

Maria: He thinks we are all thick anyway. He once asked us all what 'as well' means. We all know what 'as well' means!

Alan: Yeah, he thinks that we don't understand . . .

MC: . . . OK . . .

Alan: . . . he thinks we don't know what 'turn up' means and we do. He thinks we're thick. He made us write down what it meant. So then we had to write longer and longer lists of what words meant. It's such a waste of time.

(Corker, 2003 [forthcoming])

These Deaf children believe they are not being stretched at school and feel insulted by the teacher. They set up a 'him' and 'us' discourse that reinforces the adult vs. child divide. This separation can also be found in the language of the staff in schools, the language of academics who write about 'special' and 'inclusive' 'education', and the texts of writers in childhood studies who make too much of the separation between adult and children's rights (Davis and Watson, 2000, 2001). For example, in one form of childhood studies children are viewed as a universal minority group who are in opposition to adults (James *et al.*, 1998).

These divisions also occur between children of different ethnic backgrounds and disabled and non-disabled children. In the next examples Imran does not want to go to a mixed ethnicity youth club (his ideal friendships are with deaf 'Asian' children) and Chick wants to go to school with people like him:

M: Do you go to the Deaf Club?

I: No . . . only on a Monday when it is the deaf Asian group.

M: Do all of the deaf Asian kids go, all?

I: Yeah . . . oh no some don't, one Indian doesn't come. So, yeah, all but one does and that's a shame because it means that they are at home alone . . .

M: . . . I wondered if any of your friends talked about the [non-Asian] club?

I: I don't know about that. I think that there can be trouble there, [white] people fighting and bad behaviour. I'm not sure about that so I don't go anyway. I think they can be a bit wild and bully people and I don't want to be involved with that. I'd rather go on a Saturday when the people there are a little more sensible, that's when I go.

Chick: Yeah. I'm closer to the people I met there [at the Special Olympics], who have the same condition as me, than I've ever been to anybody. Which is why I might like to go to the school there . . . I think my greatest friends are down south and abroad not here but far away. I was only with these people for ten days and I got really close. So am waiting to hear about the new school there's a meeting on Friday probably of education, social work and health in the council and it will come down to money. They will probably say no to start with and we'll have to fight because that's what usually happens. We'll probably have to appeal . . . No, I mean what can we do. I mean what am going to say at the meeting is that you wouldn't stick an able-bodied boy in a special school and expect them to be OK, by the end of the week they'd want out. I don't want to be the one boy to conquer everything, the school or the world. Well, I would like it because a probably get loads of money but I don't think a can do that and I don't believe people want to do that. I can't do the fighting all the time. I can't wait for the day I say bye-bye to this school.

We do not want to down play these children's experiences. There are many reasons why these children emphasise their differences from other children. For example, a lot of the children had experienced bullying (Watson *et al.*, 2000). However, the difficulty with their position is that it reinforces their own isolation from mainstream experience. In the short term this may have benefits but in the long term, on leaving school, they will be confronted with the same conditions once again.

The status quo in writing on 'special education' involves writers blaming a lack of inclusion on a number of structural barriers – for example, class sizes, league tables, political intrusion on the management of schools, teachers' attitudes to change (Davis and Watson, 2001). The examples above suggest a deeper cultural division. Inclusion in both 'mainstream' and 'special' schools is interrelated with adult's and children's notions of difference and normality. Many disabled children are put under pressure in educational settings to demonstrate that they are 'different' (in order to justify special provision) and yet 'normal' (in order to obtain social acceptance). The mistreatment of disabled children in educational settings relates as much to the unreflexive imposition of discourses of difference and normality as to the financial restrictions experienced by schools.

'Real' educational inclusion is not only dependent on structural change but is also reliant on a fusion of a number of factors (e.g. equal access to educational opportunities, the development of equitable group dynamics and the presence of strong-willed individual pupils, parents and staff). At the heart of good practice is the need to recognise that disabled children are both the same as and different from other children. Irene explains that she mostly wants to be treated the same as other children, yet occasionally will want her different requirements to be understood:

> *Irene:* Yeah. It gets a bit annoying. And like 'cause they're teachers you can't just say, like you've got to be polite or whatever. You just have to, you can't just say, 'I'm not having trouble with this' . . . cause in primary, like em, it seemed like em, like everyone like goes quite close in primary and stuff like the boys and the girls and stuff like that. And then like if I fell over everyone would be like, 'Oh, Irene are you alright, you alright?' And like if someone else fell over it would be, 'Oh, are you OK?' And like maybe it was because I don't know my character or whatever I dunno. Or maybe it's my visual impairment, but everyone seemed really protective . . . It's like they don't make you feel independent. Like they want to do stuff for you. It's like you want help, but you don't want like charity . . . Like the best judge of what you can do and what you can't do is yourself, for anyone, not just if you're disabled.

> *Irene:* It wasn't the same for both of us. It was the copying. It was the copying that Maxine couldn't do. I couldn't see it (when the writing was small or the style difficult to read). And he tries to make it bigger but he doesn't understand that she can't copy it . . .

Irene wants the children to treat her the same and to stop being over-protective, yet she also wants specific support in the classroom setting. Irene does not want teachers and pupils to stereotype or stigmatise her. She points out that not all children with visual impairments are the same and that she has different wishes at different times.

Often service providers find it difficult to accommodate the perspectives of children like Irene. We believe that the vast majority of service provision for disabled children in the UK still starts from the position that services are what adults and the 'able-bodied' provide for disabled children. Despite the change in language surrounding inclusion there is little evidence that disabled children are working in partnership with service providers to develop their own solutions to their life problems. There is even less evidence that service provider 'consultation' has resulted in disabled children's own perspectives on their lives being put at the centre of service development. Social policy concerning disabled children rarely recognises the problem-solving skills of disabled children. For the most part it imposes adult solutions that are based on professional and personal prejudice that relate to essentialist notions of disability (Priestley, 1998). Very little time is spent allowing disabled children to identify and solve their own life problems.

The solution to this situation does not lie in blaming adults/ non-disabled children and idolising disabled children. The solution lies in developing social policy that promotes negotiation between adults and children and recognises the ability of children, families and service providers to develop their own localised solutions to their everyday life problems (Davis and Watson, 2000). Despite the generally bleak analysis outlined above, disabled children do encounter professionals who are receptive to their ideas and also treat them and their parents with respect (Davis and Watson, 2000, 2001; Davis *et al.*, 2000). During the course of our work we met many professionals who were not involved in defensive practice. They either felt secure as individuals or had the support of other staff and children. These people somehow managed to resist the structural pressures that their colleagues experienced. Not all adults and children are the same, and it is important that we examine the different cultures and identities of service providers as much as the different wishes of disabled children. It is from the professionals and children who do not adopt stereotypical practices that social policy can learn a lot.

Conclusion

Social policy, like law, is traditionally reactive (see Corker, 2003, forthcoming). Yet social policy, unlike law, has the potential to be proactive – to set in place a series of principles that define a just and inclusive society and practical but flexible ways of implementing them. We have argued that the social model of disability, though having many virtues, does not form as strong a basis for social policy as was first hoped. This is mainly because, like the medical model of disability, it does not easily recognise the abilities of disabled children.

In a multi-layered approach we need to:

- Change the structures of social and educational settings and address the cultures of discrimination within.
- Work more closely with children, parents and practitioners to bring forth their own local solution.

- Include the peer group and their solutions.
- Put in more resources to resolve technical rational issues that create barriers to inclusion.
- Put in more resources to enable children, parents and practitioners to engage in more meaningful discussions concerning the variability of disabled children's lives.

Many of these aims are already present in social policy guidelines; however, they are prevented from being meaningfully enacted because some professionals at different levels of seniority within specific service directorates lack the will or ability to put them into practice. Yet, at the same time many children and adults find their own ways to overcome this barrier and promote their own brand of meaningful inclusion. It is important that we, as academics, highlight these pockets of good practice so that they can form the basis for more solid and sustainable action.

Finally, many children told us that, as much as anything else, what they wanted was respect. As Anna told us: 'It's like you want help, but you don't want charity.' If an appropriate social policy response to the problems faced by disabled children is to be developed then the voices of the children themselves must be listened to and solutions to their life problems must be stimulated by family members, service providers and the children themselves. This will require open dialogue and the recognition that difference and disagreement can be the stimulus for fruitful negotiation.

Notes

1 Albeit with a number of 'get out' clauses. For example, children may be excluded from mainstream schools only if it is felt that a mainstream school is not suited to the ability or aptitude of the child; is incompatible with the provision of efficient education for the children with whom the child would be educated; or that inclusion would result in unreasonable public expenditure.
2 Although it should be noted that the essentialising of difference is critiqued within the chapter, Deaf (upper case) is used to highlight the cultural differences between deaf (lower case) people whose first language is English and Deaf people who predominantly are BSL speakers and consider themselves to be a cultural minority.
3 All names are pseudonyms.

References

Ahmad, W., Darr, A. and Jones, L. (2000) '"I send my child to school and he comes back an Englishman": minority ethnic deaf people, identity politics and services', in W. Ahmad (ed.) *Ethnicity, Disability and Chronic Illness*, Buckingham: Open University Press.

Ali, Z., Fazil, A., Bywaters, P., Wallace, L. and Singh, G. (2001) 'Disability, ethnicity and childhood: a critical review of research', *Disability and Society*, 16, 7: 949–67.

Bailey, R. (1996) 'Prenatal testing and the prevention of impairment', in J. Morris (ed.) *Encounters with Strangers: Feminism and Disability*, London: Women's Press.

Baldwin, S. and Carlisle, J. (1994) *Social Support for Disabled Children and their Families*, London: HMSO.

Begum, N., Hill, M. and Stevens, A. (1994) *Reflections: Views of Black People on their Lives and Community Care*, CCETSW, Paper 32.3, London: Central Council for Education and Training in Social Work.

Beresford, B. (1994) Positively Parents: *Caring for a Severely Disabled Child*, London: HMSO.

Bignall, T. and Butt, J. (2000) *Between Ambition and Achievement: Young Black People's Views and Experiences of Independence and Independent Living*, York: Joseph Rowntree Foundation.

Corker, M. (2002) 'Sensing disability', *Hypatia*, 16, 4: 34–52.

Corker, M. (2003, forthcoming) '"They don't know what they don't know". The social constitution of deaf childhoods in sites of learning', in S. Gabel and S. Lissner (eds) *Disability, Culture and Education*, New York: Peter Lang.

Corker, M. and Davis, J.M. (2000) 'Disabled children – (still) invisible under the law', in J. Cooper (ed.) *Law, Rights and Disability*, London: Jessica Kingsley.

Corker, M. and French, S. (1999) *Disability Discourse*, Buckingham: Open University Press.

Davis, J.M. and Corker, M. (2001) 'Disability studies and anthropology: difference troubles in academic paradigms', *Anthropology in Action*, 8, 2: 18–27.

Davis, J.M. and Watson, N. (2000) 'Disabled children's rights in everyday life: problematising notions of competency and promoting self-empowerment', *International Journal Of Children's Rights*, 8: 211–28.

Davis, J.M. and Watson, N. (2001) 'Where are the children's experiences? Analysing social and cultural exclusion in "special" and "mainstream" schools', *Disability and Society*, 16, 5: 671–87.

Davis, J.M., Watson, N. and Cunningham-Burley, S. (2000) 'Learning the lives of disabled children: developing a reflexive approach', in P. Christiensen and A. James (eds) *Conducting Research With Children*, London: Falmer.

Estes, C. (1979) *The Ageing Enterprise*, San Francisco: Jossey-Bass.

Fairbairn, G. and Fairbairn, S. (eds) (1992) *Integrating Special Children: some ethical issues*, Aldershot: Avebury.

Ingstad, B. and Reynolds-Whyte, S. (1993) *Disability and Culture*, Berkeley, Calif.: University of California Press.

James, A., Jenks, C. and Pront, A. (1998) *Theorising Childhood*, Cambridge: Polity Press.

Keith, L. and Morris, J. (1994) 'Easy targets: a disability rights perspective on the "children as carers" debate', *Critical Social Policy*, 44, 5: 36–57.

Levitas, R. (1998) *The Inclusive Society? Social Exclusion and New Labour*, London: Macmillan.

MacMurray, J. (1932) *Freedom in the Modern World*, London: Faber.

Morris, J. (1993) *Independent Lives: Community Care and Disabled People*, Basingstoke: Macmillan.

Morris, J. (1997) 'Gone missing? Disabled children living away from their families', *Disability and Society*, 12, 2: 241–58.

Oliver, M. (1990) *The Politics of Disablement*, Basingstoke: Macmillan.

Olsen, R. (1996) 'Young carers: challenging the facts and politics of research into children and caring', *Disability and Society*, 11, 1: 41–54.

Olsen, R. and Parker, G. (1997) 'A response to Aldridge and Becker – "Disability rights and the denial of young carers: the dangers of zero-sum arguments"', *Critical Social Policy*, 17: 125–33.

Phillipson, C., Bernard, M. and Strang, P. (1986) *Dependency and Independency in Later Life*, London: Croom Helm.

Priestley, M. (1998) 'Childhood disability and disabled childhoods: agendas for research', *Childhood*, 5, 2: 207–23.

Robinson, C. and Stalker, K. (1998) *Growing Up with Disability*, London: Jessica Kingsley.

Scottish Executive (1999) *New Community Schools Prospectus*, Edinburgh: Scottish Executive.

Scottish Executive (2000) *New Community Schools: A Framework for National Evaluation*, Edinburgh: Scottish Executive.

Shakespeare, T. (1999) 'Losing the plot? Discourses of disability and genetics', in J. Gabe and P. Conrad (eds), *Social Perspectives on the New Genetics*, Oxford: Blackwell Publishers.

Shakespeare, T. (2000) *Help*, Birmingham: Venture Press.

Shakespeare, T. and Watson, N. (1998) 'Theoretical principles in disabled childhood', in K. Stalker and C. Robinson (eds), *Growing Up with Disability*, London: Jessica Kingsley.

Shakespeare, T., Gillespie-Sells, K. and Davis, D. (1996) *Untold Desires: The Sexual Politics of Disability*, London: Cassell.

Swain, J., Finkelstein, V., French, S. and Oliver, M. (1993) *Disabling Barriers – Enabling Environments*, London: Sage.

Townsend, P. (1981) 'The structured dependency of the elderly', *Ageing and Society*, 1, 21: 5–28.

Vernon, A. (1996) 'A stranger in many camps: the experience of disabled black and ethnic minority women', in J. Morris (ed.) *Encounters with Strangers: Feminism and Disability*, London: Women's Press.

Wald, N. (1992) 'Antenatal maternal screening for Down's syndrome: results of a demonstration project', *British Medical Journal*, 305: 391–4.

Warnes, A.M. (1993) 'Being old, old people and the burdens of burden', *Ageing and Society*, 13: 297–338.

Wates, M. (1997) *Disabled Parents: Dispelling the Myths*, Cambridge: National Childbirth Trust.

Watson, N., Shakespeare, T., Cunningham-Burley, S., Barnes, C., Corker, M., Davis, J. and Priestley, M. (2000) *'Life as a Disabled Child: A Qualitative Study of Young People's Experiences and Perspectives'*, ESRC Research Programme, Children 5–16: Growing into the Twenty-First Century, University of Edinburgh/ University of Leeds.

Part IV
Resources for children

13 Child poverty and child health in international perspective

Jonathan Bradshaw

Introduction

In the 20 years between the end of the 1970s and the 1990s relative child poverty in the United Kingdom increased more than threefold. Child poverty increased more in the UK than any other rich country for which there is comparable data. There is survey and administrative evidence that the child poverty rate has at last begun to fall. However, throughout the years when it increased, or stayed at internationally very high levels, there were very few attempts to monitor the impact of poverty on child well-being. As part of the ESRC Children 5–16 project Bradshaw (2001a) undertook a review of the impact of child poverty on the physical and mental health of children, and their behavioural, cognitive and emotional well-being. With the support of Save the Children (UK) we have begun to produce a biennial report on the well-being of children in the UK (Bradshaw, 2002). As part of this work we have come to the conclusion that there are problems with the kind of child health indicators that have been used traditionally to make comparisons between nations or within nations over time. This chapter reviews the evidence leading to this conclusion and argues that there is a need to develop new ways of measuring child health in industrial countries – in ways that are more sensitive to picking up the impact of poverty.

The increase in child poverty in the UK

In the Households Below Average Income (HBAI) series (Department of Social Security, 2001a) the UK now has a vehicle for comparing child poverty rates more or less consistently over time. Figure 13.1 uses this source to trace the prevalence of child poverty between 1979 and the latest available date 1999/2000. It presents the proportion of children living in households with equivalent income after housing costs below three conventional thresholds relative to the average. Taking the 50 per cent of average threshold, it can be seen that the child poverty rate rose from 10 to 35 per cent between 1979 and 1998/9. Most of this

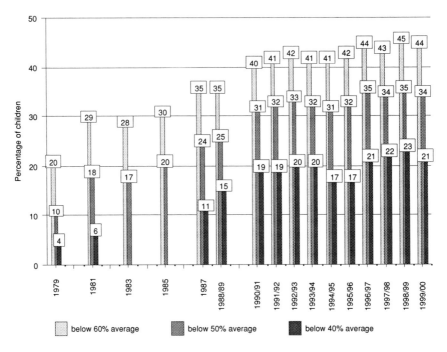

Figure 13.1 Percentage of children in poverty, contemporary terms (after housing costs)

increase occurred in the 1980s, and during the 1990s child poverty remained high but steady. This is not the place to review the causes of this increase in child poverty (but see Bradshaw, 1999, 2001a) – it was influenced by a combination of economic and demographic factors, but was mainly the result of policy decisions made by successive Conservative governments.

Child poverty in the UK has been falling since 2000. This is not yet shown very clearly in the survey evidence. The latest Family Resources Survey, used for the 1999/2000 HBAI estimates, covers only part of the period after the big tax and benefit changes of the Labour government. Administrative statistics take the picture a little further up to date and they show, for example, that the proportion of children living in families dependent on Income Support fell from over 25 per cent in 1995 to less than 18 per cent in 2001 (Department of Social Security, 2001b). Even more up-to-date evidence comes from modelling – analysis using POLIMOD, a micro-simulation model run by Sutherland (2001) at Cambridge indicates that taking into account all the tax and benefit changes announced by the government up to and including the 2001 budget, one million children will have been lifted out of poverty.

Child poverty in comparative perspective

Although, thanks to the Luxembourg Income Survey (LIS), the European Community Household Panel Survey (ECHP) and the work of Office of Economic Cooperation and Development (OECD) (using national data), there is now a good array of comparable data on child poverty – but none of it is very up to date. Most estimates from these sources are for the mid-1990s and the latest estimate (from the 1998 ECHP) uses income data for 1997. However there are three main conclusions to be drawn from this evidence.

1   In the mid-1990s the UK had a very high child poverty rate comparatively. UNICEF (2000) (based on the work of Bradbury and Jantti (1999) using LIS) found that out of 25 industrial countries, the UK had the third highest child poverty rate – only lower than the USA and Russia. The latest ECHP gives a child poverty rate for the UK, which is by far the highest in the EU (see Figure 13.2).

2   Between the mid-1980s and mid-1990s the UK child poverty rate increased more than any other country included in the OECD comparisons (Oxley *et al.*, 2001) over time. Indeed it can be seen in Figure 13.3 that a number of countries experienced a reduction in their child poverty rates.

3   Comparative evidence indicates that this was partly driven by the fact that the UK has a comparatively high rate of worklessness among families with children and that it has a high proportion of children living in lone-parent families, who, in the 1980s and 1990s, found

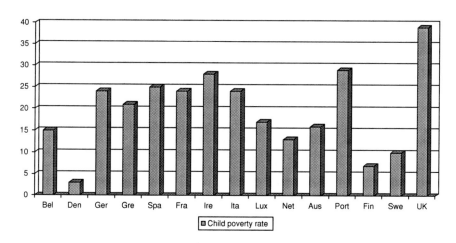

Figure 13.2 Percentage of children in households with equivalent income less than 60 per cent of the median, 1997
Source: European Community Household Panel, 1998

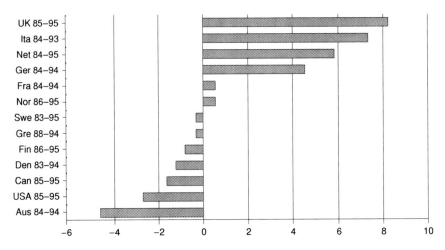

Figure 13.3 Trends in child poverty (percentage point change)
Source: Oxley *et al.* (2001)

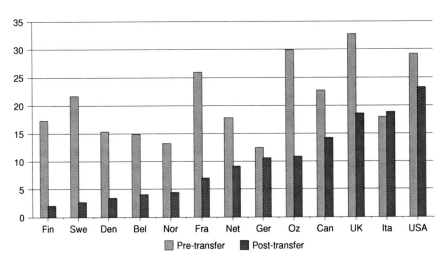

Figure 13.4 Impact of transfers on child poverty rates, mid-1990s
Source: Oxley *et al.* (2001)

it difficult to obtain paid employment. However the UK tax and benefit system is less successful than in most other countries in protecting our children from poverty. Figure 13.4 compares the pre-transfer (market incomes, before the impact of taxes and benefits) with post-transfer (after the impact of taxes and cash benefits) poverty rates. It can be seen that although the UK reduces market-generated child poverty rate more successfully than in the USA and Italy (where it increases as a result of transfers!), the UK is far less successful than other countries.

Child poverty and child health in the UK

The review undertaken as part of the ESRC Children 5–16 project sought to answer three questions about the relationship between poverty and outcomes:

1   Is there evidence that a particular outcome is associated with poverty? That is, does it vary with poverty (or its proxies) so that the poor fare worse?
2   Is there evidence that a particular outcome has got worse over the period when poverty has been increasing?
3   Is there evidence that during this period when the poverty has got worse and inequalities have grown, there has been a widening in the dispersion of a particular outcome?

The study covered a very wide range of outcomes, but in this chapter the focus is on health outcomes and health behaviours.

Certainly there is evidence (for this evidence see Bradshaw, 2001a, 2002) that many health outcome measures are associated with poverty and its proxies. Thus there is good evidence that rates of low birth-weight, infant mortality, child mortality, most morbidity (including dental health), child mental health, youth suicide and smoking among girls are all much higher among poor children.

However, during a period when poverty increased threefold most of the health indicators for which there is time series data continued to improve. Thus the rate of low birth-weight fell, as did infant and child mortality (including fatal accidents), teenage conceptions and most morbidity. There is no evidence on trends in child mental health, though male youth suicide increased (though it is now falling).

Not only did some of the health indicators continue to improve but also there was a closing of the gap between the rich and the poor. For example, class differentials in infant mortality and dental health fell.

Some other health indicators improved overall but there was a growing gap between the poor and others. Among this class of indicators are low birth-weight, child deaths (especially accidental deaths), teenage conceptions and youth suicide.

Finally there are some health indicators which appear to have got worse in the last 20 years but which do not appear to be associated with poverty. These include some morbidity such as asthma, alcohol consumption and the consumption of illicit drugs.

There are a variety of explanations that can be proposed for this lack of association between child poverty and indicators of child health outcomes.

1   As with inequalities in health there is a mix of theoretical explanations
    for any relationship found (or not found) between child poverty
    and health. Thus poor children may be unhealthy

- because they are genetically less healthy
- because the environments in which they live are less healthy
- because their behaviour (and the behaviour of their parents)
  puts them at greater risk of being unhealthy
- because they have less access to health and other services that
  would enable them to maintain their health.

It is likely that all these hypotheses explain some of the link between
child poverty and child health (or the lack of it). To take a few
examples: congenital malformations are more common in low-
income families, and a family with a child who is disabled is more
likely to have a low income. Poor children are more likely to live
in urban environments and in poorer housing conditions, where air
pollution and the risk of traffic accidents are higher. The mothers of
poor children are more likely to smoke and low-income families
are less able to provide their children with an adequately nutritious
diet (see the review by Searle, 2002). Comparative research on health
services by OECD (Or, 2000) has shown that having controlled for
GDP per capita, occupation, alcohol and tobacco consumption and
air pollution the number of doctors per 1,000 and a publicly financed
health service explain some of the variation in infant and perinatal
mortality in industrial countries.

2   The increase in child poverty is an increase in *relative* child poverty,
    actually an increase in inequality. Certainly there was for a time a
    sharp increase in the numbers of children who were absolutely worse
    off. For example in 1992/3 there were 500,000 more children living
    below the 1979 real income poverty threshold than there had been
    in 1979. However, over the whole period, children living in fam-
    ilies on Income Support had their real living standards maintained
    – they just fell further behind the average. That is not to claim that
    their living standards were ever adequate, nor that relative depriva-
    tion may be as damaging or more damaging to health (see the dis-
    cussion on pp. 224–5) than absolute poverty. However, if absolute
    poverty is the driver of ill health then there was not much increase
    in absolute poverty.

3   It is known that things other than poverty influenced some health
    indicators during this period. Take three examples:

- The *infant mortality rate* (deaths in the first year of life), the most
  classical indicator of child health. From the mid-1970s mothers
  were told to lie their babies on their backs rather than their fronts.
  This public health campaign appears to have had a remarkable

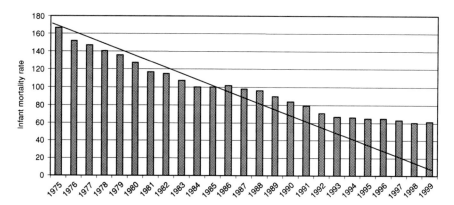

Figure 13.5 Infant mortality rate 1975–99, England and Wales (1985 = 100)
Sources: OPCS, *Mortality Statistics: Childhood and Maternity* (London: HMSO, 1979);
ONS, *Mortality Statistics: Childhood, Infant and Perinatal* (London: HMSO, 1999)

impact on the incidence of Sudden Infant Death Syndrome (SIDS), and SIDS had been one of the main contributors to infant mortality. Figure 13.5 traces the infant mortality rate between 1975 and 1999 with 1985 set at 100. It shows that the infant mortality rate fell faster than the trend line before 1985 (possibly because of the decline in SIDS) and more slowly than the trend line after 1985 (possibly because the gain from SIDS had been absorbed). This chart is a development of one originally used by Wilkinson (1996) to demonstrate the relationship between inequality and health. He took trends in infant mortality from 1975 to 1992, which 'coincided with an unprecedentedly rapid widening of income inequalities' (p. 98), and argued that the reduced rate of decline in the infant mortality rate after 1985 was an impact of rising inequality. However, child poverty (and inequality) rose most sharply before 1985, and although there may have been a delay factor, the least improvement in infant mortality occurred during the 1990s when child poverty (and inequality) were not increasing so much. Wilkinson also made comparisons of trends in the infant mortality between (equal) Sweden and (unequal) the UK. Figure 13.6 traces the infant mortality rates for Sweden, England and Wales and New Zealand. This shows that the gap between the infant mortality of Sweden and the UK diminished in the 1980s when poverty in the UK rose so rapidly. The gap grew again in the early 1990s despite child poverty increasing during Sweden's rapid recession and child poverty being more or less steady in the UK. The UK rate improved faster than that in New Zealand. This was a

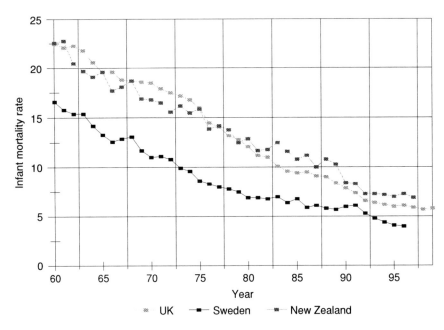

Figure 13.6 Infant mortality rates: trends over time

period when New Zealand's zeal to dismantle her welfare state was out-Thatchering Thatcher.

- The rate of *low birth-weight*. There are well-known class differentials in low birth-weight (Botting, 1997). The rate of low birth-weight has increased over time. The UK has a comparatively high rate of low birth-weight. Can it be concluded that the increase in low birth-weight has been due to rising child poverty and/or to the increase in the numbers of mothers who are having their babies while dependent on Income Support (by the mid-1990s a third of children were being born to mothers on Income Support in Britain)? Possibly, but the picture is complicated by a host of other factors influencing the rate of low birth-weight. Among these are the high rates of births to Asian mothers who 'naturally' have low birth-weight babies – Japan the richest, most equal and arguably most healthy country has the highest low birth-weight rate in the industrial world. Also fertility treatment has led to an increase in multiple births, which are more likely to result in low birth-weight. Also the technical skills of doctors have succeeded in delivering very small and premature babies and keeping them alive. All this complicates the trend picture. The best evidence of the link between poverty and low birth-weight is not the trend in prevalence but that differentials by social class have grown (ONS, 1997).

- *Child accidental deaths.* There is clear evidence of a steep class gradient in accidental deaths. However, during a period when poverty was rising rapidly, accidental deaths were falling for all classes. The UK has one of the highest child poverty rates in the industrial world, at the same time as having one of the lowest rates of accidental death (UNICEF, 2001). Clearly a nation's child accidental death rate is not merely a function of living standards or relative poverty. Policy, the environment, behaviour, and the extent to which children are protected from risk, all play a part. Better-off children live in safer environments in the UK. Their parents are able to drive them to school (on the way killing poor children walking to school).

Child poverty and child health in international perspective

There is no doubt that if this chapter had had a global perspective, the relationship between child poverty and child health would be easier to draw. There are a number of excellent sources, which on a global scale provide the evidence for a close relationship between child poverty and child health, albeit with countries that buck the trend (UNICEF, 1999; UNDP, 1999).

There is also some very good evidence (Hutton and Redmond, 2000; Flemming and Micklewright, 1999; Micklewright and Stewart, 2000; Forster and Toth, 1999), that children in the transitional countries experienced a significant deterioration in their health and well-being, partly as a result of the implementation of free market economic policies imposed by the IMF and World Bank (and of course this has also been true of developing countries in Africa and other parts of the world).

We have seen also that there is considerable evidence at a national level that differentials in child health are associated with poverty. For example Mitchell *et al.* (2000) have estimated that 1,400 lives would be saved each year amongst those under 15 if child poverty were abolished in Britain (as the government intends).

So it is known that child health is associated with poverty and that child health can suffer as the result of social and economic change. So is it also possible to find the same associations using comparative evidence? The next part of the chapter takes a variety of measures of poverty and inequality and plots them against a variety of health outcomes. The picture obtained is rather mixed.

Figure 13.7 plots the relative child poverty rate against the infant mortality rate. It can be seen that there is a reasonably strong positive correlation, which would have been stronger if the USA had not been

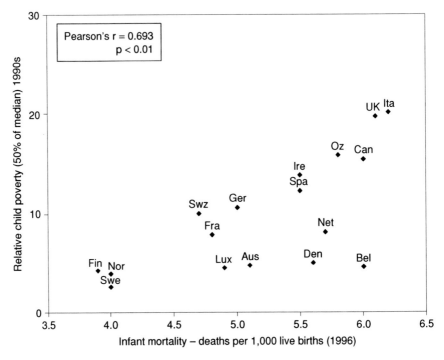

Figure 13.7 Relative child poverty (50 per cent of median) and infant mortality (deaths/1,000 live births)
Source: OECD, *Health Data 1999* (Paris: OECD, 2000)

taken out of the analysis. Italy, the UK (and the USA) have the highest child poverty rates and the highest infant mortality rates. Finland, Norway and Sweden have the lowest child poverty and infant mortality rates. However, there are some interesting outliers. Denmark and particularly Belgium have higher infant mortality rates than would be expected given their level of relative poverty. The perinatal and under-five child death rates were also plotted against the relative child poverty rate, and their relationship was much less strong. The perinatal mortality rate correlated $r = 0.35$ (ns) and the under-five death rate $r = 0.59$ $p < 0.01$ (including the USA).

Figure 13.8 plots the relative child poverty rate against another classical child health indicator: the low birth-weight rate. The UK and the USA, with their high low-birth-weight rates and high child poverty rates, contribute to a fairly strong positive correlation. However, if they were excluded the relationship would be much weaker. Ireland is an outlier with a much lower low birth-weight rate than would be expected, given its child poverty rate, and also Belgium with a much higher low

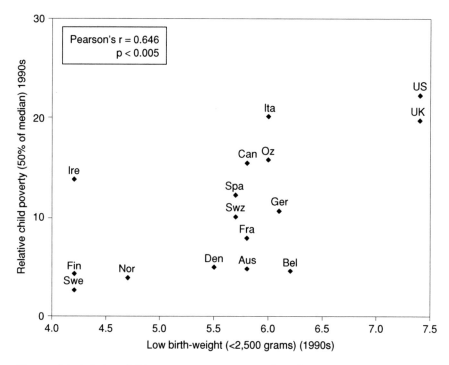

Figure 13.8 Relative child poverty (50 per cent of median) and low birth-weight
(<2,500 grams) – percentage of live births
Source: OECD, *Health Data 1999* (Paris: OECD, 2000)

birth-weight rate than would be expected. Given the problems with low birth-weight discussed above, and the fact that there is so little variation in this indicator among industrial countries, perhaps it is no longer a useful health outcome measure.

It may be argued that this is because these comparisons use a relative measure of poverty, and that what matters to health is the absolute level of living of children. This is explored using the child poverty rates derived by Bradbury and Jantti (UNICEF, 2000), using the US Poverty standard which was originally (nearly forty years ago) based on a budget standard and has been up-rated only in line with prices since then. Figure 13.9 shows the relationship between absolute child poverty and infant mortality, again excluding the USA. There is a positive correlation but it is heavily influenced by Spain, Italy and the UK and is weaker than the one obtained with the relative poverty measure. Canada and Belgium are outliers with higher infant mortality rates than would be expected. The relationship between absolute child poverty and perinatal mortality is again low and not significant ($r = 0.19$), nor is the under-five mortality rate ($r = 0.16$). Also the relationship between absolute

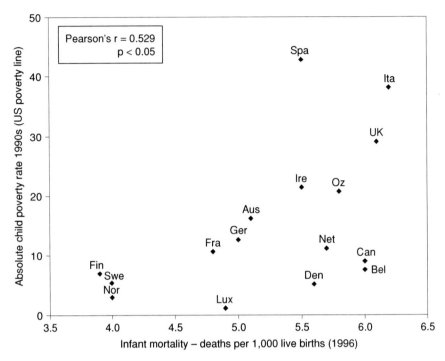

Figure 13.9 Absolute child poverty (US poverty line) and infant mortality (deaths/ 1,000 live births)

Sources: B. Bradbury and M. Jänti, *Child Poverty Across Industrialised Countries*, Innocenti Occasional Paper, Economic and Social Policy Series No. 71 (Florence: UNICEF International Child Development Centre, 1999); OECD, *Health Data 1999* (Paris: OECD, 2000)

poverty and low birth-weight is lower than that achieved with relative poverty and not significant (r = 0.38 ns).

Alternatively, it may be argued (after Wilkinson) that what matters is not poverty or child poverty but inequality. Wilkinson (1996), in his book *Unhealthy Societies*, has argued that the main health gains to be achieved now in industrial societies are not to be found in economic growth, nor in increased expenditure on health, nor even in the population behaving more healthily – but in reducing inequality and poverty. Poverty is the engine of sickness, operating through stress. Figure 13.10 shows that there is a relationship between the Gini coefficient of inequality and infant mortality. The correlation is slightly higher than that achieved with the relative child poverty rate but that is because the USA is not excluded, as it was in Figure 13.7, and also New Zealand and Japan are included – for the first time because there is inequality data for them but no child poverty data (they are not in LIS). If they were excluded the correlation would be no better than using the child

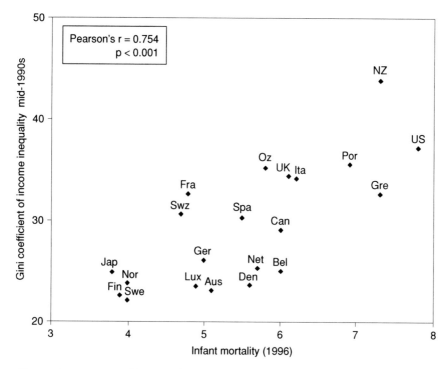

Figure 13.10 Gini coefficient of income inequality and infant mortality (deaths/ 1,000 live births)

Sources: World Bank, *World Development Report 2000/2001* (2001: www.worldbank.org/ poverty/wdrpoverty/report); OECD, *Health Data 1999* (Paris: OECD, 2000)

poverty rate. The correlation between the Gini coefficient and the perinatal mortality rate was 0.24 (ns), with the low birth-weight rate 0.56 (p = 0.05); if Japan was excluded it would have been higher r = 0.74 (p = 0.01).

Income-based measures of poverty are indirect indicators. For EU countries it is possible to use the data from the European Community Household Panel Survey as more direct indicators of the economic well-being of children. As well as income poverty that survey collects data on the proportion of children in households:

1   dissatisfied with their financial situation;
2   having difficulties in making ends meet;
3   unable to save regularly;
4   unable to afford three or more basic necessities;
5   financial situation deteriorated since the previous year;
6   income required to make ends meet more than 105 per cent of actual income;

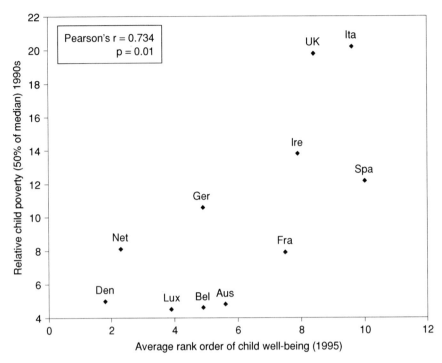

Figure 13.11 Average rank order of child well-being and relative child poverty
(50 per cent of median)

Sources: LIS (www.lisbweb.oeps.lu/publications/incomeproject/povertytable.htm);
Eurostat, *European Community Household Panel Survey 1995* (Eurostat, 1999)

7   with three or more housing problems;
8   with financial burdens or debts.

An index of child well-being can be derived from these questions in
the ECHPS by ranking each of the indicators and producing an overall
average rank (see Bradshaw, 1999). It is interesting that the rank order
index derived from these measures produces a different ranking to the
EU income-based child poverty index (Figure 13.11).

Figure 13.12 shows that there is a positive relationship between the
infant mortality rate and the proportion of families with children unable
to afford three or more necessities – though the strength of the relationship is heavily influenced by Greece and Portugal. There is a positive
relationship between the average rank order on this index and the infant
mortality rate (see Figure 13.13), but it was again influenced by Portugal
and Greece. There was no relationship between either of these direct
indicators of child poverty and low birth-weight.

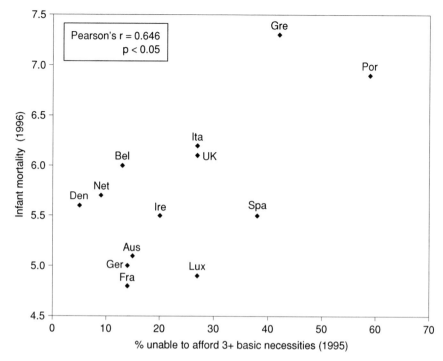

Figure 13.12 The infant mortality rate (deaths/1,000 live births) and the proportion
of families with children unable to afford three or more basic necessities
Sources: OECD, *Health Data 1999* (Paris: OECD, 2000); Eurostat, *European Community Household Panel Survey 1995* (Eurostat, 1999)

There are other health or quasi-health indicators for which comparative data is available. Following Micklewright and Stewart (1999), who made comparisons within the European Union, there is no relationship between child poverty and child accident mortality for 15 countries ($r = -0.10$ $p < 0.74$) or the teenage birth rate ($r = 0.21$ $p < 0.49$). As Figure 13.14 shows there is if anything a negative correlation between child poverty and the youth suicide rate – though the correlation is not statistically significant.

The need for new child health indicators

Using international data some statistically significant relationships have been found between some child health indicators and some measures of child poverty. Infant mortality appears to be the most clearly correlated with poverty measures, and the relationship between low birth-weight and inequality is quite strong if Japan is excluded. Relative child poverty

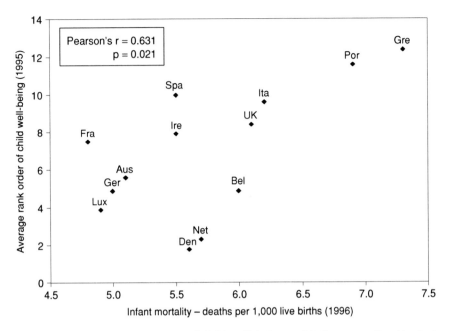

Figure 13.13 Average rank order of child well-being and infant mortality (deaths/
      1,000 live births)
Sources: OECD, *Health Data 1999* (Paris: OECD, 2000); Eurostat, *European Community Household Panel Survey 1995* (Eurostat, 1999)

and inequality are both more closely correlated with health outcomes
than absolute poverty, which supports the Wilkinson thesis.

However, the main conclusion of this chapter is that there is a need
for an international effort to establish new health indicators, useful in
monitoring the impact on children of social and economic change in
industrialised countries. Work is going on.

For example, there has been a programme of work originally known
as the 'Jerusalem Initiative' (Ben Arieh and Wintersberger, 1997; Ben
Arieh *et al.*, 2001) to develop indicators for cross-country comparisons
of children's well-being covering five domains – safety and physical
status; personal life skills; civic life; economic resources; and activities.
For each domain a set of indicators are specified, including a set of
health and well-being indicators. An international team are seeking to
collect comparable data on these indicators for a variety of countries,
but they are faced with the problem that beyond the conventional
international health indicators they do not exist. At present there is
really only one source of data.

The WHO Cross-National Study, *The Health Behaviour of School
Children* (HBSC), has now grown to 30 countries collecting data from
samples of school age children (11–15) every four years. The HBSC

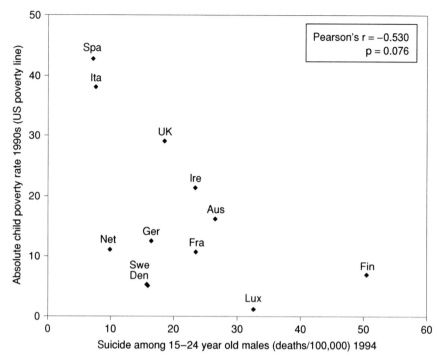

Figure 13.14 Absolute child poverty (US poverty line) and suicide rates among 15- to 24-year-old males (deaths/100,000)
Sources: B. Bradbury and M. Jänti, *Child Poverty Across Industrialised Countries*, Innocenti Occasional Paper, Economic and Social Policy Series No. 71 (Florence: UNICEF International Child Development Centre, 1999); J. Micklewright and K. Stewart, *The Welfare of Europe's Children: Are EU Member States Converging?* (Bristol: Policy Press, 2000)

does not collect data on income, but in the 1997/8 surveys developed a Family Affluence Score (based on the number of cars or vans; the child having an unshared bedroom; and the number of holidays in the past month). There is also a question on how wealthy the young people think that their family is. Currie (2001) has taken these questions and related them to two measures of subjective health and well-being: *How healthy do you think you are?* and *In general how do you feel about your life at present?* In addition there are questions covering experience of symptoms, psychosocial adjustment (including perceived self-confidence), loneliness and helplessness. The Family Affluence Score has not been used here; instead, the health results that are in the public domain have been taken for each country and related to the child poverty rates. Figure 13.15 shows the relationship (ns) between the child poverty rate and the proportion of 15-years-olds in each country reporting not being very happy. The strongest relationship found using this dataset, with

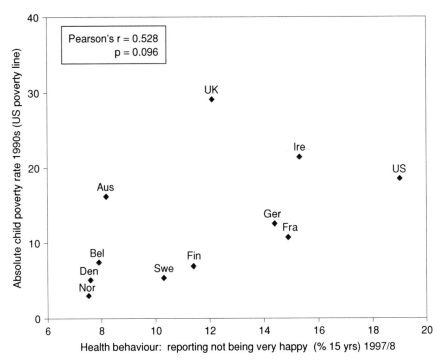

Figure 13.15 Absolute child poverty (US poverty line) and percentage of 15-year-
olds reporting not being very happy
Sources: B. Bradbury and M. Jänti, *Child Poverty Across Industrialised Countries*,
Innocenti Occasional Paper, Economic and Social Policy Series No. 71 (Florence:
UNICEF International Child Development Centre, 1999); *Health Behaviour of School
Aged Children 1997/8* (www.ruhbc.ed.ac.uk/hbsc)

all the poverty and inequality measures, is shown in Figure 13.16 – the
relationship between the relative child poverty rate and the percentage
of 11- to 15-year-olds reporting feeling low is positive and very nearly
statistically significant.

Following the announcement by the Prime Minister in 1999 that the
UK government intended to abolish child poverty within 20 years, the
government committed themselves to producing an annual report on
progress towards their goal. Three annual reports have been produced
so far and Table 13.1 summarises the findings relating to children and
young people from the third and latest report. There are 15 indicators
relating to children (in fact there are more because there are more than
one statistic for each indicator). It can be seen that generally the indicators
are moving in the right direction. All indicators show either a stable
situation or an improvement.

Scotland, which now has its own Parliament and Executive, has
produced a different list of child and young people outcome measures.[1]

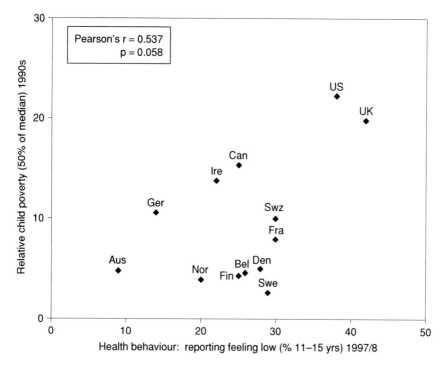

Figure 13.16 Relative child poverty (50 per cent of median) and percentage of
11- to 15-year-olds reporting feeling low
Sources: LIS (www.lisbweb.oeps.lu/publications/incomeproject/povertytable.htm);
Health Behaviour of School Aged Children 1997/8 (www.ruhbc.ed.ac.uk/hbsc)

The US Bureau of Labor Statistics publishes *America's Children: Key
National Indicators of Well-Being* (Johnson, 1999, and http://childstats.gov/
americaschildren/). In 1998 the New Zealand Department of Social
Welfare published a set of 22 'Strengthening Families' Target Measures,
which had a baseline for 1995, and targets for 2000 and 2010.

What is interesting about all these lists of indicators is the difficulty
that countries have had in coming up with good health outcome indicators. The health indicators in the first two *Opportunities for All* reports
changed in the third one. It is also aggravating that in this selection of
other countries' monitoring efforts the health indicators they are employing are so different.

Conclusion

There is a lot to learn from international comparisons. It is possible to
discover a great deal about child poverty and why and how it varies
between countries. It is possible to learn how it is that some countries

Table 13.1 Summary of the opportunity for all indicators for children and young people

	Indicator	Data (value / year)
1.	Percentage children living in workless households	17.9 (1997); 17.8 (1998); 17.3 (1999); 15.7 (2000); 15.3 (2001)
2a.	Percentage children living in households with income below 60% of the contemporary median before housing costs	26 (1996–7); 25 (1997–8); 24 (1998–9); 23 (1999–0)
2a.	Percentage children living in households with income below 60% of the median after housing costs	34 (1996–7); 33 (1997–8); 33 (1998–9); 32 (1999–0)
2b.	Percentage children living in households with income below 60% of the 1996–7 median held constant in real terms before housing costs	26 (1996–7); 24 (1997–8); 22 (1998–9); 19 (1999–0)
2b.	Percentage children living in households with income below 60% of the 1996–7 median held constant in real terms after housing costs	34 (1996–7); 32 (1997–8); 31 (1998–9); 28 (1999–0)
2c.	Percentage of children experiencing persistent low income in at least three out of four years	19 (1991–4); 16 (1994–7); 17 (1995–8); 16 (1996–9)
2c.	Percentage children experiencing persistent low income – below 70% median household income in at least three out of four years	28 (1991–4); 25 (1994–7); 26 (1995–8); 26 (1996–9)
3.	Percentage of 7-year-old children in Sure Start areas achieving Key Stage 1 English and maths tests	
4a.	Percentage of those aged 11 achieving level 4 or above in Key Stage 2 tests for literacy	57 (1996); 63 (1997); 65 (1998); 71 (1999); 75 (2000); 75 (2001)
4b.	Percentage of those aged 11 achieving level 4 or above in Key Stage 2 tests for numeracy	54 (1996); 62 (1997); 59 (1998); 69 (1999); 72 (2000); 71 (2001)
5.	Percentage of 16-year-olds with at least one GCSE A★-G	92.2 (1996); 92.3 (1997); 93.4 (1998); 94.0 (1999); 94.4 (2000)
6.	Percentage of 19-year-olds with at least a level 2 qualification or equivalent	79.7 (1996); 72.3 (1997); 73.9 (1998); 74.9 (1999); 75.3 (2000)

	1995–6 / 1996	1996–7	1997–8	1998–9	1999–0	2001
7. Percentage truancies and school exclusions	0.17 1995–6	0.17 1996–7	0.16 1997–8	0.14 1998–9	0.11 1999–0	
8. Percentage of children who live in a home which falls below the set standard of decency	23 1996					
9. Admission rates (per thousand) to hospital as a result of an unintentional injury resulting in a stay of longer than three days for children aged under 16		1.20 1996–7	1.12 1997–8	1.02 1998–9	1.02 1999–0	
10. Percentage of 16- to 18-year-olds in learning	76.3 1996	74.9 1997	74.9 1998	75.0 1999	75.8 2000	
11. Percentage of young people leaving care with one or more GCSE (grade A★-G) or a vocational qualification				31 1999		
12a. Under 18 conception rates per 1,000 aged 15–17	45.9 1996	45.5 1997	46.5 1998	44.7 1999		
12b. Percentage of teenage parents who are not in education, employment or training	83.5 1996	82.1 1997	72.6 1998	72.9 1999	68.4 2000	71.0 2001
13. Percentage re-registered on the child protection register			19 1997–8	15 1998–9	14 1999–0	
14. A reduction in the gap in mortality for children under one year between manual groups and the population as a whole	0.50 1996	0.42 1997	0.49 1998			
15. A reduction in smoking rates: During pregnancy					18 2000	
Among children 11–15	13 1996		11 1998	9 1999	10 2000	

Source: Department for Work and Pensions (2001)

are more successful than others in mitigating market-generated child poverty. Comparative research demonstrates very clearly that rich nations with high child poverty rates only have to blame themselves for their failure to protect their children using social policies. But at the moment there is not much to learn about the relationship of poverty and health from comparing industrialised countries. Our indicators are just too weak, lacking in differentiation and explanatory power.

At a national level there is a good deal of activity designed to monitor the well-being of children, and in some countries some of it purports to be particularly concerned with the outcomes of poor children. It is to be hoped that this work will eventually lead to the development of a set of internationally agreed indicators which can be used for cross-country comparisons. But this is not yet the position. There is clearly scope for an international body – the World Health Organisation, UNICEF, in the context of children, or for European countries the European Commission – to take on this task. There is certainly scope in the UK for learning how other countries monitor the well-being of children.

Note

1 *Scotland Milestones* (Scottish Executive, 2000)
    1 Percentage of children in working households.
    2 Below 60 per cent of median income.
    3 Reading, writing and maths at primary 2 and primary 7.
    4 All in quality childcare/learning before school.
    5 Decline in pregnant women smoking, decline in low birth-weight, decline in dental decay, increase in women breastfeeding.
    6 Households with children in temporary accommodation.
    7 Halving 16- to 19-year-olds not in education, training and employment.
    8 All young people leaving care achieve English and maths standard grades and have appropriate housing.
    9 Bringing bottom 20 per cent closer to average.
    10 Reducing by one-third days lost each year through exclusion and truancy.
    11 Reducing smoking among 12- to 15-year-olds, teenage pregnancy 13- to 15-year-olds, suicides among young people.
    12 No one sleeps rough.

References

Ben Arieh, A. and Wintersberger, H. (eds) (1997) *Monitoring and Measuring the State of Children: Beyond Survival*, Eurosocial Reports, No. 62, Vienna: European Centre.

Ben Arieh, A. *et al.* (2001) *Measuring and Monitoring Children's Well-being*, Social Indicators Research Series vol. 7, Dordrecht: Kluwer Academic Publishing.

Botting, B. (1997) 'Mortality in childhood', in F. Drever and M. Whitehead (eds) *Health Inequalities: Decennial supplement*, Series DS No. 15, London: The Stationery Office.

Bradbury, B. and Jantti, M. (1999) *Child Poverty Across Industrialised Countries*, Innocenti Occasional Paper, Economic and Social Policy Series, No. 71, Florence: UNICEF International Child Development Centre.

Bradshaw, J. (1999) 'Child poverty in comparative perspective', *Journal of European Social Security*, 1, 4: 383–404.

Bradshaw, J. (ed.) (2001a) *Poverty: The Outcomes for Children*, London: Family Policy Studies Centre/National Children's Bureau.

Bradshaw, J. (2001b) 'Poor children better off under Labour: but much too slowly', in G. Fimister (ed.) *Child Poverty and Labour*, London: Child Poverty Action Group.

Bradshaw, J. (ed.) (2002) *The Well-being of Children in the United Kingdom*, London: Save the Children (UK).

Currie, C. (2001) 'Socio-economic circumstances among school age children in Europe and North America', in K. Vleminckx and T. Smeeding (eds) *Child Well-being, Child Poverty and Child Policy*, Bristol: Policy Press.

Department for Work and Pensions (2001) *Opportunity for All – Making Progress*, London: The Stationery Office.

Department of Social Security (DSS) (2001a) *Households Below Average Income. A Statistical Analysis, 1994/95–1999/00*, London: The Stationery Office.

Department of Social Security (2001b) *Income Support, Quarterly Statistical Enquiry*, London: The Stationery Office.

Flemming, J. and Micklewright, J. (1999) *Income Distribution, Economic Systems and Transition*, Innocenti Occasional Paper 70, Florence: UNICEF.

Forster, M. and Toth, I.G. (1999) *Trends in Child Poverty and Social Transfers in the Czech Republic, Hungary and Poland: Experiences from the Years after Transition*, Paper for the Child Well-being in Rich and Transition Countries, Luxembourg: LIS.

Hutton, S. and Redmond, G. (eds) (2000) *Poverty in Transition Economies*, London: Routledge.

Johnson, D. (1999) *America's Children: Key National Indicators of Well-Being 1999*, US Bureau of Labor Statistics and Federal Interagency Forum on Child and Family Statistics, Washington.

Micklewright, J. and Stewart, K. (1999) *Is Child Welfare Converging in the European Union?*, Innocenti Occasional Papers, Economic and Social Policy Series, 69, Florence: UNICEF International Child Development Centre.

Micklewight, J. and Stewart, K. (2000) *Child Well-being in the EU and Enlargement to the East*, Innocenti Working Paper 74, Florence: UNICEF.

Mitchell, M., Shaw, M. and Dorling, D. (2000) *Inequalities in Life and Death*, Bristol: The Policy Press.

New Zealand Department of Social Welfare (1998) New Zealand 'Strengthening Families Target Measures' (copied).

Office for National Statistics (ONS) (1997) *Health Inequalities: Decennial Supplement*, Series DS, No. 15. London.

Or, Z. (2000) *Exploring the Effects of Health Care on Mortality Across OECD Countries*, Labour Market and Social Policy Occasional Papers 46, Paris: OECD.

Oxley, H., Dang, T., Forster, M. and Pellizzari, M. (2001) 'Income inequalities and poverty among children and households with children in selected OECD countries', in K. Vleminckx and T. Smeeding (eds) *Child Well-being, Child Poverty and Child Policy*, Bristol: Policy Press.

Scottish Executive (2000) *Social Justice: a Scotland where everyone matters, Annual Report 2000*, Edinburgh: Scottish Executive.

Searle, B. (2002) 'Diet and nutrition', in J. Bradshaw (ed.) *The Well-being of Children in the UK*, London: Save the Children.

Sutherland, H. (2001) *Five Labour Budgets (1997–2001): Impacts on the Distribution of Household Incomes and on Child Poverty*, Microsimulation Unit Research Note no. 41.

UNDP (1999) *Human Development Report 1999*, Oxford: Oxford University Press.

UNICEF (1999) *The State of the World's Children*, Oxford: Oxford University Press.

UNICEF (2000) *A League Table of Child Poverty in Rich Nations*, Innocenti Report Card 1, Florence: UNICEF.

UNICEF (2001) *A League Table of Child Deaths by Injury in Rich Nations*, Innocenti Report Card 2, Florence: UNICEF.

Wilkinson, R. (1996) *Unhealthy Societies: The Afflictions of Inequality*, London: Routledge.

14 Children's share of household consumption[1]

Hannele Sauli

Introduction

The cost of children is a crucial element in evaluations of the living standards of families. For one thing, conceptions about and measures of the cost of children have direct implications for practical social policy: child support, alimony and other income transfers in a society. At the same time, they form a conceptual and measurement problem in quantitative empirical research on economic well-being at the micro and macro levels. Not only are children's costs an interesting research area in their own right, but measurements of how much families spend on children or what they are supposed to spend affect empirical analyses of income distribution and poverty through their impact on equivalence scales. In general, perceptions about the cost of children are compressed into the weights in equivalence scales. Since researchers have developed a lot of different scales, one wonders whether all their implications are fully understood among the users of research results. In the first part of this chapter I therefore discuss different scales and their uses. Since they may turn into self-fulfilling norms through political decisions and social policy practices, it is important to understand what kinds of standpoints they reflect.

In the second part of this chapter I try to find and test empirical evidence which would support the various claims about the economic status of children in their families. With the aid of household expenditure data I focus on a narrow issue – the internal distribution of resources within a family – that, however, is a central aspect of the theoretical basis of income measurement. Empirical research on the distribution of resources between generations – that is, children and adults – suffers from lack of suitable empirical data. I will show that even if we do have empirical observations about what actually is spent on (or by) children, the researcher still faces questions on how to process, classify and interpret the data.

Third, I will raise a question of the appropriateness of the use of statistics on the cost of children as an argument in negotiations of the maintenance agreements in connection with legal actions for divorce. A courtroom, of all places, should be the place where people are heard. But, instead of hearing the voice of the child, statistics are used by opposing sides to give numerical expression to what is supposed to be normal. Thus, statistics can turn into self-fulfilling norms even in such a private situation.

Political facts versus hearing the voices of children

Almost any debate about income distribution, poverty or the economic state of the child population involves arguments for proper measurement. There are many problems of measurement, but the question of which equivalence scale should be used seems to be one with no solution. Since results in income and poverty research are sensitive to the choice of scale (among a vast literature on this, see e.g. Coulter *et al.*, 1992b: 1081; Citro and Michael, 1995: 160; Canberra Group, 2001: 56), lack of consensus about this issue leads to endless political and expert debates about facts.

The choice and effects of equivalence scales seems a distant issue in an effort to hear the voices of children. The scales represent a form of knowledge that can be criticised as stereotyping, symbolically violent and meaningful neither locally nor in comparative contexts, and especially not sensitive to children's voices!

Alan Prout (1998: 90) has made an effort to reconnect different forms of knowledge. He suggests a distinction between two sets of research practices in accounting for childhood diversity: the 'distal' and the 'proximal' presentations of childhood (see also James *et al.*, 1999: 142). While distal knowledge is generalising and, being so, appealing to social debates and policy-making, the proximal knowledge shows the complexities of local variations and meanings and is less prone to generalisations.

Mainstream income distribution and poverty studies are an example of the application of distal knowledge: the internal variances in the groups studied are overlooked – or practically taken care of by regression techniques and then forgotten by less-informed users – and the structures observed may often be interpreted as relatively stable. Behavioural invariances ('coded without reference to its local meaning' (Prout, 1998: 90)) are looked after 'distally' in order to make research results feasible for political decision-making. The immediate aim of the users of this kind of knowledge is more often social engineering than increasing our understanding about the world. The distal nature of this knowledge is not changed by close examination of how scientific procedures include children, but our understanding of these procedures as a discourse positioning children in the society may be improved.

Child poverty became a popular topic in micro-economic poverty research in the 1990s. Certain studies received world-wide attention

(Rainwater and Smeeding, 1995; Bradbury and Jäntti, 1999), revealing the hitherto hidden prevalence of children's poverty even in the developed world. Their observations are based on conventional statistical data and methods, and on the innovative choice of the child as the statistical unit instead of families.

The indicators on child poverty have had political relevance. All income studies are politically highly interesting, especially when they produce results in the form of *indicators* of economic well-being. Politicians operate with indicators, assuming that indicators give clear answers based on firm, generally accepted concepts and agreed methods of arriving at conclusions. Indicators should be products of, as Isaiah Berlin (2000: 60) aptly puts it, 'organised observation'.

In our societies, organised observation should be the aim of empirical social science and official statistics. They give us insight into the state of the society, about what causes this state, how it can be influenced and the effects of it. But, how often do the results of such organised observation mistakenly mix the empirical and the normative, unable to distinguish between observations and normative conceptions of what the state of affairs *should* be?

Equivalence scales: normative, but for what purpose?

Equivalence scales are research tools that evidently involve normative judgements. Even though they can be constructed in many ways, there is no single correct way. Researchers justify their choice of scale on the one hand by the purpose of the research in question, and on the other hand by using and comparing the effects of different variants (sensitivity analyses are strongly recommended by Canberra Group (2001: 40), the often cited authority on measurement of income).

With the ultimate target of trying to assess the standard of living of individuals, almost all efforts to measure it empirically in the form of income or consumption are based on observation of household units. The usual assumption is that household members pool and share their incomes thereby reaching an equal standard of living (Bradbury *et al.*, 2001: 39; Lazear and Michael, 1988: 1). But since there are differences in household size and composition, the pooled income has to be adjusted for differences in need due to those disparities. And, to complicate matters even more, the *economies of scale* have to be taken account of in the adjustment; that is, the decreasing amount of resources needed for each additional member.

Equivalence scales are based on the idea of *needs* of household members – children's and adults'. Each member is assigned a weight that reflects his needs in terms of expenditure needs in relation to others. For example, a person living alone has the scale value of 1.0 unit. If another adult joins the same household, he would add less than 1.0 unit to the scale value since two persons can share some of the expenditures (the dwelling, energy, furniture, etc.). The relative need of two adults could be estimated to, say, 1.7 units. A child's expenditure is usually assumed to be less than that of an adult and therefore to amount to smaller-scale values, say 0.5 units. Thus a family of two adults and two children would need 2.7 times the amount of one adult.

The pooled income of the household will be divided by the sum of these weights in the household. The resulting measure is called equivalent income. With this measure we are now able to compare the income situations in households of different size and composition, assuming that our scale has some validity. But how do we judge validity?

Equivalence scales represent practical solutions: deciding the children's weights (between 0 and 1) in the scale means deciding whether the child needs more or less resources. If a child is added to a family, how much has to be added to family income to maintain the family's well-being? With high weights for children, a family with children is more likely to be classified as poor since their income needs would be judged higher, while the opposite would be true with low weights. In the end, the way families with children rank on the income distribution of a nation is highly affected by the scale chosen, which makes the choice a politically relevant issue.

A typology by Coulter *et al.* (1992a: 79) of five types of equivalence scales according to their foundations is revealing:

- econometric scales (based on what people buy)
- subjective scales (based on what people say)
- budget standard scales (based on what experts say)
- social assistance benefit scales (based on what society pays), and
- pragmatic scales (which are precisely that).

Atkinson *et al.* (1995: 18–21) studied the variation of economies of scale embedded in 54 equivalence scales developed for different uses in research or national official statistics in various countries. They found that highest economies of scale are implied in subjective scales. In other words, subjective scales are 'flat', they implicate low relative levels of needs per person. A family of four persons would be treated as equivalent to 1.4 adults on average by subjective scales. Scales in the other extreme of 'generosity' might treat the same family as equivalent to 2.7 adults (ibid., 21). In general, budget standard and pragmatic scales are 'steeper'.

Subjective scales are often derived from surveys asking minimum income needs or income evaluation questions, such as 'Living where you are now and meeting the expenses that you consider necessary, what would be the very smallest income you and your family would need to make ends meet?' (Citro and Michael, 1995: 175). This might explain why the economies of scale are often deemed quite high in subjective scales: poor circumstances may bring about readiness to share in the family. In other words, lower incomes may lead to lowered expectations. Asking about the minimum income to make ends meet implies an entirely different concept of need than the need concept revealed, for instance, in actual consumer spending, the latter actually not being a concept of need at all, but preferences. But all subjective scales are not flat – Van den Bosch has shown that asking about income satisfaction instead of the minimum income needs results in scales that are a lot steeper (Van den Bosch, 1999; see also an overview in Citro *et al.*, 1995: 134–6, about the wide variations of subjective poverty resulting from small differences in the wording of the question).

Econometric scales are usually based on expenditure studies. They do not distinguish whether observed consumption behaviour is based on needs or not. Consumption patterns can be functions of taste, income level, life cycle or reallocation of resources in the family, among other things. Second, budgetary constraints set the limit to most consumption behaviour and, therefore, a person's actual needs are not observable.

According to Atkinson *et al.* (1995) budget standard scales and social assistance benefit scales imply middle-range economies of scale. It is understandable, as they often involve normative notions of necessities. Even the names of the standards often illustrate this, being such as 'basic minimum standard' or 'modest-but-adequate standard' (see, for instance, Carney *et al.*, 1994). Coulter *et al.* (1992a: 99–101) note that such scales are defined with reference to a subsistence or poverty standard of living: 'Although the scales may be relevant for analysis of poverty, it is not obvious that they are the relevant ones for analysis of inequality across the whole income distribution.'

Pragmatic scales – called 'expert statistical' by Atkinson *et al.* (1995: 19) or 'normative or statistical' by Hagenaars *et al.* (1994: 18) – often rank as the most generous ones, and are notably steeper than the scales based on observed consumption expenditure studies.

The widely adopted OECD social indicators scale represents the pragmatic scales. It is not based on any budget norm, but solely on agreement by OECD experts (OECD 1982). According to Coulter *et al.* (1992a: 101), it simply prescribes an equivalence scale to be used for distributional comparisons. This scale was criticised by Hagenaars *et al.* (1994: 18) for being too generous in giving relatively greater weight to additional persons; in other words, assuming small economies of scale in households. In the search for a politically more acceptable, less generous scale for European Union poverty studies, they created the so-called OECD modified scale by simply lowering the weights. In the Hagenaars *et al.*'s modified scale, the weight of an additional adult in a household would be 0.5 instead of 0.7, and children's (aged less than 14) weights were lowered from 0.5 to 0.3. Hence, a family of two parents and two children would correspond to 2.1 equivalent adults instead of the traditional scale value of 2.7 equivalent adults. The European Union has decided to use the OECD modified scale in all its statistics on income and poverty (European Commission, 2001).

The fact that the modified scale has been adopted as the recommended main reference scale for all European Union income and expenditure statistics will have an impact on the conclusions that are drawn from statistics and research. In EU policy, a strong emphasis is placed on the eradication of poverty. Estimates of the extent of inequality and poverty are sensitive to the choice of equivalence scale. Coulter *et al.* (1992a: 104–9) show that the effects of different scales are not intuitively clear: intermediate scales between two extremes will not necessarily result in intermediate inequality and poverty measures.

The change from steeper (e.g. OECD traditional) to flatter equivalence scale (e.g. OECD modified) affects the measured income situation of a household depending on its size and structure. In a large household, the flatter scale leads to a higher equivalent income since the number of equivalent adults will fall from 2.7 to 2.1. Larger households will thus move upwards on the relative income distribution. The equivalent income in a small household is not as much affected by the change of the scale. The position of small households on the relative income distribution will be relatively worse since larger households 'pass' them. Also, the poverty threshold will rise as a consequence of the rise in median equivalent income. The flattening of the scale will necessarily raise the median since the number of equivalent adults diminishes.

Ritakallio (2001) has calculated empirically how the change from the OECD traditional scale to the OECD modified scale affects the poverty rates in different countries. Not unexpectedly, in countries with many large families the overall poverty rate decreased (Ireland, UK, Spain, Germany, France) when the modified scale was adopted, whereas it increased in countries like the Northern European countries where one-person households are quite common (Norway, Denmark, Finland). Apart from the fact that the rates in general will change, scales have effects on who is considered poor: the flatter the scale, the higher the relative poverty of small households. As a consequence of the change of the scale, the old-age poverty rate increased in the European Union and poverty rates for large families decreased. In policy choices, there are (at least) two lines of thinking: emphasis on *not supporting* someone who doesn't need to be supported or emphasis on *not neglecting* someone who actually is in need. The first approach calls for more wariness in assessments of the necessary economic needs than does the latter. The line chosen may lead on to a choice of the equivalence scale, too.

Many writers explicitly state the need to form conservative scales (Citro and Michael, 1995: 48–50, 51; Hagenaars *et al.*, 1994: 23–4) in establishing policy-relevant methodology for identifying the poor. Conservative scales are not too 'generous', which means that the economies of scale may be assessed as substantial and the income needs of children and extra household members as modest. There are two different concepts involved in welfare comparisons: subsistence level versus the Townsendian concept of 'exclusion from ordinary way of life', which comes close to the concept of inequality. Most poverty research is about 'minimum acceptable way of life' in a specific community context. That explains the low budget emphasis in equivalence scaling.

It seems fair to sum up this discussion about the underlying normative assumptions in the equivalence scales by saying that many scales estimate children's costs from a minimum or necessary needs perspective. The subjective, budget standard and social assistance scales set the child's costs in general on a lower level than the actual cost of an average child. Other scales that use spending patterns as their starting point are also constrained by the income levels of families. A cost norm based on observed spending patterns at lower income levels may lead us to accept something less than optimal as a standard.

The myth of equal sharing

Statistical conventions such as equivalence scales are constructed and applied to compensate for the lack of practical information on complex real life situations. For instance, the concept of economies of scale is based on an assumption of income sharing in households – that all members of the household are supposed to reach similar living standards – even though this assumption is known to be an oversimplification.

In spite of criticisms that the assumption of equality does not hold in reality, there have been relatively few attempts to find new solutions, mostly because of the scarcity of empirical data on the intra-household economy. Economists are well aware that intra-family income and consumption inequalities exist. They are also aware of the fact that the relative needs of households are not necessarily the same in, for example, small or large, low-income or high-income households. For instance, it is widely believed that parents limit their consumption in favour of their children. Empirical evidence of gender differences show that wives are sometimes worse off than their husbands (Nordberg, 1998: 8 – but see also Cantillon and Nolan, 1998).

Equal sharing has been an adult-centred notion in economists' theories. Discussions of the parents' utility of having children (which compensates part of the cost of children) have been used without considering what it might mean to children themselves. It is obvious that the 'joys of parenthood' cannot be shared (Bradbury *et al.*, 2001: 40) – deprived children in poor large households are not compensated for their deprivation by their happiness at having siblings (Boijer and Nelson, 1999: 533)!

One of the construction methods for scales resting on empirical observations of differences in the consumption behaviour of children and adults is called the Rothbarth Method. This method derives scales directly from the actual household expenditure. In this method, expenditure is split into collective expenditure, adults' personal[2] expenditure and children's personal expenditure. The basic assumption is that all children's personal expenditure should be compensated for in the equivalence scales and the adults' expenditure levels should be identical whether they have children or not. (For criticism of this method, see Hagenaars *et al.*, 1994: 21.)

The basic idea, in practice, is that since there is no way of knowing children's actual private expenditure, changes in families' consumption patterns could be estimated by comparing households with and without children at the same income level with the help of goods that children do not consume. Alcohol and tobacco would be the best examples of such adult goods. If the consumption of adult goods declines when a child is added to a family, the child's needs are met by making cuts in the expenditure on adult goods. Citro and Michael (1995: 172–4) state that 'the decline in the expenditure on adult goods does not show the decline in the living standards of the parents, but the amount of money that the parents have diverted to the child, which is the information needed'.

Lazear and Michael (1988) used US expenditure survey data in their analysis of intra-household consumption inequality. They focused on spending differences between adults and children, assuming that household expenditures can be divided into private adult expenditures (that are distributed equally among the adults) and private expenditures for children (that are also equally distributed among the household's children). Common goods are consumed by family members in the same ratios as private goods. Since they did not have direct data on private expenditures, their estimates are based on the condition that adults' expenditure (patterns estimated from expenditure on adult clothes, alcohol and tobacco) is at the same level in families with and without children. They found – using data from two time periods – that an average household spent $38–40 per child for every $100 spent per adult, but also noted substantial deviation around this mean. Children benefited remarkably less than adults from any increase in income. They were also able to point to several household characteristics that change the relative resource allocation patterns between adults and children (ibid., 6–11).

A problem of most of the studies attempting to use household expenditure data to estimate the cost of children, or the cost of individual household members in general, is that there is no information about who gets what in a household. However, even if there were such data, much household expenditure consists of common consumption, which must be allocated by the analyst. To do that, one has to ask again who benefits and by how much from the common goods. And, furthermore, even if we had perfect, member-specific data on household expenditure, broad assumptions have to be made to translate the observed spending patterns into individual costs or welfare. In fact, we do have such unique data in the Finnish Household Expenditure Survey since 1985. In the following, I use these data to illustrate intra-household unequal sharing in 1994–96 and 1998 data.[3] (More details in Kartovaara and Sauli, 2001: 82–8; Sauli, 1998a.)

Private expenditure as evidence of unequal sharing

In the Finnish household budget survey, the purpose of which is to compile official statistics on household expenditure, the data are collected from the households by a diary method. In recording all expenditures during a fortnight, the household member for whom each commodity or service has been purchased is also coded in the diary. Of course, all expenditure cannot be specified in this way: in fact, only about 35 per cent of all household expenditure is personal in this sense. On average, 65 per cent of the household's expenditure is common.

Data collection in the survey is designed so that one group of commodities has been pre-determined by the researcher as items for which allocation to a household member is compulsory. Clothing and footwear, meals eaten outside the home, education, health and day care, travel, cultural, sports and other leisure activities, insurance, infant-care articles, personal items such as wristwatches, jewellery, and so on, are goods that always have to be linked to a named person in the household. The person who provides the information in the diary is asked to specify the recipient of each item purchased whenever it is possible.

Nevertheless, if a household purchases a large number of, say, toothbrushes – for which member-specific information would be compulsory – without specifying which household members they were bought for, the processor of the data will divide the expenditure between the household members. This ensures that personal expenditure, for which information about the beneficiary must be made available, is specified as accurately as possible.

Another group of commodities consists of goods and services that are member-specified only if the household chooses to define the item as individual expenditure. The commodity groups typically include different household articles, automobile expenses, personal goods, pets, food, papers and magazines, etc. Among the problematic items to specify are expenditures on the family motor car, a substantial item of expenditure in a family's economy. The car and its operational costs are often specified as personal expenditure of men, yet they serve the whole family's transportation needs although, according to time-use surveys for example, men use the motor car more. Looking at these items, the specification of which is 'non-compulsory', we are able to study *varieties of commonness*: do different households act differently in specifying these commodities as individual or common?

Member-specific allocation would be impossible for dwelling costs, most of the food purchased for the home, kitchen utensils and furnishings, as well as consumer durables. (For a good description of the collection procedure and some descriptions of consumption patterns, see Ruuskanen, 1997: 64–76 and Appendix 1.)

Apart from the quality problems of data collection and processing, the analyst has to solve classification problems such as who benefits from different kinds of consumption, like the example of a family car mentioned above. If something is procured for a child, does it automatically enhance the child's welfare or his choice? A good example of this would be the question on day care: who benefits from this expenditure? As a consumer, a child is not in the same position as an adult because a child's independence in, for example, making decisions about consumption depends greatly on age, among other things. Day care could be interpreted as a prerequisite to the adult's ability to go out to work; that is, part of the adult's living costs. Education benefits a child more clearly, although decisions about that, too, are not always based on the child's own choice.

Due to the fact that children are dependent on decisions made by others about consumption, it is somewhat unclear as to whose consumption really is in question when we measure and study children's consumption. One should be careful in making the simple assumption that any goods, services and other commodities purchased for a child, as well as the family's common goods, increase the child's well-being – much in the same way as material consumption is also considered to increase the well-being of adults. The 'cost of a child' is a lot easier concept than 'well-being' since one doesn't have to take a stand whether the costs increase its well-being.

Varieties of commonness

The degree of commonness could be taken as an indicator of shared utilities. For example, in a normal case, all household members can enjoy the warmth of the dwelling, food is served to everyone, a washing machine is useful for all members of the household, a TV set offers entertainment to all, and so on.

As we have data on the household's total consumption expenditures, as well as data on what items are perceived as somebody's personal consumption, it is possible to make observations on what householders understand as 'common' and whether this perception is patterned by household composition.

The subjectivity that has been allowed in data collection on this point, may give us some clues about how the respondents actually see the shared utilities. Since several items of consumption are allowed to be recorded as either personal or common, we may observe differences in the perception of 'commonness' between, for example, families with and without children. We can look at a few examples of adults' and children's goods, such as cars and car-related expenditures, alcohol, toys, and sweets. The interesting observation is that there certainly are differences in perceptions of commonness, perhaps even in actual commonness, but the differences are smaller than what one would expect.

Cars and car-related expenditures, for example, make about 10 per cent of total expenditure in an average household. One-third of this is coded as common on average. In two-parent families with children, these expenditures are less often recorded as personal than in families with a single parent and children. The presence of two possible drivers seems to make it more likely that expenditure on the car is recorded as being common, not the idea that car rides add to the well-being of the whole family.

In families comprising of more than two adults – i.e. parents and grown-up children – cars are more often seen as personal. Also alcohol expenses are more often personal than common in these families. In this case, this might reflect a real situation of a less-shared lifestyle: in households with parents and adult children, the lifestyle and stage of life can be expected to differ from those of families with children.

In about 50 per cent of the cases, couples without and couples with children do not at all record alcohol as personal (see Table 14.1, Alcohol column; median = 0 or almost 0). When they do make this distinction, couples without children have recorded a much-lower proportion of total alcohol consumption as personal. In other words, alcohol consumption is perceived as common by couples without children.

Table 14.1 Mean and median percentage of the total household expenditure on cars and alcohol which is seen as personal

	Car		Alcohol	
	Mean	*Median*	*Mean*	*Median*
Childless couples	57.5	55.4	30.6	0.0
Couple with children	58.3	59.2	37.5	6.3
One parent with children	64.2	74.6	47.5	50.0
Couple with only grown-up children	69.8	85.1	45.8	41.2
One parent with only grown-up children	74.4	95.7	50.4	57.1
Average all households	59.8	63.5	36.5	0.0

Source: Household Budget Survey 1994–6, Statistics Finland; author's calculations
Note: Households with spouse/parent older than 50 years excluded

Alcohol is an adult commodity: a higher proportion of alcohol expenditure was perceived as private when the household included children. And again, in single-parent families alcohol expenditures are more often recorded as private than in families with two adults and children.

The observations on how adults' goods are perceived and coded in the data give us reason to question the comparability of the concept of commonness of consumption in different households. Perceptions of privacy as to adults' and children's goods seem to differ more between single- and two-parent families with children than between families with children and childless households. In families with children and two adults, the adults form a *collective of adults* who consume adults' goods together and distinguish themselves from children as a group of adults. That's why they also report the adult goods they consume as common. In the same way, a *collective of children* is formed in families with more than one child. Sweets, comic books, toys and other children's goods may be bought for all children. There seems to be an intra-family children's sphere for economies of scale. Clustering adults and children into two consumption groups forms a well-grounded alternative to looking at each member of the family separately.

Childless couples, on the other hand, perceive more of these expenditures as common than personal. Childless couples perceive their car-related expenses as being in common more often than do families with children.

What is important here is the notion that childless couples have a lot more common goods – adults' and other goods (Sauli, 1998b: 57) – than other households. This weakens our willingness to use the method of comparing childless couples' common expenditure as a starting point for trying to allocate common goods to parents. If the structure of personal and common expenditures varies in different households by lifestyle or other, more practical, considerations, there is not much sense to compare these structures between childless couples and parents. But can we compare the overall level of expenditures in these groups?

It is obvious that childless couples as a group are structurally different from parents. First, there are quite a few childless couples in the lowest three income quintile groups. Those in the first quintile group with the lowest income have higher expenditures than couples in the second quintile. By age, the youngest childless couples have relatively high expenditure regardless of income level. All comparisons of expenditure patterns should take these structural differences into account.

To conclude: the method of using childless couples' expenditure as a standard reference for parents' expenditure is subject to criticism – first, in light of these empirical findings of what is perceived as personal vs. common; second, in light of structural socio-economic differences between parents and the childless couples. In the next section I narrow my focus on distributions of personal expenditure inside the family with children.

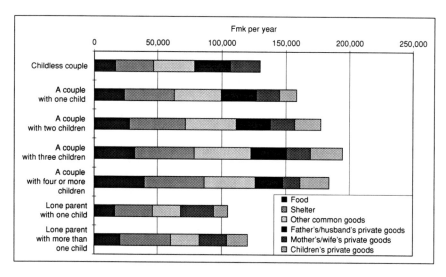

Figure 14.1 Personal and shared expenditure in different families, Finnish marks per year

Source: Household Budget Survey 1994–6, Statistics Finland; author's calculations

Note: Households with spouse/parent older that 50 years excluded

Children's and parents' share of household expenditures

Figure 14.1 shows how expenditures vary on common goods (shelter, food and other common goods) in different households and on private goods of husbands, wives and children. Total expenditure increases quite modestly as the size of the households grows. There is no way of knowing whether it is a sign of increasing economies of scale or budgetary constraints. Couples with four or more children seem to consume less than smaller families, and, according to income information in the same data, large families with children actually are hardly represented at all in the two top income quintiles.

Wives spend less than husbands on private goods in all couple families. A closer look at the gender differences inside the families (not documented here) reveals, not unexpectedly, that personal expenditure of mothers, wives and grown-up daughters are lower than that of their male counterparts. Gender differences were not as clear for younger children, because small boys consume more than small girls, but teenage girls spend more than teenage boys (Sauli, 1997).

Parents amend their consumption in favour of children, but less than expected. Fathers' and mothers' consumption remains pretty much at the same level as the number of children increases from one to three. However, there is a marked reduction in the personal expenditure of

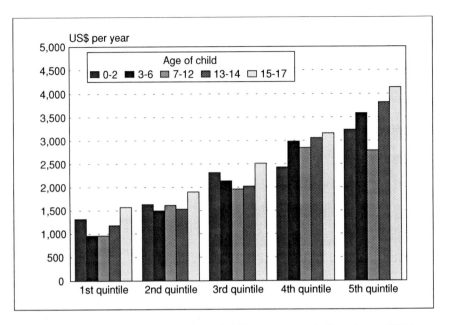

Figure 14.2 Personal expenditure of one child by income quintile and age, US$/year
Source: Household Budget Survey 1998; author's calculations
Note: Income quintiles are based on equivalent disposable household income

both fathers and mothers where there are four or more children
(Figure 14.1).

Household income has a strong effect on the level of spending by or
for a child. In Figure 14.2, children's private expenditure is expressed
in US dollars by household income (equivalent disposable household
income quintiles). In the 1st quintile (the lowest-income group) spending on a child is less than a third of the spending on a child in the
5th quintile (the highest-income group of households).

The number of siblings also has a strong impact on spending on
children. In Figure 14.3, private expenditure is expressed in US dollars
by number of children in a household. A child with two or more siblings
seems to have approximately 50 per cent less money for his personal
consumption than another child with no siblings. In absolute money
terms, a child's spending is more strongly associated with his family's
income level than the size of the family. But, if we look at the same
spending as a share of households' total resources used for consumption
(measured here as the total expenditure of the household), we see that
income has less impact than the number of siblings (Table 14.2).

A child with two or more siblings, regardless of age, gets a smaller
share of the total expenditure of his household than an only child. The
number of children in the family has the strongest effect on a child's

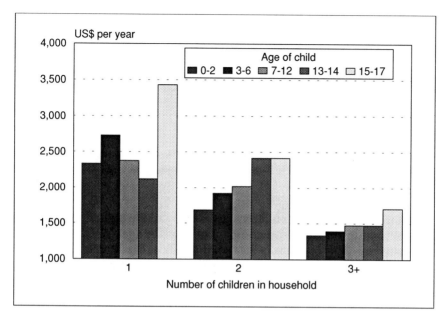

Figure 14.3 Personal expenditure of one child by age and number of children in household, US$/year
Source: Household Budget Survey 1998, Statistics Finland; author's calculations

Table 14.2 Average personal expenditure per child as a percentage of total household expenditure by age and number of children in the household, and by age and income quintile

Age	Number of children in household			Income quintile					Average
	1	*2*	*3+*	*I*	*II*	*III*	*IV*	*V*	
0–2	8.1	5.0	3.1	4.2	4.8	6.4	5.8	6.7	5.4
3–6	8.3	5.4	3.4	2.9	4.2	5.6	6.3	6.3	4.9
7–12	5.2	5.4	3.5	2.8	4.1	4.7	6.3	5.0	4.5
13–14	6.8	4.9	3.6	3.4	4.0	4.7	6.2	6.5	4.9
15–17	7.8	5.8	3.9	4.5	4.8	6.0	6.9	7.4	6.1

Source: Household Budget Survey 1998, Statistics Finland; author's calculations

share of household expenditure (Table 14.2, left-hand panel). Variation caused by income group seems to be weaker (Table 14.2, right-hand panel).

Relative expenditure per child, measured as a proportion of total household expenditure, is surprisingly similar in different income levels and age groups. The lowest proportion, 2.8 per cent, is found in the

Table 14.3 Ratio of personal spending of mothers and children to the personal spending of fathers (indexed at 1.00)

	Total	Number of children in family			Income quintile				
		1	2	3+	Lowest	II	III	IV	Highest
Father	1.00	1.00	1.00	1.00	1.00	1.00	1.00	1.00	1.00
Mother	0.74	0.80	0.77	0.61	0.64	0.70	0.74	0.81	0.74
An average child	0.47	0.56	0.46	0.36	0.37	0.45	0.52	0.55	0.52

Source: Household Budget Survey 1994–6, Statistics Finland; author's calculations

lowest income quintile of children aged 7–12, and the highest proportion, 7.4 per cent, in the highest income quintile at the ages 15–17. Although the share per child in a family's expenditure was the lowest in the low-income families, the totalled up share of private expenditures on all the family's children was relatively similar in low-income and high-income families (Table 14.2). This is explained by the fact that large families usually have low equivalent incomes.

A simple calculation of the ratio between the medians of fathers', mothers' and children's personal expenditure (sum of compulsory and non-compulsory) is presented in Table 14.3. If fathers' private expenditure is set to 1.00, then mothers' private expenditure seems to be 0.7 on average, and children's private expenditures set around the 0.5 level. This scale, naively and directly extracted by comparing the medians, is quite similar to the OECD social indicators equivalence scale!

Conclusions

With these unique data, we have been able to analyse the differences between household members as to their personal consumption, which makes up only one-third of all consumption in the household. Common consumption is only assumed as common, and inequalities between household members are not ruled out. These inequalities are difficult to observe empirically. It has been demonstrated in comparisons between childless couples and couples with children, for example, that scales are quite different depending on the consumption items compared – a scale based on food consumption would be steep in comparison with a scale based on housing costs, for instance. Atkinson (1998: 41) suggests that the appropriate equivalence scale may vary according to, for example, the price level of the fixed costs, such as for housing, heating, etc. If they are low, then standard of living considerations may point to a scale which is close to per capita, and, if they are larger, then the costs of additional household members may be less.

A simpler approach, used by Lazear and Michael (1988), applies the relations implied in the personal expenditures to allocating common costs for each member. But doing so, we would implicitly assume that all common expenditure – food, housing, equipment for the home, etc. – benefits children and adults alike, which would be a false assumption. It would also give an implicit normative approval to actual practices which are probably constrained by available incomes.

Nordberg (1998) experimented using the data on personal spending in the Finnish household budget survey by comparing the effects of equivalence scales derived from private expenditure to effects of the OECD scale on different poverty and income distribution indicators. Equivalence scales derived from private expenditure relations lead only to a slight increase in poverty rates, Gini coefficients and other inequality measures of individuals. As private expenditure ratios of family members seem to be rather similar to the widely used OECD equivalence scale, the result is of no surprise.

Epilogue: how a distal concept changes into reality

I have, however, been surprised by reactions of numerous lawyers and divorcing parents who have contacted me to discuss the implementation of these statistics in legal proceedings involving child alimony payment suits. I have opposed the use of averages in individual situations on the grounds that they do not reveal needs, and take no account of the great variations behind the averages.

Since the Finnish authorities have not created universally applicable good practices for defining child alimony in confrontational situations, the demand for information of children's costs is noteworthy. Well-to-do parents, in particular, have been able to reduce their alimony payments by referring to statistics on the cost of children. In fact, there is no legislation on the amount of alimony, but the existing norms do not vest children with rights to luxurious consumption (Taskinen, 2001: 34). Lack of discursive practices that would structure argumentation in these difficult negotiations thus make room for attaching 'price tags' on children and therefore strengthens the tendency towards the commoditisation of children (see Zelizer, 1994). The statistician's nightmare of averages becoming norms, of distal knowledge replacing proximal and *becoming* reality through this normative process, is actually happening.

Notes

1 I am grateful to Markus Jäntti from Statistics Finland, Caroline Lakin from ONS in Britain and Dorothy Watson from ESRI in Ireland for their comments on this chapter. I am of course responsible for the content.
2 In this chapter, I use 'personal expenditure', 'private expenditure' or 'individual expenditure' as synonyms.

3 The 1994–6 data include 6,700 households, of which 2,200 are two-parent families, and 250 single-parent families. The 1998 data include 4,300 households, of which 1,400 are two-parent families, and 175 single-parent families.

References

Atkinson, A.B. (1998) *Poverty in Europe*, Blackwell Publishers, Oxford.

Atkinson, Anthony B., Rainwater, Lee and Smeeding, Timothy M. (1995) *Income Distribution in OECD Countries: Evidence from Luxembourg Income Study*, OECD, Paris.

Berlin, Isaiah (2000) *Does Political Theory Still Exist?* (first published in 1961), in Isaiah Berlin, *The Proper Study of Mankind. An Anthology of Essays*, Farrar, Straus and Giroux, New York.

Boijer, Hilde and Nelson, Julie A. (1999) 'Equivalence Scales and the Welfare of Children: A Comment on "Is there Bias in the Economic Literature on Equivalence Scales?"', *Review of Income and Wealth*, 45, 4, 531–4.

Bradbury, Bruce and Jäntti, Markus (1999) *Child Poverty across Industrial Nations*, Innocenti Occasional Papers, Economic and Social Policy Series 71, UNICEF, Florence.

Bradbury, Bruce, Jenkins, Stephen P. and Micklewright, John (2001) 'Conceptual and Measurement Issues', in Bruce Bradbury, Stephen P. Jenkins and John Micklewright (eds) *The Dynamics of Child Poverty in Industrial Countries*, Cambridge University Press, Cambridge.

The Canberra Group: Expert Group on Household Income Statistics (2001) *Final Report and Recommendations*, Ottawa.

Cantillon, Sara and Nolan, Brian (1998) 'Are Married Women More Deprived Than Their Husbands?', *Journal of Social Policy*, 27, 151–71.

Carney, Claire, Fitzgerald, Eithne, Kiely, Gabriel and Quinn, Paul (1994) *The Cost of a Child. A Report on Financial Cost of Child-rearing in Ireland*. Combat Poverty Agency, Research Report Series No. 17, Dublin.

Citro, Constance F. and Michael, Robert T. (eds) (1995) *Measuring Poverty. A New Approach*, National Academic Press, Washington, DC.

Coulter, Fiona A.E., Cowell, Frank A. and Jenkins, Stephen P. (1992a) 'Differences in Needs and Assessment of Income Distributions', *Bulletin of Economic Research*, 44, 77–124.

Coulter, Fiona A.E., Cowell, Frank A. and Jenkins, Stephen P. (1992b) 'Equivalence Scale Relativities and the Extent of Inequality and Poverty', *The Economic Journal*, 1067–82.

European Commission (2001) 'Structural Indicators', Communication from the Commission, 30.10.2001, COM(2001) 619.

Hagenaars, Aldi J.M., de Vos, Klas and Zaidi, M. Ashgar (1994) *Poverty Statistics in the Late 1980s: Research Based on Micro-data*, Eurostat Theme 3, Series C, VII. Luxembourg.

James, Allison, Jenks, Chris and Prout, Alan (1999) *Theorizing Childhood*, Polity Press, Cambridge.

Kartovaara, Leena and Sauli, Hannele (2001) *Children in Finland*. Statistics Finland, Population 2001: 9, Yliopistopaino, Helsinki.

Lazear, Edward P. and Michael, Robert T. (1988) *Allocation of Income within the Household*, University of Chicago Press, Chicago.

Nordberg, Leif (1998) 'Inequality, Poverty and the Intra-household Distribution of Income', Paper prepared for the 25th General Conference of the International Association for Research in Income and Wealth, Cambridge, England, 23–29 August.

OECD (1982) *The OECD List of Social Indicators*, OECD, Paris.

Prout, Alan (1998) 'Objective vs. Subjective Indicators or Both? Whose Perspective Counts? or The Distal, the Proximal and Circuits of Knowledge', in Asher Ben-Arieh and Helmut Wintersberger (eds) *Monitoring and Measuring the State of Children – Beyond Survival*, European Centre for Social Welfare Policy and Research, Vienna.

Rainwater, Lee and Smeeding, Timotty M. (1995) *Doing Poorly. The Real Income of American Children in Comparative Perspective*, Luxemburg Income Study, Working Paper 127, August.

Ritakallio, Veli-Matti (2001) 'Tilastointikäytännön muutos muuttaa kuvaa eurooppalaiseta köyhyydestä' [The change in statistical procedure changes the landscape of poverty in Europe], *Hyvinvointikatsaus* [Welfare Bulletin], 4/01, 44–8, Statistics Finland.

Ruuskanen, Olli-Pekka (1997) 'Testing Different Hypotheses of Household Decision-making with the Finnish Household Expenditure Survey', Licentiate thesis, Helsinki School of Economics and Business Administration, Helsinki.

Sauli, Hannele (1997) 'Lapsen kulutus osana perheen kulutusta' [Children's spending in proportion to family expenditure], *Hyvinvointikatsaus* [Welfare Bulletin], 4/97, 22–9, Statistics Finland.

Sauli, Hannele (1998a) 'Children's Share in Household Consumption', Paper presented in the session of the Political Economy of Childhood Working Group 03, Sociology of Childhood 14th ISA World Congress, Montreal, Canada, 30 July. Available from the author.

Sauli, Hannele (1998b) 'Minun, sinun ja meidän kulutus' [My expenditure, yours and ours], *Hyvinvointikatsaus* [Welfare Bulletin] spesiaali: *Hyvä, paha kulutus*, 54–67, Statistics Finland.

Taskinen, Sirpa (2001) *Lapsen etu erotilanteissa. Opas sosiaalitoimelle* [Child's best interest in divorce and separation. Handbook for social services], Stakes, Oppaita 46, Saarijärvi.

Van den Bosch, Karel (1999) 'How People View the Cost of Children: Two Similar Methods, Very Different Results', Paper presented in the conference on Child Well-Being in Rich and Transition Countries, Luxembourg, 30 September to 2 October.

Zelizer, Viviane A. (1994) *Pricing the Priceless Child* (first published 1985), Princeton, New Jersey.

Index

Lightning Source UK Ltd.
Milton Keynes UK
20 August 2009

142867UK00003B/100/A